Advances in Topological Materials

Advances in Topological Materials

Editor

Artem Pronin

MDPI • Basel • Beijing • Wuhan • Barcelona • Belgrade • Manchester • Tokyo • Cluj • Tianjin

Editor
Artem Pronin
Universitaet Stuttgart
Germany

Editorial Office
MDPI
St. Alban-Anlage 66
4052 Basel, Switzerland

This is a reprint of articles from the Special Issue published online in the open access journal *Crystals* (ISSN 2073-4352) (available at: https://www.mdpi.com/journal/crystals/special_issues/Advances_Topological_Materials).

For citation purposes, cite each article independently as indicated on the article page online and as indicated below:

LastName, A.A.; LastName, B.B.; LastName, C.C. Article Title. *Journal Name* **Year**, *Volume Number*, Page Range.

ISBN 978-3-0365-4235-5 (Hbk)
ISBN 978-3-0365-4236-2 (PDF)

© 2022 by the authors. Articles in this book are Open Access and distributed under the Creative Commons Attribution (CC BY) license, which allows users to download, copy and build upon published articles, as long as the author and publisher are properly credited, which ensures maximum dissemination and a wider impact of our publications.

The book as a whole is distributed by MDPI under the terms and conditions of the Creative Commons license CC BY-NC-ND.

Contents

About the Editor vii

Artem V. Pronin
Advances in Topological Materials
Reprinted from: *Crystals* **2021**, *11*, 680, doi:10.3390/cryst11060680 1

Elena S. Zhukova, Hongbin Zhang, Victor P. Martovitskiy, Yurii G. Selivanov, Boris P. Gorshunov and Martin Dressel
Infrared Optical Conductivity of Bulk Bi_2Te_2Se
Reprinted from: *Crystals* **2020**, *10*, 553, doi:10.3390/cryst10070553 5

Wenlong Gao and Yao-Ting Wang
Ideal Photonic Weyl Nodes Stabilized by Screw Rotation Symmetry in Space Group 19
Reprinted from: *Crystals* **2020**, *10*, 605, doi:10.3390/cryst10070605 13

Dmytro L. Kamenskyi, Artem V. Pronin, Hadj M. Benia, Victor P. Martovitskii, Kirill S. Pervakov and Yurii G. Selivanov
Bulk Cyclotron Resonance in the Topological Insulator Bi_2Te_3
Reprinted from: *Crystals* **2020**, *10*, 722, doi:10.3390/cryst10090722 23

Monica Ciomaga Hatnean, Talha Ahmad, Marc Walker, Martin R. Lees and Geetha Balakrishnan
Crystal Growth by the Floating Zone Method of Ce-Substituted Crystals of the Topological Kondo Insulator SmB_6
Reprinted from: *Crystals* **2020**, *10*, 827, doi:10.3390/cryst10090827 31

Sascha Polatkan and Ece Uykur
Optical Response of Chiral Multifold Semimetal PdGa
Reprinted from: *Crystals* **2021**, *11*, 80, doi:10.3390/cryst11020080 45

Sergey Nikolaev, Dmitry Pshenay-Severin, Yuri Ivanov and Alexander Burkov
Effect of Deformation on Topological Properties of Cobalt Monosilicide
Reprinted from: *Crystals* **2021**, *11*, 143, doi:10.3390/cryst11020143 53

Alexey Shuvaev, Lei Pan, Peng Zhang, Kang L. Wang and Andrei Pimenov
Faraday Rotation Due to Quantum Anomalous Hall Effect in Cr-Doped $(Bi,Sb)_2Te_3$
Reprinted from: *Crystals* **2021**, *11*, 154, doi:10.3390/cryst11020154 73

Rebecca L. Dally, Daniel Phelan, Nicholas Bishop, Nirmal J. Ghimire and Jeffrey W. Lynn
Isotropic Nature of the Metallic Kagome Ferromagnet Fe_3Sn_2 at High Temperatures
Reprinted from: *Crystals* **2021**, *11*, 307, doi:10.3390/cryst11030307 83

M. B. Schilling, C. X. Wang, Y. G. Shi, R. K. Kremer, M. Dressel and A. V. Pronin
Fractional Power-Law Intraband Optical Conductivity in the Low-Dimensional Dirac Material $CaMnBi_2$
Reprinted from: *Crystals* **2021**, *11*, 428, doi:10.3390/cryst11040428 93

Shujie Cheng and Xianlong Gao
Topological Properties in a Λ/V-Type Dice Model
Reprinted from: *Crystals* **2021**, *11*, 467, doi:10.3390/cryst11050467 101

Alexander Yaresko and Artem V. Pronin
Low-Energy Optical Conductivity of TaP: Comparison of Theory and Experiment
Reprinted from: *Crystals* **2021**, *11*, 567, doi:10.3390/cryst11050567 111

About the Editor

Artem Pronin graduated from the Moscow Physics and Engineering Institute, Russia, in 1994. His PhD research was conducted at the General Physics Institute of the Russian Academy of Sciences, Moscow. In 1998, he received a PhD degree in solid-state physics. Afterwards, he held positions at McMaster University, Canada; Leiden University, the Netherlands; the University of Leeds, UK; and the High Magnetic Field Laboratory in Dresden, Germany. Since 2015, he has been leading a group at the 1st Physics Institute of the University of Stuttgart, Germany. The group investigates the optical properties of different topological materials, particularly, of Weyl and Dirac semimetals.

Editorial

Advances in Topological Materials

Artem V. Pronin

Physikalisches Institut, Universität Stuttgart, Pfaffenwaldring 57, 70569 Stuttgart, Germany; artem.pronin@pi1.physik.uni-stuttgart.de

Citation: Pronin, A.V. Advances in Topological Materials. *Crystals* **2021**, *11*, 680. https://doi.org/10.3390/cryst11060680

Received: 10 June 2021
Accepted: 11 June 2021
Published: 14 June 2021

Publisher's Note: MDPI stays neutral with regard to jurisdictional claims in published maps and institutional affiliations.

Copyright: © 2021 by the author. Licensee MDPI, Basel, Switzerland. This article is an open access article distributed under the terms and conditions of the Creative Commons Attribution (CC BY) license (https://creativecommons.org/licenses/by/4.0/).

Materials with electronic bands that possess nontrivial topology have remained a focal point of condensed matter physics since 2005, when topological insulators were theoretically discovered by Kane and Mele [1,2]. In parallel to this remarkable discovery, Haldane and Raghu [3] realized that topological phases are a universal phenomenon of waves in periodic media. Thus, topological concepts can also be applied, for example, to electromagnetic waves in photonic crystals [4], magnons in magnetic materials [5], and sound waves in different periodic structures [6]. This Special Issue of *Crystals* represents a collection of 11 papers devoted to different aspects of experimental and theoretical studies on topological materials.

Five papers from the Special Issue focus on the theory side. Gao and Wang [7] propose a new design for an ideal photonic Weyl metacrystal ("ideal" means that there are no additional states at the Weyl-node energy). The Weyl nodes of this metacrystal are stabilized by the screw rotation symmetry of space group 19. The authors argue that this design might be advantageous for further experimental studies of photonic Weyl materials. Cheng and Gao [8] study a non-interacting Λ/V-type dice model composed of three triangular sublattices. By considering certain nearest-neighbor and next-nearest-neighbor hopping terms, as well as a quasi-staggered on-site potential, they acquire the full phase diagrams for different energy band fillings. They find abundant topologically nontrivial phases with different Chern numbers and a metallic phase in several regimes. Nikolaev et al. [9] study the influence of uniaxial deformation on the band structure and topological properties of the multifold semimetal CoSi with large topological charges. The $\mathbf{k}\cdot\mathbf{p}$ Hamiltonian, which takes the deformation into account, is constructed from symmetry considerations near the Γ and R points of the Brillouin zone. The transformation of the multifold band crossings into nodes of other types with different topological charges, their shift in energy and in reciprocal space, and the tilt of the dispersion around the nodes are studied in detail, depending on the direction of uniaxial deformation. Polatkan and Uykur [10] present a theoretical study of the band structure and optical conductivity for another multifold semimetal, PdGa. They identify several characteristic features in the optical conductivity and relate their origin to the band structure. Yaresko and Pronin [11] calculate the *ab*-plane optical conductivity of the Weyl semimetal TaP and compare it to the experimental data. Based on these calculations, they propose an explanation of the strong low-energy peak observed in the experimental spectra: this peak originates from transitions between the almost parallel non-degenerate electronic bands split by spin-orbit coupling.

The other papers in this Special Issue report experimental findings. Dally et al. [12] present small-angle inelastic neutron scattering measurements of Fe_3Sn_2. Fe_3Sn_2 has recently been discovered to host room temperature skyrmionic bubbles and is known to have competing magnetic exchange interactions, correlated electron behavior, weak magnetocrystalline anisotropy, and lattice anisotropy. The results of Dally et al. reveal that, at elevated temperatures, there is an absence of significant magnetocrystalline anisotropy and that the system behaves as a nearly ideal isotropic exchange interaction ferromagnet. Hatnean et al. [13] report on the growth of large high-quality Ce-substituted SmB_6 crystals via the floating zone method. The topological properties of SmB_6 are currently being intensively discussed in relation to Kondo physics. Hence, the investigation of substituted

SmB$_6$ samples is of interest. The structural, magnetic and transport properties of single crystals with different Ce contents are investigated by Hatnean et al. using X-ray diffraction techniques, electrical resistivity and magnetization measurements. The authors find that the substitution of Sm with magnetic Ce does not lead to long-range magnetic ordering.

The remaining experimental reports focus on optics. Shuvaev et al. [14] present sub-terahertz measurements of the quantum anomalous Hall effect (QAHE). In the static regime, the QAHE is observed as a step in Hall resistivity. At optical frequencies, it is transformed into a step in the polarization rotation, with the size of this step being equal to the fine structure constant, $\alpha \approx 1/137$. The authors measure the polarization rotation in thin films of the topological insulator (Bi,Sb)$_2$Te$_3$ doped with Cr and observe the expected steps at temperatures below 20 K. However, due to material issues, the size of the steps only reaches up to 20% of the theoretical value (at 1.85 K). At millikelvin temperatures, full-size steps are anticipated. Kamenskyi et al. [15] perform magneto-optical measurements of the topological insulator Bi$_2$Te$_3$ in the terahertz frequency range in magnetic fields up to 10 T. They report on the observation of a cyclotron resonance mode and ascribe it to free bulk carriers. The width of the mode demonstrates a non-monotonous behavior in the magnetic field. The authors propose that the mode width is defined by two competing factors: impurity scattering and electron–phonon scattering, which exhibit opposite behaviors in applied magnetic fields. Another topological insulator, Bi$_2$Te$_2$Se, is investigated by Zhukova et al. [16] by mid- and near-infrared optical measurements. The optical conductivity of Bi$_2$Te$_2$Se is found to be dominated by bulk carriers and shows a linear-in-frequency increase at 0.5 to 0.8 eV. This linearity might be interpreted as a signature of the three-dimensional (bulk) Dirac bands; however, the band structure-based calculations performed by the authors show that transitions between bands with complex dispersions contribute instead to the inter-band optical conductivity at these frequencies and, hence, the observed linearity is accidental. These results warn against oversimplified interpretations of optical conductivity measurements in different Dirac materials. Finally, Schilling et al. [17] investigate the broadband optical conductivity of the two-dimensional Dirac material CaMnBi$_2$. They find that both components of the intraband conductivity follow a universal power law as a function of frequency at low temperatures. This conductivity scaling differs from the standard Drude-like behavior and might point toward quantum criticality in this system.

Overall, this Special Issue represents a few recent developments in the broad and growing field of topological material studies.

Acknowledgments: I am grateful to Dancy Yu for her editorial assistance in the production of this Special Issue and to Ece Uykur for proofreading the draft of this paper.

Conflicts of Interest: The author declares no conflict of interest.

References

1. Kane, C.L.; Mele, E.J. Z_2 Topological Order and the Quantum Spin Hall Effect. *Phys. Rev. Lett.* **2005**, *95*, 146802. [CrossRef] [PubMed]
2. Kane, C.L.; Mele, E.J. Quantum Spin Hall Effect in Graphene. *Phys. Rev. Lett.* **2005**, *95*, 226801. [CrossRef] [PubMed]
3. Haldane, F.D.M.; Raghu, S. Possible Realization of Directional Optical Waveguides in Photonic Crystals with Broken Time-Reversal Symmetry. *Phys. Rev. Lett.* **2008**, *100*, 013904. [CrossRef] [PubMed]
4. Wang, H.; Gupta, S.K.; Xie, B.; Lu, M. Topological photonic crystals: A review. *Front. Optoelectron.* **2020**, *13*, 50–72. [CrossRef]
5. McClarty, P. Topological Magnons: A Review. *arXiv* **2021**, arXiv:2106.01430.
6. Zhang, X.; Xiao, M.; Cheng, Y.; Lu, M.-H.; Christensen, J. Topological sound. *Commun. Phys.* **2018**, *1*, 97. [CrossRef]
7. Gao, W.; Wang, Y.-T. Ideal Photonic Weyl Nodes Stabilized by Screw Rotation Symmetry in Space Group 19. *Crystals* **2020**, *10*, 605. [CrossRef]
8. Cheng, S.; Gao, X. Topological Properties in a Λ/V-Type Dice Model. *Crystals* **2021**, *11*, 467. [CrossRef]
9. Nikolaev, S.; Pshenay-Severin, D.; Ivanov, Y.; Burkov, A. Effect of Deformation on Topological Properties of Cobalt Monosilicide. *Crystals* **2021**, *11*, 143. [CrossRef]
10. Polatkan, S.; Uykur, E. Optical Response of Chiral Multifold Semimetal PdGa. *Crystals* **2021**, *11*, 80. [CrossRef]
11. Yaresko, A.; Pronin, A.V. Low-Energy Optical Conductivity of TaP: Comparison of Theory and Experiment. *Crystals* **2021**, *11*, 567. [CrossRef]

12. Dally, R.L.; Phelan, D.; Bishop, N.; Ghimire, N.J.; Lynn, J.W. Isotropic Nature of the Metallic Kagome Ferromagnet Fe_3Sn_2 at High Temperatures. *Crystals* **2021**, *11*, 307. [CrossRef]
13. Hatnean, M.C.; Ahmad, T.; Walker, M.; Lees, M.R.; Balakrishnan, G. Crystal Growth by the Floating Zone Method of Ce-Substituted Crystals of the Topological Kondo Insulator SmB_6. *Crystals* **2020**, *10*, 827. [CrossRef]
14. Shuvaev, A.; Pan, L.; Zhang, P.; Wang, K.L.; Pimenov, A. Faraday Rotation Due to Quantum Anomalous Hall Effect in Cr-Doped $(Bi,Sb)_2Te_3$. *Crystals* **2021**, *11*, 154. [CrossRef]
15. Kamenskyi, D.L.; Pronin, A.V.; Benia, H.M.; Martovitskii, V.P.; Pervakov, K.S.; Selivanov, Y.G. Bulk Cyclotron Resonance in the Topological Insulator Bi_2Te_3. *Crystals* **2020**, *10*, 722. [CrossRef]
16. Zhukova, E.S.; Zhang, H.; Martovitskiy, V.P.; Selivanov, Y.G.; Gorshunov, B.P.; Dressel, M. Infrared Optical Conductivity of Bulk Bi_2Te_2Se. *Crystals* **2020**, *10*, 553. [CrossRef]
17. Schilling, M.B.; Wang, C.X.; Shi, Y.G.; Kremer, R.K.; Dressel, M.; Pronin, A.V. Fractional Power-Law Intraband Optical Conductivity in the Low-Dimensional Dirac Material $CaMnBi_2$. *Crystals* **2021**, *11*, 428. [CrossRef]

Article

Infrared Optical Conductivity of Bulk Bi$_2$Te$_2$Se

Elena S. Zhukova [1,2,*], **Hongbin Zhang** [3], **Victor P. Martovitskiy** [4], **Yurii G. Selivanov** [4], **Boris P. Gorshunov** [1,2] **and Martin Dressel** [1,2,*]

[1] Moscow Institute of Physics and Technology, National Research University, 141701 Dolgoprudny, Moscow Region, Russia; gorshunov.bp@mipt.ru
[2] 1. Physikalisches Institut, Universität Stuttgart, Pfaffenwaldring 57, 70569 Stuttgart, Germany
[3] Institute of Materials Science, Technische Universität Darmstadt, Jovanka-Bontschits-Str. 2, 64287 Darmstadt, Germany; hzhang@tmm.tu-darmstadt.de
[4] P. N. Lebedev Physical Institute of the RAS, 119991 Moscow, Russia; victormart@yandex.ru (V.P.M.); selivan@lebedev.ru (Y.G.S.)
* Correspondence: zhukova.es@mipt.ru (E.S.Z.); martin.dressel@pi1.physik.uni-stuttgart.de (M.D.)

Received: 8 June 2020; Accepted: 24 June 2020; Published: 28 June 2020

Abstract: Mid- and near-infrared measurements reveal that the optical conductivity of the three-dimensional topological insulator, Bi$_2$Te$_2$Se, is dominated by bulk carriers and shows a linear-in-frequency increase at 0.5 to 0.8 eV. This linearity might be interpreted as a signature of three-dimensional (bulk) Dirac bands; however, band-structure calculations show that transitions between bands with complex dispersion contribute instead to the inter-band optical conductivity at these frequencies and, hence, the observed linearity is accidental. These results warn against the oversimplified interpretations of optical-conductivity measurements in different Dirac materials.

Keywords: topological insulators; optical conductivity; Dirac materials

1. Introduction

Spin-orbit coupling often leads to the formation of linear bands in solids. Electrons in such bands (the Dirac electrons) manifest themselves in special ways in different experiments [1–5]. One of these manifestations is in their optical response: the contribution of a *d*-dimensional Dirac band to the inter-band optical conductivity, which is calculated to follow a simple power–law frequency dependence [6,7]:

$$\sigma(\omega) \propto \omega^{d-2}. \quad (1)$$

Such optical-conductivity behavior—unusual for conventional materials—has indeed been confirmed for (quasi)-2D electrons in graphene, graphite, and the line-node semimetal ZrSiS, where $\sigma(\omega) \approx const(\omega)$ was reported [8–10]. In turn, the 3D Dirac electrons in Dirac and Weyl semimetals, such as ZrTe$_5$, Cd$_3$As$_2$, and TaAs, provide the inter-band optical conductivity to be proportional to frequency, $\sigma(\omega) \propto \omega$ [11–13]. The linearity in $\sigma(\omega)$ over a broad frequency range in a 3D electron system is often considered as a "smoking gun" for Dirac physics. For example, Timusk et al. [14] suggested the presence of 3D Dirac fermions in a number of quasicrystals, based entirely on the observation of a linear $\sigma(\omega)$ in these materials.

Besides, enormous efforts have been made to investigate the symmetry-protected surface states of topological insulators [2,3]. However, the dominant physics of the bulk often obscures the surface properties and hence is generally considered as an obstacle for experiments targeting the surface states. Achieving dissipationless surface spin currents may be of primary importance for potential applications of topological insulators, nevertheless, investigations into bulk electronic properties are essential for understanding the complete picture of the topological-state formation [15].

Our experiments reveal that the bulk optical conductivity of Bi_2Te_2Se follows a linear frequency dependence in an appreciably broad spectral range. Based on band-structure calculations, we argue that this linearity is not due to transitions within (a) particular 3D linear band(s), but instead a result of contributions from the transitions between the bands with complex dispersion.

2. Materials and Methods

Bi_2Te_2Se bulk crystals were synthesized by a modified Bridgman method [16]. Highly purified (99.9999%) elemental starting materials (Bi, Te, and Se) (Chimmed, Moscow, Russia) were loaded in quartz ampules inside an inert-gas glove box in the stoichiometric ratio 2:2:1. The sealed evacuated ampules were kept at 850 °C for 24 h with periodic stirring to ensure the homogeneity of the melt, followed by a cooldown to 520 °C with a rate of 5 °C/h. The crystals were then annealed at 520 °C for six days. The typical crystal sizes obtained in this way were in the centimeter range. The crystals were cut into appropriate pieces for X-ray, Hall, and optical measurements (and kept in vacuum until the measurements).

Utilizing an X'Pert Pro Extended MRD X-ray diffractometer (PANalytical, Almelo, the Netherlands) we have confirmed the high structural quality of the crystals, see Figure 1. The free-carrier concentration and mobility were measured in a standard Hall geometry. Indium-soldered contacts were applied to razor-cut Hall bars with typical dimensions of $2 \times 0.5 \times 0.2$ mm^3. For all samples, the conduction was by n-type carriers. The properties of the sample, used in our infrared studies, are listed in Table 1.

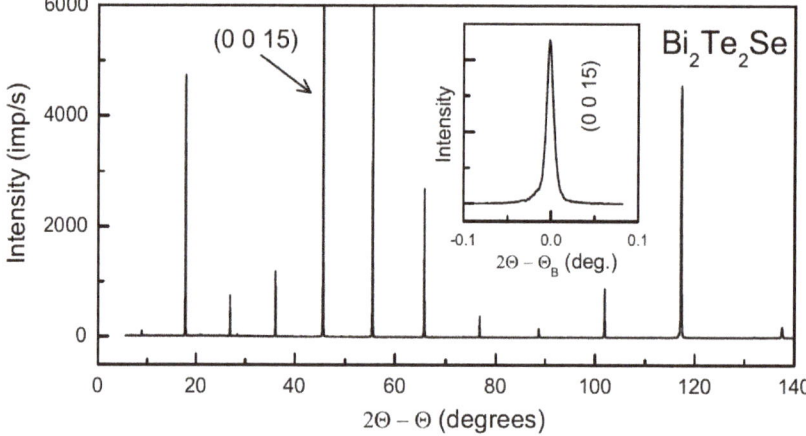

Figure 1. Bi_2Te_2Se X-ray diffraction pattern. Inset: Rocking curve for the (0 0 15) reflection peak.

Table 1. Room-temperature properties of the single-crystalline Bi_2Te_2Se sample used for the optical measurements. The mobility value is typical for the samples with such electron densities [17].

Lateral Dimensions	Thickness	Bulk electron Density	Mobility	Lattice Constant
5×5 mm^2	350 µm	1.0×10^{18} cm^{-3}	330 cm^2/Vs	29.766 Å

Optical reflectivity was measured from the (001) plane on freshly cleaved surfaces. The room-temperature experiments were performed in the mid- and near-infrared spectral ranges (600–8000 cm^{-1}, 75 meV–1 eV) with a Bruker Vertex 80v Fourier-transform infrared spectrometer (Bruker Corporation, Billerica, MA, USA). Freshly evaporated gold mirrors served for reference measurements. We used unpolarized light, because Bi_2Te_2Se possesses C_3 rotational symmetry along the [001] direction and hence the (001)-plane response, expressed via a second-rank tensor, such as optical conductivity, is isotropic.

3. Results and Discussion

In the top panel of Figure 2, we plot the raw reflectivity data recorded at 300 K. The reflectivity is very flat between 4000 and 8000 cm^{-1}. In order to obtain the optical conductivity from the reflectivity data, we first tried to fit the measured spectra using a standard Drude–Lorentz procedure [18]. However, we found that such flat reflectivity is impossible to fit in an acceptable way with a physically meaningful number of Lorentzians. In an alternative approach, we used Kuzmenko's variational dielectric function method [19], which produces optical functions with an accuracy equivalent to Kramers–Kronig. For the sake of convenience, the variable part of the dielectric response function was described by a large number of Lorentzians. Justification and details of this approach can be found in [20]. Similar to the Kramers–Kronig analysis, this method gives less accurate results near the edges of the experimental window. Thus, the results below approximately 2000 cm^{-1} and above 7000 cm^{-1} cannot be considered as accurate.

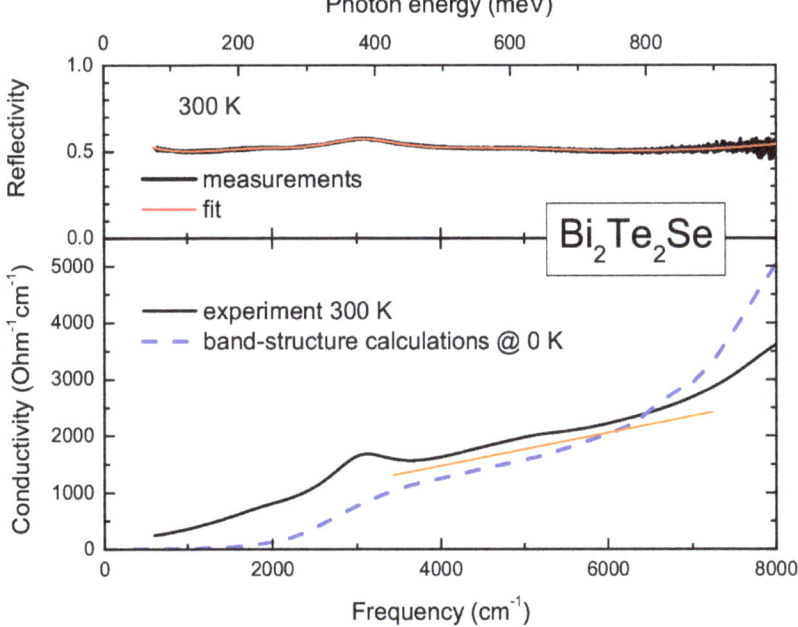

Figure 2. Top panel: [001]-plane reflectivity of Bi$_2$Te$_2$Se at 300 K: measurements (black line) and fit (red line). Bottom panel: bulk optical conductivity (real part) of Bi$_2$Te$_2$Se, as obtained from the reflectivity fit (black straight line) and the inter-band portion of optical conductivity, computed from the band structure of Figure 3 at 0 K (dashed line), as detailed in the text. The thin orange line is to mimic a linear increase in frequency.

The real part of the optical conductivity obtained from this fit is plotted in the bottom panel of Figure 2. The eye-catching feature of the figure is the linear increase in $\sigma(\omega)$ at 4000 to 7000 cm^{-1} (~0.5–0.8 eV).

Let us first argue that the observed optical conductivity originates from the bulk of Bi$_2$Te$_2$Se. In Bi$_2$Te$_2$Se, the surface Dirac point lies inside the bulk band gap [21,22] and metallic surface states have been experimentally confirmed [21–27]. Nevertheless, Bi$_2$Te$_2$Se samples usually possess a significant concentration of bulk charges due to the basically unavoidable presence of defects, the so-called self-doping [26–30]. This is also the case for our sample—its bulk carrier concentration is rather large, as shown in Table 1. Furthermore, the skin depth, calculated from the complex optical conductivity, is above 30 nm at any measurement frequency, while the thickness of the topologically non-trivial surface layer is believed to be around 1 nm [3]. Hence, the response detected by our optical measurements is due to the bulk.

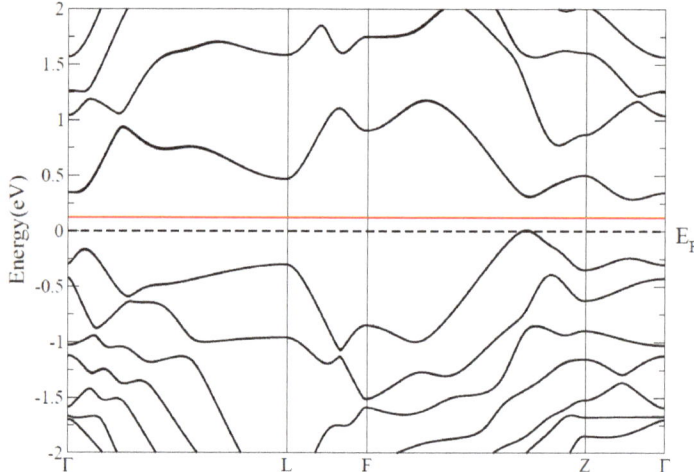

Figure 3. Band structure of Bi_2Te_2Se. Black dashed (red solid) horizontal line indicates the original (shifted) Fermi energy.

Let us also note that, at elevated temperatures, the optical detection of surface carriers in Bi_2Te_2Se, as well as in similar compounds, such as Bi_2Te_3 and Bi_2Se_3, remains so far elusive, while bulk carriers clearly manifest themselves in the optical response of Bi_2Te_2Se [16,28–30] and related compounds [31–35]. Reijnders et al. have reported on a mixed (surface plus bulk) optical response in Bi_2Te_2Se for low frequencies at temperatures below some 40 K [30]. However, at room temperature, as well as at frequencies above 2000 cm^{-1}, their data are perfectly reconciled with entirely bulk response.

Coming back to the linear $\sigma(\omega)$, it is tempting to interpret it in terms of Equation (1), namely, as a signature of a 3D Dirac band (because our $\sigma(\omega)$ reflects the bulk response). Such a band, however, is not expected to appear in the bulk of Bi_2Te_2Se [36]. We would like to point out that all the available optical conductivity spectra (ours and those previously reported in [16,28–30]) are rather similar to each other, although the linearity of $\sigma(\omega)$ is most apparent in our data. The deviations between the data sets can be assigned, for example, to the abovementioned difference in the exact Fermi-level position in different samples of Bi_2Te_2Se. In order to check the origin of the linear frequency increase in $\sigma(\omega)$, we performed band-structure calculations for Bi_2Te_2Se and then calculated its inter-band optical conductivity.

The band-structure and optical-conductivity calculations were performed using the full potential linear augmented plane-wave method, as implemented in the WIEN2k code [37]. The exchange-correlation functional is parameterized using the GGA approximation [38]. The self-consistent charge-densities and optical-conductivity calculations were done with 400 and 2000 k-points in the whole Brillouin zone, respectively. The results of the calculations are shown in Figures 2 and 3. The obtained band structure is basically identical to the one reported in [36]. In order to be reconciled with the bulk electron concentration (the self-doping problem mentioned above), the Fermi level needs to be shifted upwards, as compared to the undoped situation, as shown in Figure 3. From the figure, it is apparent that there is no truly Dirac band in the bulk of Bi_2Te_2Se.

The calculated optical conductivity is shown as a dashed line in Figure 2. Taking into account the generally poor reproducibility of the experimental infrared optical conductivity by first-principles calculations (cf., e.g., in [39,40]), the agreement between theory and experiment can be considered as fairly good. Further, we should point out that the computed σ(ω) has no intra-band (free-carrier) contribution. Thus, it is not surprising that the low-frequency experimental σ(ω) is larger than the theoretical line. Additionally, the effect of temperature broadening is absent in the calculations. Such broadening would make the smooth step at around 3000 cm^{-1} even broader [10]. Taking into account the mentioned issues in the computations of σ(ω) is outside of our capacity and beyond the scope of the paper. The important result of our computations is that the linear σ(ω) is nicely reproduced at 4000 to 6000 cm^{-1} (~0.5–0.75 eV). Thus, we can conclude that this linearity comes as a cumulative effect of transitions between the bands, which do not have a simple linear dispersion. We note that recent measurements of $BaCoS_2$ and GdPtBi provide other examples of linear σ(ω) not due to a simple 3D Dirac band [41,42].

4. Conclusions

We have experimentally found that the bulk optical conductivity of Bi_2Te_2Se is linear in frequency at 4000 to 7000 cm^{-1} (~0.5–0.8 eV). Our computations demonstrate that this linearity is not due to transitions within a 3D Dirac band, but emerges as a cumulative effect of transitions between the bands with complex dispersion. Obviously, similar situations can appear in other systems and, thus, suggestions for Dirac physics based on optical-conductivity measurements have to be made cautiously.

Author Contributions: Infrared measurements, E.S.Z. and B.P.G.; sample preparation, V.P.M. and Y.G.S.; data analysis, E.S.Z.; writing—original draft preparation, E.S.Z.; writing—review and editing, H.Z., M.D., and B.P.G.; project administration, B.P.G.; funding acquisition, Y.G.S. M.D., and B.P.G. All authors have read and agreed to the published version of the manuscript.

Funding: This work was supported by the Ministry of Science and Higher Education of the Russian Federation (Program "5 top 100"), by the Russian Science Foundation (grant No. 17-12-01544) and by the Deutsche Forschungsgemeinschaft (DFG) via grants No. DR228/51 and No. ZH559/2-1.

Conflicts of Interest: The authors declare no conflict of interest. The funders had no role in the design of the study; in the collection, analyses, or interpretation of data; in the writing of the manuscript, or in the decision to publish the results.

References

1. Neto, A.C.; Guinea, F.; Peres, N.; Novoselov, K.S.; Geim, A.K. The electronic properties of graphene. *Rev. Mod. Phys.* **2009**, *81*, 109. [CrossRef]
2. Hasan, M.Z.; Kane, C.L. Colloquium: Topological insulators. *Rev. Mod. Phys.* **2010**, *82*, 3045. [CrossRef]
3. Qi, X.L.; Zhang, S.C. Topological insulators and superconductors. *Rev. Mod. Phys.* **2011**, *83*, 1057. [CrossRef]
4. Wehling, T.O.; Black-Schaffer, A.M.; Balatsky, A.V. Dirac materials. *Adv. Phys.* **2014**, *63*, 1. [CrossRef]
5. Armitage, N.P.; Mele, E.J.; Vishwanath, A. Weyl and Dirac semimetals in three-dimensional solids. *Rev. Mod. Phys.* **2018**, *90*, 015001. [CrossRef]
6. Hosur, P.; Parameswaran, S.A.; Vishwanath, A. Charge transport in Weyl semimetals. *Phys. Rev. Lett.* **2012**, *108*, 046602. [CrossRef] [PubMed]
7. Bacsi, A.; Virosztek, A. Low-frequency optical conductivity in graphene and in other scale-invariant two-band systems. *Phys. Rev. B* **2013**, *87*, 125425. [CrossRef]
8. Kuzmenko, A.B.; van Heumen, E.; Carbone, F.; van der Marel, D. Universal Optical conductance of graphite. *Phys. Rev. Lett.* **2008**, *100*, 117401. [CrossRef]
9. Mak, K.F.; Sfeir, M.Y.; Wu, Y.; Lui, C.H.; Misewich, J.A.; Heinz, T.F. Measurement of the Optical conductivity of graphene. *Phys. Rev. Lett.* **2008**, *101*, 196405. [CrossRef]
10. Schilling, M.B.; Schoop, L.M.; Lotsch, B.V.; Dressel, M.; Pronin, A.V. Flat Optical Conductivity in ZrSiS due to two-dimensional Dirac bands. *Phys. Rev. Lett.* **2017**, *119*, 187401. [CrossRef]
11. Chen, R.Y.; Zhang, S.J.; Schneeloch, J.A.; Zhang, C.; Li, Q.; Gu, G.D.; Wang, N.L. Optical spectroscopy study of the three-dimensional Dirac semimetal $ZrTe_5$. *Phys. Rev. B* **2015**, *92*, 075107. [CrossRef]
12. Neubauer, D.; Carbotte, J.P.; Nateprov, A.A.; Löhle, A.; Dressel, M.; Pronin, A.V. Interband optical conductivity of the [001]-oriented Dirac semimetal Cd_3As_2. *Phys. Rev. B* **2016**, *93*, 121202. [CrossRef]

13. Xu, B.; Dai, Y.M.; Zhao, L.X.; Wang, K.; Yang, R.; Zhang, W.; Liu, J.Y.; Xiao, H.; Chen, G.F.; Taylor, A.J.; et al. Optical spectroscopy of the Weyl semimetal TaAs. *Phys. Rev. B* **2016**, *93*, 121110. [CrossRef]
14. Timusk, T.; Carbotte, J.P.; Homes, C.C.; Basov, D.N.; Sharapov, S.G. Three-dimensional Dirac fermions in quasicrystals as seen via optical conductivity. *Phys. Rev. B* **2013**, *87*, 235121. [CrossRef]
15. Xu, S.-Y.; Xia, Y.; Wray, L.A.; Jia, S.; Meier, F.; Dil, J.H.; Osterwalder, J.; Slomski, B.; Bansil, A.; Lin, H.; et al. Topological phase transition and texture inversion in a tunable topological insulator. *Science* **2011**, *332*, 560. [CrossRef]
16. Aleshchenko, Y.A.; Muratov, A.V.; Pavlova, V.V.; Selivanov, Y.G.; Chizhevskii, E.G. Infrared spectroscopy of Bi_2Te_2Se. *JETP Lett.* **2014**, *99*, 187. [CrossRef]
17. Jia, S.; Ji, H.; Climent-Pascual, E.; Fuccillo, M.K.; Charles, M.E.; Xiong, J.; Ong, N.P.; Cava, R.J. Low-carrier-concentration crystals of the topological insulator Bi_2Te_2Se. *Phys. Rev. B* **2011**, *84*, 235206. [CrossRef]
18. Dressel, M.; Grüner, G. *Electrodynamics of Solids*; Cambridge University Press: Cambridge, UK, 2002.
19. Kuzmenko, A.B. Kramers–Kronig constrained variational analysis of optical spectra. *Rev. Sci. Instrum.* **2005**, *76*, 083108. [CrossRef]
20. Chanda, G.; Lobo, R.P.S.M.; Schachinger, E.; Wosnitza, J.; Naito, M.; Pronin, A.V. Optical study of superconducting Pr_2CuO_x with x≃4. *Phys. Rev. B* **2014**, *90*, 024503. [CrossRef]
21. Xu, S.-Y.; Wray, L.A.; Xia, Y.; Shankar, R.; Petersen, A.; Fedorov, A.; Lin, H.; Bansil, A.; Hor, Y.S.; Grauer, D.; et al. Discovery of several large families of topological insulator classes with backscattering-suppressed spin-polarized single-Dirac-cone on the surface. *arXiv* **2010**, arXiv:1007.5111.
22. Ren, Z.; Taskin, A.A.; Sasaki, S.; Segawa, K.; Ando, Y. Large bulk resistivity and surface quantum oscillations in the topological insulator Bi_2Te_2Se. *Phys. Rev. B* **2010**, *82*, 241306. [CrossRef]
23. Xiong, J.; Petersen, A.C.; Qu, D.; Hor, Y.S.; Cava, R.J.; Ong, N.P. Quantum oscillations in a topological insulator Bi_2Te_2Se with large bulk resistivity (6 Ωcm). *Physica E* **2012**, *44*, 917. [CrossRef]
24. Li, Z.; Chen, T.; Pan, H.; Song, F.; Wang, B.; Han, J.; Qin, Y.; Wang, X.; Zhang, R.; Wan, J.; et al. Two-dimensional universal conductance fluctuations and the electron-phonon interaction of surface states in Bi_2Te_2Se microflakes. *Sci. Rep.* **2012**, *2*, 595. [CrossRef] [PubMed]
25. Tian, J.; Miotkowski, I.; Hong, S.; Chen, Y.P. Electrical injection and detection of spin-polarized currents in topological insulator Bi_2Te_2Se. *Sci. Rep.* **2015**, *5*, 14293. [CrossRef]
26. Arakane, T.; Sato, T.; Souma, S.; Kosaka, K.; Nakayama, K.; Komatsu, M.; Takahashi, T.; Ren, Z.; Segawa, K.; Ando, Y. Tunable Dirac cone in the topological insulator $Bi_{2-x}Sb_xTe_{3-y}Se_y$. *Nat. Commun.* **2011**, *3*, 636. [CrossRef]
27. Neupane, M.; Xu, S.-Y.; Wray, L.A.; Petersen, A.; Shankar, R.; Alidoust, N.; Liu, C.; Fedorov, A.; Ji, H.; Allred, J.M.; et al. Topological surface states and Dirac point tuning in ternary topological insulators. *Phys. Rev. B* **2012**, *85*, 235406. [CrossRef]
28. di Pietro, P.; Vitucci, F.M.; Nicoletti, D.; Baldassarre, L.; Calvani, P.; Cava, R.; Hor, Y.S.; Schade, U.; Lupi, S. Ab initio studying of topological insulator Bi_2Se_3 under the stress. *Phys. Rev. B* **2012**, *86*, 045439. [CrossRef]
29. Akrap, A.; Tran, M.; Ubaldini, A.; Teyssier, J.; Giannini, E.; van der Marel, D.; Lerch, P.; Homes, C.C. Optical properties of Bi_2Te_2Se at ambient and high pressures. *Phys. Rev. B* **2012**, *86*, 235207. [CrossRef]
30. Reijnders, A.A.; Tian, Y.; Sandilands, L.J.; Pohl, G.; Kivlichan, I.D.; Zhao, S.Y.F.; Jia, S.; Charles, M.E.; Cava, R.J.; Alidoust, N.; et al. Optical evidence of surface state suppression in Bi-based topological insulators. *Phys. Rev. B* **2014**, *89*, 075138. [CrossRef]
31. LaForge, A.D.; Frenzel, A.; Pursley, B.C.; Lin, T.; Liu, X.; Shi, J.; Basov, D.N. Optical characterization of Bi_2Se_3 in a magnetic field: Infrared evidence for magnetoelectric coupling in a topological insulator material. *Phys. Rev. B* **2010**, *81*, 125120. [CrossRef]
32. Sushkov, A.B.; Jenkins, G.S.; Schmadel, D.C.; Butch, N.P.; Paglione, J.; Drew, H.D. Far-infrared cyclotron resonance and Faraday effect in Bi_2Se_3. *Phys. Rev. B* **2010**, *82*, 125110. [CrossRef]
33. Dordevic, S.V.; Wolf, M.S.; Stojilovic, N.; Lei, H.; Petrovic, C. Signatures of charge inhomogeneities in the infrared spectra of topological insulators Bi_2Se_3, Bi_2Te_3 and Sb_2Te_3. *J. Phys. Condens. Matter* **2013**, *25*, 075501. [CrossRef] [PubMed]
34. Chapler, B.C.; Post, K.W.; Richardella, A.R.; Lee, J.S.; Tao, J.; Samarth, N.; Basov, D.N. Infrared electrodynamics and ferromagnetism in the topological semiconductors Bi_2Te_3 and Mn-doped Bi_2Te_3. *Phys. Rev. B* **2014**, *89*, 235308. [CrossRef]

35. Post, K.W.; Lee, Y.S.; Chapler, B.C.; Schafgans, A.A.; Novak, M.; Taskin, A.A.; Segawa, K.; Goldflam, M.D.; Stinson, H.T.; Ando, Y.; et al. Infrared probe of the bulk insulating response in $Bi_{2-x}Sb_xTe_{3-y}Se_y$ topological insulator alloys. *Phys. Rev. B* **2015**, *91*, 165202. [CrossRef]
36. Wang, L.-L.; Johnson, D.D. Ternary tetradymite compounds as topological insulators. *Phys. Rev. B* **2011**, *83*, 241309. [CrossRef]
37. Available online: http://www.wien2k.at (accessed on 6 June 2020).
38. Perdew, J.P.; Burke, K.; Ernzerhof, M. Generalized gradient approximation made simple. *Phys. Rev. Lett.* **1996**, *77*, 3865. [CrossRef]
39. Frenzel, A.J.; Homes, C.C.; Gibson, Q.D.; Shao, Y.M.; Post, K.W.; Charnukha, A.; Cava, R.J.; Basov, D.N. Anisotropic electrodynamics of type-II Weyl semimetal candidate WTe_2. *Phys. Rev. B* **2017**, *95*, 245140. [CrossRef]
40. Neubauer, D.; Yaresko, A.; Li, W.; Löhle, A.; Hübner, R.; Schilling, M.B.; Shekhar, C.; Felser, C.; Dressel, M.; Pronin, A.V. Optical conductivity of the Weyl semimetal NbP. *Phys. Rev. B* **2018**, *98*, 195203. [CrossRef]
41. Santos-Cottin, D.; Klein, Y.; Werner, P.; Miyake, T.; Medici, L.d.; Gauzzi, A.; Lobo, R.P.S.M.; Casula, M. Linear behavior of the optical conductivity and incoherent charge transport in $BaCoS_2$. *Phys. Rev. Materials* **2018**, *2*, 105001. [CrossRef]
42. Hütt, F.; Yaresko, A.; Schilling, M.B.; Shekhar, C.; Felser, C.; Dressel, M.; Pronin, A.V. Linear-in-frequency optical conductivity in GdPtBi due to transitions near the triple points. *Phys. Rev. Lett.* **2018**, *121*, 176601. [CrossRef]

© 2020 by the authors. Licensee MDPI, Basel, Switzerland. This article is an open access article distributed under the terms and conditions of the Creative Commons Attribution (CC BY) license (http://creativecommons.org/licenses/by/4.0/).

Article

Ideal Photonic Weyl Nodes Stabilized by Screw Rotation Symmetry in Space Group 19

Wenlong Gao [1],* and Yao-Ting Wang [2,3],*

1. Department of Physics, Paderborn University, Warburger Straße 100, 33098 Paderborn, Germany
2. Department of Physics, Imperial College London, London SW7 2AZ, UK
3. Department of Mathematics, Imperial College London, London SW7 2AZ, UK
* Correspondence: bhamwxg334@gmail.com (W.G.); ywang14@ic.ac.uk (Y.-T.W.)

Received: 20 April 2020; Accepted: 6 July 2020; Published: 12 July 2020

Abstract: Topological photonics have developed in recent years since the seminal discoveries of topological insulators in condensed matter physics for electrons. Among the numerous studies, photonic Weyl nodes have been studied very recently due to their intriguing surface Fermi arcs, Chiral zero modes and scattering properties. In this article, we propose a new design of an ideal photonic Weyl node metacrystal, meaning no excessive states are present at the Weyl nodes' frequency. The Weyl node is stabilized by the screw rotation symmetry of space group 19. Group theory analysis is utilized to reveal how the Weyl nodes are spawned from line nodes in a higher symmetry metacrystal of space group 61. The minimum four Weyl nodes' complex for time reversal invariant systems is found, which is a realistic photonic Weyl node metacrystal design compatible with standard printed circuit board techniques and is a complement to the few existing ideal photonic Weyl node designs and could be further utilized in studies of Weyl physics, for instance, Chiral zero modes and scatterings.

Keywords: Weyl nodes; screw rotation symmetry; line node; space group 19; space group 61

1. Introduction

Weyl nodes (WN) are linear band crossings existing in odd dimensions [1–3]. Three dimensional WN have been extensively exploited in recent years for their intriguing physics. As a drain/source of Berry curvatures, WN hold a quantized topological index, Chern number, of ±1. Due to the stability of the topological index, WN are extremely tolerant to disorders and can be gapped only by the coalesce and annihilation between WN with opposite Chern numbers. WN are also renowned for their Chiral Anomaly Magnetoresistance [4–6], Fermi arc surface states [7–15] and nonlinear Hall effects [16–18]. More recently, topological nodes beyond WN [19], for instance, Dirac points [20–26], spin-1, spin-2/3 WN and double WN [27–30] have also gained significant progress in research.

In photonics, WN have been exploited in photonic crystals [31–34], metamaterials [35–37], magnetized plasma [38,39] and in synthetic spaces [40,41]. Despite substantial studies, there have been only a few ideal WN designs. Ideal WN are salient because no excessive modes are present at the WN frequency, which is beneficial for revealing the properties of WN without disturbance coming from excessive bands [42]. In this article, we proposed a printed circuit board (PCB) technique compatible ideal WN metacrystal functioning in the millimeter wavelength regime (~36 GHz). Group theory analysis shows that the WN are stabilized by screw rotation symmetry in space group (SG) 19, and are spawned from ideal line nodes (LN) in SG 61. Fermi arcs connecting WN with opposite Chern numbers are also found.

2. Results

The metacrystals we propose comprise two double-layer PCB boards in one primitive cell. The primitive cell's dimension is $3 \times 3 \times 3$ mm^3. Each PCB board layer's thickness is 1 mm, hence, thickness of the dielectric layer between the PCB boards is 0.5 mm and has a relative permittivity of 2.2, which is within the common PCB board material Teflon's parameter range. The PCB board's relative permittivity is 2.2 as well. All the metallic layers have the standard 37 μm thickness and are assumed to work as perfect electric conductors within the frequency range of interest. The metacrystal is shown in Figure 1a. Each PCB layer consists of double-layer metallic wire-like structures and the layers are electrically connected by metal-coated 0.2 mm radius through holes. The metallic pads connecting the through holes to the wires have radii of 0.4 mm. Note that in the figures, the primitive cell in the x–y direction is denoted by the red dashed lines. For clarity, the two layers are not drawn together, though it should be remembered that in the real structure, the two layers are gapped by a merely 0.5 mm thickness dielectric board. The designed structure belongs to SG 61 (Pbca). It will be shown later in the article that this metacrystal could be reduced to SG 19 (P2$_1$2$_1$2$_1$) by introducing a deformation, as shown in Figure 2a, of which the inversion symmetry and glide symmetries are broken, and are later essential for the creation of the WN.

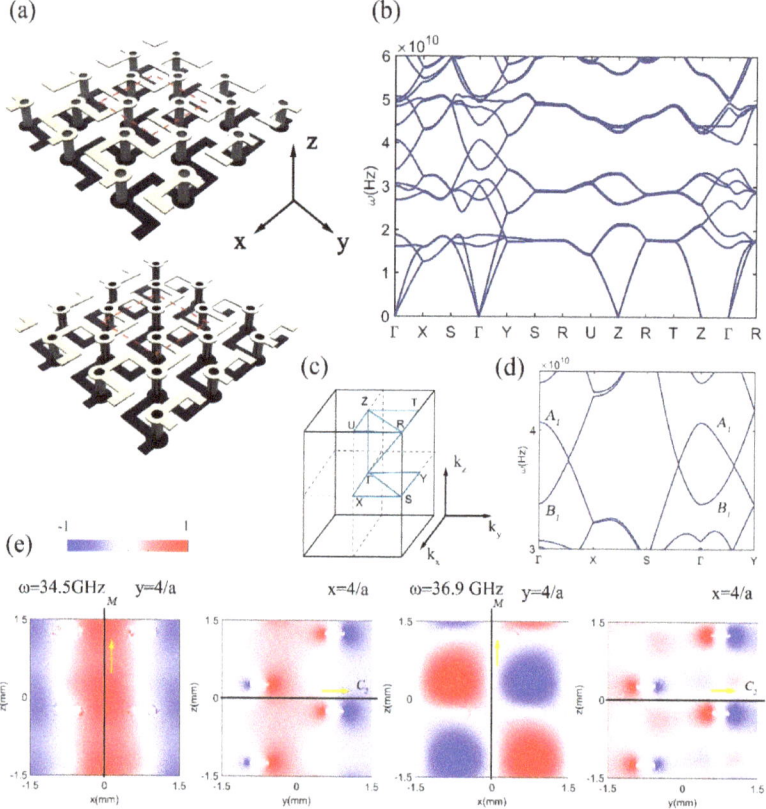

Figure 1. (a) First and second layer structure of the line node metacrystal. (b) Band diagram of the line node structure. (c) Detailed band diagram of the line node. (d) Brillouin zone and the path for band diagram. (e) E_x field components of the line nodes eigen modes found at $k_y = \frac{\pi}{2a}$, $k_x = 0$, $k_z = 0$ and the frequency ω at 34.5 and 36.9 GHz, respectively.

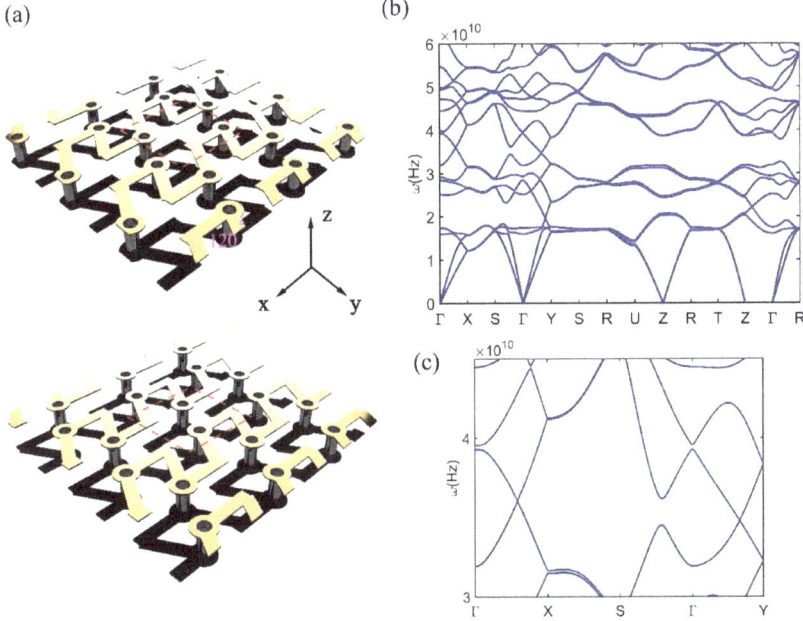

Figure 2. (a) First and second layer of the perturbed metacrystal structure. (b) Band diagram of the perturbed metacrystal. (c) Detailed band diagram of the metacrystal around the Weyl node frequency. The Weyl nodes are found on the ΓX and ΓY high symmetry lines, and the band crossings at other momentums are gapped.

2.1. Line Node from SG 61

Without the deformation, the metacrystal structure belongs to SG 61, whose group representatives are translational symmetry **T**, three glide symmetries $G_{x,y,z}$, three screw rotation symmetries $S_{2,x,y,z}$, and inversion symmetry P. The nonsymmorphic group operations are expressed explicitly as:

$$G_x(x,y,z) \to \left(-x, y, z+\frac{1}{2}\right)$$

$$G_y(x,y,z) \to \left(x+\frac{1}{2}, -y, z\right)$$

$$G_z(x,y,z) \to \left(x, y+\frac{1}{2}, -z\right)$$

$$S_{2x}(x,y,z) \to \left(x+\frac{1}{2}, -y, -z+\frac{1}{2}\right)$$

$$S_{2y}(x,y,z) \to \left(-x, y+\frac{1}{2}, -z\right)$$

$$S_{2z}(x,y,z) \to \left(-x+\frac{1}{2}, -y, z+\frac{1}{2}\right)$$

Nonsymmorphic group operations have been extensively used to protect degeneracies at the boundaries of the Brillouin zone beyond the capabilities of point group [43,44]. A band diagram of the metacrystal is given in Figure 1b, whose sweeping path is given in Figure 1c, and presents band crossings along the high symmetry lines ΓX $S\Gamma$ and ΓY that is line node (LN) degeneracy. Noticeably, the band diagram is pseudo-gapped for the LN, meaning no other excessive bands can be found around the LN frequency at other sites in the Brillouin zone. Furthermore, on the edge of the Brillouin zone (RS, RU and RT high symmetry lines), Dirac nodal lines are found, featuring four-fold degeneracy on the whole edges [45].

2.2. Group Theory Analysis

Since the LN is due to an accidental degeneracy that resides on the high symmetry line/plane, the two bands consisting of LN degeneracy are expected to belong to different irreducible group representations. On the high symmetry lines ΓX and ΓY, the little group reduced to $G_{\Gamma X} = \{E, S_{2y}, G_x, G_z, T\}$ and $G_{\Gamma Y} = \{E, S_{2x}, G_y, G_z, T\}$, respectively. Despite the existence of the half unit cell translations within the nonsymmorphic operations, the coset groups $G_{\Gamma X}/T$, $G_{\Gamma Y}/T$ of the little groups are found to be isomorphic to simple point group C_{2v}, whose character and compatability tables are given below in Tables 1 and 2. Note that on the ΓX and ΓY high symmetry lines, the σ_v mirror operation are σ_y and σ_x while σ'_v is σ_z.

Table 1. Character table of group C_{2v}.

C_{2v}	E	C_2	σ_v	σ'_v
A_1	1	1	1	1
A_2	1	1	-1	-1
B_1	1	-1	1	-1
B_2	1	-1	-1	1

Table 2. Compatibility table of group C_{2v}.

C_{2v}	C_2	C_v	C'_v
A_1	A	A'	A'
A_2	A	A''	A''
B_1	B	A'	A''
B_2	B	A''	A'

Field distributions of the electrical component $e_x = E_x e^{-ikr}$ on the momentums half way on ΓX and ΓY are given in Figure 1e. Note that after multiplying the phase factor e^{-ikr}, e_x is the periodic function in the primitive cell. The left two and the right two images belong to the same frequency, respectively. In the figures, the mirror plane and the rotation axis are illustrated by the solid black lines, and the half unit cell translations related to the nonsymmorphic group operations are illustrated by the yellow arrow. In the left two figures in Figure 1e, it can be inspected that the state is an even state under the glide operation, and an odd state under the screw rotation operation from their (0 1 0) and (1 0 0) direction's fields. The group representation is, thus, B_1 according to Table 1. Whereas, for the other state consisting the LN, it is odd under the glide operation and even under the screw rotation operation, meaning the group representation is A_1.

2.3. Weyl Point from SG 19

What the group theory analysis can show is that after introducing certain structure deformation, whether the band crossing is kept or gapped can be predicted. Introducing the deformation shown in Figure 2a will essentially reduce the original SG 61 to SG 19, since the only remaining symmetries are the three screw rotations. Therefore, on the ΓX and ΓY high symmetry lines, the little groups are isomorphic to point group C_2 (Table 2). In the compatibility relation in Table 2, A_1 and B_1 can be reduced to different irreducible representations A and B, meaning the band crossings are kept, while gapped when k is away from the high symmetry lines.

Instead, if the original metacrystal is reduced to SG 29 by keeping $S_{x,y}$ and G_z, the isomorphic point group is C'_v in the compatibility relation in Table 2. The irreducible representations are A' for both the bands, meaning the LN is immediately gapped. This is consistent with the fact that Weyl nodes cannot be found on mirror planes since mirror operations can flip the chirality of the Weyl nodes. The band structure of the SG 29 metacrystal is given in Figure 3, showing a full band gap around 36 GHz.

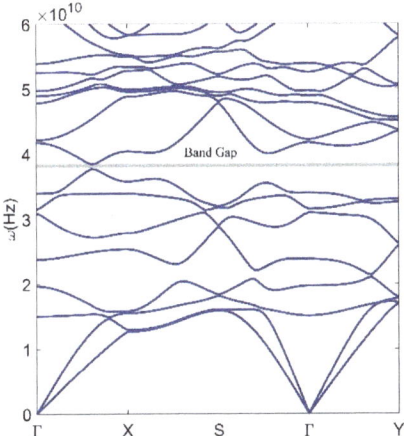

Figure 3. Band structure of the SG 29 metacrystal.

2.4. Surface States of the LN and the WN

It has been well understood that LN and WN hold surface states. LN hold the 'drumhead' surface states and are normally flat bands that could enhance interactions and are promising for high temperature superconductivity. The WN, on the other hand, hold the so-called Fermi arcs that have been exploited in their intriguing transport properties and unconventional quantum Hall effects [14].

To explore the surface states of the metacrystal, we created super cell configurations that are periodic in the x and y direction and are confined with perfect electrical conductors (PEC) with 10 unit cells in the z-direction. The results are illustrated in Figure 4 and the configuration of the projected surface Brillouin is give in Figure 5. For the unperturbed LN metacrystal, surface states that are reminiscences of the drumhead surface states are found, while for the WN metacrystal, Fermi arcs are found around the momentums where LN are found (red dots in Figure 4b).

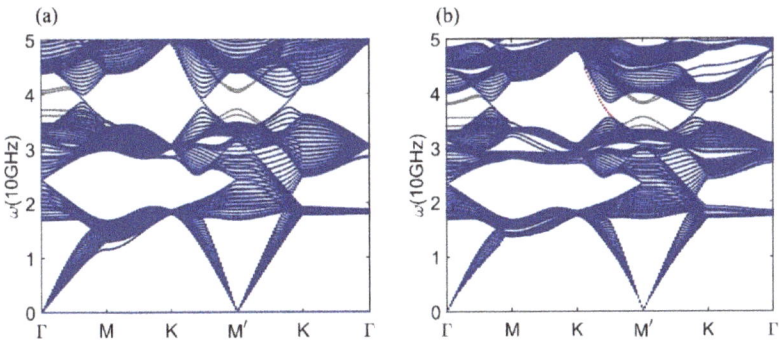

Figure 4. (**a**) Surface states (gray) and projected bulk band structure of the line node metacrystal in SG 61. (**b**) Surface states (gray/red) and projected bulk band structure of the line node metacrystal in SG 61; the topological Fermi arcs connecting the Weyl nodes are in red.

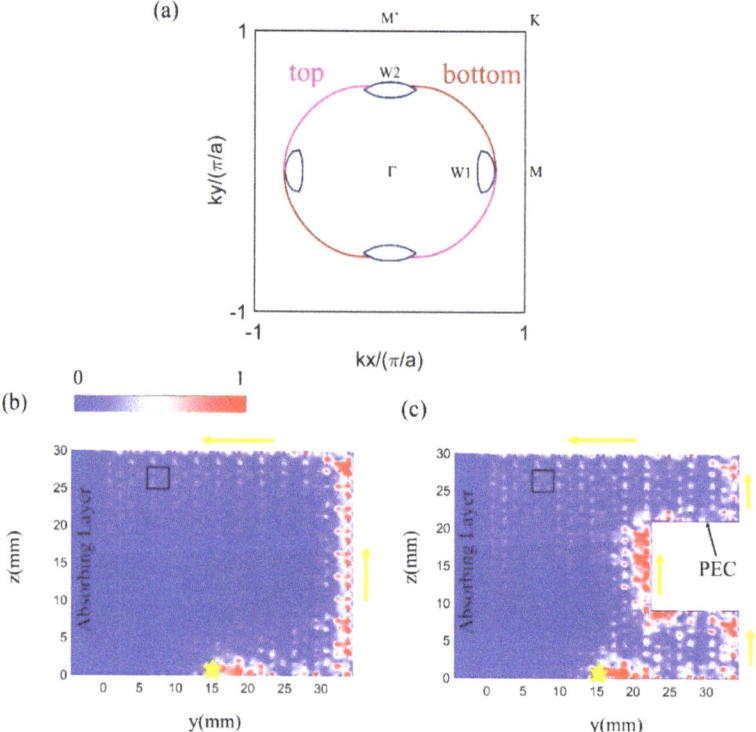

Figure 5. (a) Equi-frequency contour of the projected Weyl nodes and the Fermi arcs. Red and Magenta lines are on the top and bottom surface, respectively. (b,c) Excitation of topological fermi arc surface states with and without a square-shaped defect. Source is an x direction line current fixing the k_x at $0.2\pi/a$, marked by the yellow pentagram. The metacrystals are bounded by the perfect electric conductor (PEC) boundary condition. The unit cell is outlined by the solid black line box.

At a fixed frequency (36.5 GHz in Figure 5), Fermi arcs are found to connect WN with opposite Chern numbers (WN1 and WN2 located on the k_x and k_y axis, respectively), which are the results of the integral of Berry curvatures on a closed surface that include a WN [1]. The Fermi arcs are illustrated by the magenta and red lines that are residing on the top and the bottom surfaces, respectively. Figure 5b shows the real space field distribution of the topological surface state excited by a line current source that fixes the k_x at $0.2\pi/a$. The unidirectionality of the surface state propagation is consistent to the calculated equi-frequency contour in Figure 5a. Figure 5c shows the same surface state excitation simulation with an extra square-shaped defect. Again, the unidirectionality demonstrates the topological robustness of the fermi arc surfaces.

3. Discussion

Our design has shown how to obtain WN in SG 19 from LN in SG 61. The pure PCB layered design could also benefit the tunings of the WN. In Figure 6, we show the band diagrams of the WN metacrystal with various z-direction periods. Note that the PCB layers' thicknesses are conserved at 1 mm and only the interlayer dielectric boards' thickness is changed. Intriguingly, locations of the WN in the Brillouin zone can be effectively tuned by the periodicity. Note that when the thickness is reduced to below 4.8 mm, the WN coalesce and annihilate. The highly sensitive locations of the WN to the periodicity could be used to generate giant effective magnetic fields in the WN metacrystal by introducing a gradually changing thickness. Since photons do not respond to actual magnetic fields, effective magnetic fields are crucial for mimicking the physical effects of real magnetic fields, for example, Landau quantization and chiral zero modes [46,47].

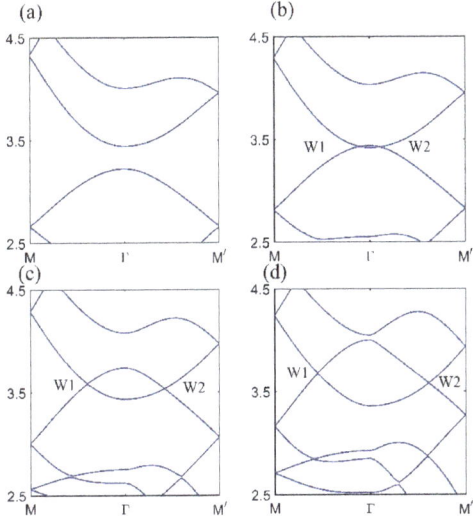

Figure 6. Band diagrams of the Weyl node for various unit cell z-direction periods. (**a**) The Weyl nodes coalesce and annihilate at 4.6 mm. (**b**) Weyl nodes are in the proximity of Γ point in the Brillouin zone at 4.8 mm. (**c**,**d**) Weyl node at 5 and 5.5 mm period.

Author Contributions: Conceptualization, W.G. and Y.-T.W.; software, W.G.; validation, W.G. and Y.-T.W.; formal analysis, W.G. and Y.-T.W.; writing—original draft preparation, W.G.; writing—review and editing, W.G. and Y.-T.W.; supervision, W.G. and Y.-T.W. All authors have read and agreed to the published version of the manuscript.

Funding: This project has received funding from the European Research Council (ERC) under the European Union's Horizon 2020 research and innovation programme (grant agreement No 724306); Engineering and Physical Science Research Council (EP/T002654/1); Leverhulme Trust (Topologically protected flexural waves in thin elastic plates).

Conflicts of Interest: The authors declare no conflict of interest.

References

1. Wan, X.; Turner, A.M.; Vishwanath, A.; Savrasov, S.Y. Topological semimetal and Fermi-arc surface states in the electronic structure of pyrochlore iridates. *Phys. Rev. B* **2011**, *83*, 205101. [CrossRef]
2. Burkov, A.A.; Balents, L. Weyl semimetal in a topological insulator multilayer. *Phys. Rev. Lett.* **2011**, *107*, 127205. [CrossRef] [PubMed]
3. Armitage, N.P.; Mele, E.J.; Vishwanath, A. Weyl and Dirac semimetals in three-dimensional solids. *Rev. Mod. Phys.* **2018**, *90*, 015001. [CrossRef]
4. Huang, X.; Zhao, L.; Long, Y.; Wang, P.; Chen, D.; Yang, Z.; Liang, H.; Xue, M.; Weng, H.; Fang, Z.; et al. Observation of the chiral-anomaly-induced negative magnetoresistance: In 3D Weyl semimetal TaAs. *Phys. Rev. X* **2015**, *5*, 031023. [CrossRef]
5. Li, Q.; Kharzeev, D.E.; Zhang, C.; Huang, Y.; Pletikosić, I.; Fedorov, A.V.; Zhong, R.D.; Schneeloch, J.A.; Gu, G.D.; Valla, T. Chiral magnetic effect in ZrTe$_5$. *Nat. Phys.* **2016**, *12*, 550–554. [CrossRef]
6. Xiong, J.; Kushwaha, S.K.; Liang, T.; Krizan, J.W.; Hirschberger, M.; Wang, W.; Cava, R.J.; Ong, N.P. Evidence for the chiral anomaly in the Dirac semimetal Na3Bi. *Science* **2015**, *350*, 413–416. [CrossRef]
7. Fang, C.; Lu, L.; Liu, J.; Fu, L. Topological semimetals with helicoid surface states. *Nat. Phys.* **2016**, *12*, 936–941. [CrossRef]

8. Xu, S.-Y.; Belopolski, I.; Sanchez, D.S.; Guo, C.; Chang, G.; Zhang, C.; Bian, G.; Yuan, Z.; Lu, H.; Feng, Y.; et al. Experimental discovery of a topological Weyl semimetal state in TaP. *Sci. Adv.* **2015**, *1*, e1501092. [CrossRef]
9. Lv, B.Q.; Xu, N.; Weng, H.M.; Ma, J.Z.; Richard, P.; Huang, X.C.; Zhao, L.X.; Chen, G.F.; Matt, C.E.; Bisti, F.; et al. Observation of Weyl nodes in TaAs. *Nat. Phys.* **2015**, *11*, 724–727. [CrossRef]
10. Weng, H.; Fang, C.; Fang, Z.; Andrei Bernevig, B.; Dai, X. Weyl semimetal phase in noncentrosymmetric transition-metal monophosphides. *Phys. Rev. X* **2015**, *5*, 011029. [CrossRef]
11. Yang, L.X.; Liu, Z.K.; Sun, Y.; Peng, H.; Yang, H.F.; Zhang, T.; Zhou, B.; Zhang, Y.; Guo, Y.F.; Rahn, M.; et al. Weyl semimetal phase in the non-centrosymmetric compound TaAs. *Nat. Phys.* **2015**, *11*, 728–732. [CrossRef]
12. Hasan, M.Z.; Xu, S.-Y.; Belopolski, I.; Huang, S.-M. Discovery of Weyl fermion semimetals and topological Fermi arc states. *Annu. Rev. Condens. Matter Phys.* **2017**, *8*, 289–309.
13. Sanchez, D.S.; Belopolski, I.; Cochran, T.A.; Xu, X.; Yin, J.X.; Chang, G.; Xie, W.; Manna, K.; Süß, V.; Huang, C.Y.; et al. Topological chiral crystals with helicoid-arc quantum states. *Nature* **2019**, *567*, 500–505. [CrossRef]
14. Wang, C.M.; Sun, H.P.; Lu, H.Z.; Xie, X.C. 3D Quantum Hall Effect of Fermi Arc in Topological Semimetals. *Phys. Rev. Lett.* **2017**, *119*, 136806. [CrossRef] [PubMed]
15. Deng, K.; Wan, G.; Deng, P.; Zhang, K.; Ding, S.; Wang, E.; Yan, M.; Huang, H.; Zhang, H.; Xu, Z.; et al. Experimental observation of topological Fermi arcs in type-II Weyl semimetal MoTe$_2$. *Nat. Phys.* **2016**, *12*, 1105–1110. [CrossRef]
16. Burkov, A.A. Anomalous hall effect in weyl metals. *Phys. Rev. Lett.* **2014**, *113*, 187202. [CrossRef]
17. Sodemann, I.; Fu, L. Quantum Nonlinear Hall Effect Induced by Berry Curvature Dipole in Time-Reversal Invariant Materials. *Phys. Rev. Lett.* **2015**, *115*, 216806. [CrossRef]
18. Ma, Q.; Xu, S.Y.; Shen, H.; MacNeill, D.; Fatemi, V.; Chang, T.R.; Mier Valdivia, A.M.; Wu, S.; Du, Z.; Hsu, C.H.; et al. Observation of the nonlinear Hall effect under time-reversal-symmetric conditions. *Nature* **2019**, *565*, 337–342. [CrossRef]
19. Bradlyn, B.; Cano, J.; Wang, Z.; Vergniory, M.G.; Felser, C.; Cava, R.J.; Bernevig, B.A. Beyond Dirac and Weyl fermions: Unconventional quasiparticles in conventional crystals. *Science* **2016**, *353*, aaf5037. [CrossRef]
20. Yang, B.J.; Nagaosa, N. Classification of stable three-dimensional Dirac semimetals with nontrivial topology. *Nat. Commun.* **2014**, *5*, 1–10. [CrossRef]
21. Hu, J.; Tang, Z.; Liu, J.; Liu, X.; Zhu, Y.; Graf, D.; Myhro, K.; Tran, S.; Lau, C.N.; Wei, J.; et al. Evidence of Topological Nodal-Line Fermions in ZrSiSe and ZrSiTe. *Phys. Rev. Lett.* **2016**, *117*, 016602. [CrossRef]
22. Gibson, Q.D.; Schoop, L.M.; Muechler, L.; Xie, L.S.; Hirschberger, M.; Ong, N.P.; Car, R.; Cava, R.J. Three-dimensional Dirac semimetals: Design principles and predictions of new materials. *Phys. Rev. B* **2015**, *91*, 205128. [CrossRef]
23. Young, S.M.; Zaheer, S.; Teo JC, Y.; Kane, C.L.; Mele, E.J.; Rappe, A.M. Dirac semimetal in three dimensions. *Phys. Rev. Lett.* **2012**, *108*, 140405. [CrossRef] [PubMed]
24. Neupane, M.; Xu, S.Y.; Sankar, R.; Alidoust, N.; Bian, G.; Liu, C.; Belopolski, I.; Chang, T.R.; Jeng, H.T.; Lin, H.; et al. Observation of a three-dimensional topological dirac semimetal phase in high-mobility cd3 as2. *Nat. Commun.* **2014**, *5*, 1–8. [CrossRef] [PubMed]
25. Wang, Z.; Weng, H.; Wu, Q.; Dai, X.; Fang, Z. Three-dimensional Dirac semimetal and quantum transport in Cd 3As2. *Phys. Rev. B* **2013**, *88*, 125427. [CrossRef]
26. Borisenko, S.; Gibson, Q.; Evtushinsky, D.; Zabolotnyy, V.; Büchner, B.; Cava, R.J. Experimental realization of a three-dimensional dirac semimetal. *Phys. Rev. Lett.* **2014**, *113*, 027603. [CrossRef]
27. Chang, G.; Xu, S.Y.; Wieder, B.J.; Sanchez, D.S.; Huang, S.M.; Belopolski, I.; Chang, T.R.; Zhang, S.; Bansil, A.; Lin, H.; et al. Unconventional Chiral Fermions and Large Topological Fermi Arcs in RhSi. *Phys. Rev. Lett.* **2017**, *119*, 206401. [CrossRef]
28. Wang, R.; Xia, B.W.; Chen, Z.J.; Zheng, B.B.; Zhao, Y.J.; Xu, H. Symmetry-Protected Topological Triangular Weyl Complex. *Phys. Rev. Lett.* **2020**, *124*, 105303. [CrossRef]
29. Tang, P.; Zhou, Q.; Zhang, S.C. Multiple Types of Topological Fermions in Transition Metal Silicides. *Phys. Rev. Lett.* **2017**, *119*, 206402. [CrossRef]
30. Zhang, T.; Song, Z.; Alexandradinata, A.; Weng, H.; Fang, C.; Lu, L.; Fang, Z. Double-Weyl Phonons in Transition-Metal Monosilicides. *Phys. Rev. Lett.* **2018**, *120*, 016401. [CrossRef]
31. Lu, L.; Wang, Z.; Ye, D.; Ran, L.; Fu, L.; Joannopoulos, J.D.; Soljačić, M. Experimental observation of Weyl points. *Science* **2015**, *349*, 622–624. [CrossRef] [PubMed]

32. Lu, L.; Fu, L.; Joannopoulos, J.D.; Soljacic, M. Weyl points and line nodes in gyroid photonic crystals. *Nat. Photonics* **2013**, *7*, 294. [CrossRef]
33. Chang, M.L.; Xiao, M.; Chen, W.J.; Chan, C.T. Multiple Weyl points and the sign change of their topological charges in woodpile photonic crystals. *Phys. Rev. B* **2017**, *95*, 125136. [CrossRef]
34. Chen, W.J.; Xiao, M.; Chan, C.T. Photonic crystals possessing multiple Weyl points and the experimental observation of robust surface states. *Nat. Commun.* **2016**, *7*, 1–10. [CrossRef] [PubMed]
35. Yang, B.; Guo, Q.; Tremain, B.; Liu, R.; Barr, L.E.; Yan, Q.; Gao, W.; Liu, H.; Xiang, Y.; Chen, J.; et al. Ideal Weyl points and helicoid surface states in artificial photonic crystal structures. *Science* **2018**, *359*, 1013–1016. [CrossRef]
36. Yang, B.; Guo, Q.; Tremain, B.; Barr, L.E.; Gao, W.; Liu, H.; Béri, B.; Xiang, Y.; Fan Di Hibbins, A.P.; Zhang, S. Direct observation of topological surface-state arcs in photonic metamaterials. *Nat. Commun.* **2017**, *8*, 1–7. [CrossRef]
37. Xiao, M.; Lin, Q.; Fan, S. Hyperbolic Weyl Point in Reciprocal Chiral Metamaterials. *Phys. Rev. Lett.* **2016**, *117*, 057401. [CrossRef]
38. Gao, W.; Yang, B.; Lawrence, M.; Fang, F.; Béri, B.; Zhang, S. Photonic Weyl degeneracies in magnetized plasma. *Nat. Commun.* **2016**, *7*, 1–8. [CrossRef]
39. Wang, D.; Yang, B.; Gao, W.; Jia, H.; Yang, Q.; Chen, X.; Wei, M.; Liu, C.; Navarro-Cía, M.; Han, J.; et al. Photonic Weyl points due to broken time-reversal symmetry in magnetized semiconductor. *Nat. Phys.* **2019**, *15*, 1150–1155. [CrossRef]
40. Lin, Q.; Xiao, M.; Yuan, L.; Fan, S. Photonic Weyl point in a two-dimensional resonator lattice with a synthetic frequency dimension. *Nat. Commun.* **2016**, *7*, 1–7. [CrossRef]
41. Wang, Q.; Xiao, M.; Liu, H.; Zhu, S.; Chan, C.T. Optical interface states protected by synthetic weyl points. *Phys. Rev. X* **2017**, *7*, 031032. [CrossRef]
42. Ruan, J.; Jian, S.K.; Yao, H.; Zhang, H.; Zhang, S.C.; Xing, D. Symmetry-protected ideal Weyl semimetal in HgTe-class materials. *Nat. Commun.* **2016**, *7*, 1–6. [CrossRef] [PubMed]
43. Wang, S.S.; Liu, Y.; Yu, Z.M.; Sheng, X.L.; Yang, S.A. Hourglass Dirac chain metal in rhenium dioxide. *Nat. Commun.* **2017**, *8*, 1–7. [CrossRef] [PubMed]
44. Young, S.M.; Kane, C.L. Dirac Semimetals in Two Dimensions. *Phys. Rev. Lett.* **2015**, *115*, 126803. [CrossRef]
45. Li, S.; Liu, Y.; Wang, S.S.; Yu, Z.M.; Guan, S.; Sheng, X.L.; Yao, Y.; Yang, S.A. Nonsymmorphic-symmetry-protected hourglass Dirac loop, nodal line, and Dirac point in bulk and monolayer X_3SiTe_6 (X = Ta, Nb). *Phys. Rev. B* **2018**, *97*, 045131. [CrossRef]
46. Fang, K.; Yu, Z.; Fan, S. Realizing effective magnetic field for photons by controlling the phase of dynamic modulation. *Nat. Photonics.* **2012**, *6*, 782–787. [CrossRef]
47. Jia, H.; Zhang, R.; Gao, W.; Guo, Q.; Yang, B.; Hu, J.; Bi, Y.; Xiang, Y.; Liu, C.; Zhang, S. Observation of chiral zero mode in inhomogeneous three-dimensional Weyl metamaterials. *Science* **2019**, *363*, 148–151. [CrossRef]

© 2020 by the authors. Licensee MDPI, Basel, Switzerland. This article is an open access article distributed under the terms and conditions of the Creative Commons Attribution (CC BY) license (http://creativecommons.org/licenses/by/4.0/).

Article

Bulk Cyclotron Resonance in the Topological Insulator Bi$_2$Te$_3$

Dmytro L. Kamenskyi [1,2,*], Artem V. Pronin [3,*], Hadj M. Benia [4], Victor P. Martovitskii [5], Kirill S. Pervakov [5] and Yurii G. Selivanov [5]

1. High Field Magnet Laboratory (HFML-EMFL), Radboud University, 6525 ED Nijmegen, The Netherlands
2. Experimentalphysik V, Center for Electronic Correlations and Magnetism, University of Augsburg, 86159 Augsburg, Germany
3. Physikalisches Institut, Universität Stuttgart, 70569 Stuttgart, Germany
4. Centre de Développement des Technologies Avancées (CDTA), Baba Hassen, 16081 Algiers, Algeria; h.benia@fkf.mpg.de
5. P. N. Lebedev Physical Institute of the RAS, 119991 Moscow, Russia; victormart@yandex.ru (V.P.M.); pervakovks@lebedev.ru (K.S.P.); selivanovyg@lebedev.ru (Y.G.S.)
* Correspondence: dmytro.kamenskyi@physik.uni-augsburg.de (D.L.K.); artem.pronin@pi1.physik.uni-stuttgart.de (A.V.P.)

Received: 28 July 2020; Accepted: 16 August 2020; Published: 20 August 2020

Abstract: We investigated magneto-optical response of undoped Bi$_2$Te$_3$ films in the terahertz frequency range (0.3–5.1 THz, 10–170 cm^{-1}) in magnetic fields up to 10 T. The optical transmission, measured in the Faraday geometry, is dominated by a broad Lorentzian-shaped mode, whose central frequency linearly increases with applied field. In zero field, the Lorentzian is centered at zero frequency, representing hence the free-carrier Drude response. We interpret the mode as a cyclotron resonance (CR) of free carriers in Bi$_2$Te$_3$. Because the mode's frequency position follows a linear magnetic-field dependence and because undoped Bi$_2$Te$_3$ is known to possess appreciable number of bulk carriers, we associate the mode with a bulk CR. In addition, the cyclotron mass obtained from our measurements fits well the literature data on the bulk effective mass in Bi$_2$Te$_3$. Interestingly, the width of the CR mode demonstrates a behavior non-monotonous in field. We propose that the CR width is defined by two competing factors: impurity scattering, which rate decreases in increasing field, and electron-phonon scattering, which exhibits the opposite behavior.

Keywords: topological insulators; cyclotron resonance; Dirac materials

1. Introduction

From the theory point of view, a three-dimensional (3D) topological insulator (TI) possesses insulating bulk and conducting surfaces, the conduction channels at surfaces being spin-polarized [1–4]. Since the spin polarization can potentially be utilized in spintronic devices, topological insulators have attracted a lot of attention in the past years [5,6]. In practice, the real samples of 3D topological insulators often conduct not only on their surfaces, but also in the bulk. Considerable efforts have been made to understand and separate the properties of surface and bulk charge carriers. These properties can particularly be studied via different spectroscopic techniques, such as angle-resolved photoemission spectroscopy (ARPES) or optical and magneto-optical spectroscopy. The optical conductivity and cyclotron resonance (CR) of a number of 3D TI materials have been reported in the literature. Perhaps the most studied family of such TIs is the bismuth selenide: bismuth telluride series, Bi$_2$(Te$_{1-x}$Se$_x$)$_3$, which also includes the undoped members, Bi$_2$Te$_3$ and Bi$_2$Se$_3$ [7–9]. In this study, we concentrate on Bi$_2$Te$_3$. Namely, we investigate experimentally the CR in this compound. Surprisingly, the published cyclotron-resonance measurements performed on this well-studied TI produce rather diverging results [10–13] with the absorption features being generally of rather complex shapes. One of the reasons for such diversity might be the sample-dependent variation between the surface and bulk contributions, which, in turn, greatly depend on the exact position of the Fermi level.

Unlike in the majority of previous reports [11–13], the CR absorption observed in our study can be well described by a single Lorentzian-shaped mode (which is rather consistent with the earliest study on this issue from 1999 [10]). We believe the absorption we detect is of bulk origin. Thus, our findings might be useful for the proper interpretations of the CR modes in doped Bi_2Te_3, where the balance between the surface and bulk-states contributions can be shifted towards the former, but the bulk still cannot be completely ignored.

2. Materials and Methods

We grew thin layers of Bi_2Te_3 on (111)-oriented BaF_2 substrates by molecular beam epitaxy [14]. For the growth, we used binary Bi_2Te_3 and elemental Te. This is different from the standard practice, when elemental (Bi and Te) sources are utilized with the typical flux ratio of Te/Bi being about 10 to 20. Using Bi_2Te_3 and Te allowed us to reduce this ratio to the values below 1 and, hence, to precisely control the stoichiometry of the growing layer. Along with the employed "ramp up" growth procedure [15], these two approaches successfully suppress twin formation in the growing films. X-ray diffraction (XRD) φ scans about the [0 0 1] axis on the asymmetric (1 0 10) reflection revealed only 120°-periodic peaks and confirmed that the films obtained by this method are either single-domain or have a very small twin volume fraction (3–7% for the films with 1 cm^2 area) with the c axis of Bi_2Te_3 being perpendicular to the substrate surface. To the best of our knowledge, this thin-film growth method is unique.

In order to prevent possible influence of atmospheric oxygen and water, we have developed a method to cover the TI films in situ with optically-friendly protecting layers of BaF_2 [16]. We have found that 30–50 nm of BaF_2 provide the optimal protection. Our measurements have shown that the BaF_2 cap layers affect neither crystal-structure parameters nor optical properties at the frequencies of interest.

The sample used in this study was thoroughly characterized by XRD, scanning electron microscopy (SEM), atomic force microscopy (AFM), and angle-resolved photoemission spectroscopy (ARPES). The results of these investigations, presented in the Supplementary Materials, confirm high structural and morphological quality of the film and show that the film possesses the topological surface electronic states as well as the states in the bulk conduction band.

For optical measurements, we utilized the infrared optical setup available at the High Field Magnet Laboratory in Nijmegen [17]. This setup consists of a commercial Fourier-transform infrared (FTIR) spectrometer (Bruker IFS113v) (Bruker Optik GmbH, Ettlingen, Germany) combined with a continuous-field 33-Tesla Bitter magnet. A detailed description of this setup could be found elsewhere [18]. The measurements were performed in the Faraday geometry [19] at 2 K. A mercury lamp was used as a radiation source. The far-infrared radiation was detected using a custom-made silicon bolometer operating at 1.4 K. The FTIR spectra were recorded in a number of magnetic fields from 0 to 30 T. The optical data were collected between 10 and 170 cm^{-1} (300–5100 GHz), using a 200-μm Mylar beamsplitter and a scanning velocity of 50 kHz. At each field, at least 100 scans were averaged. As will be seen below, the data obtained in the fields above 10 T cannot be used in our analysis because of a low signal-to-noise ratio. Thus, in this study we concentrate on the measurements performed between 0 and 10 T.

3. Results and Discussion

In Figure 1, we show raw transmission data measured though the 115-nm-thick Bi_2Te_3 film on a 0.49-mm-thick BaF_2 substrate (cf. S2 in the Supplemental Material) in magnetic fields B up to 10 T. We note that all the measurements reported in this study are performed on a single sample. As seen from Figure 2, the substrate has no detectable field dependence. Hence, all the field-inducted changes come from the film. We note that the BaF_2 substrate has intense phonon modes at roughly 50 and

140 cm^{-1} [20]. Thus, accurate measurements around these frequencies are impossible. The spectra of Figure 1 are dominated by a single broad mode, which position shifts to higher frequencies in increasing field. The spectra can be fitted by a single Lorentzian, as exemplified in Figure 3 for 2, 4, and 6 T. In zero field, the Lorentzian central frequency is zero, i.e., the observed absorption mode is due to free carriers (Drude conductivity). The field evolution of the mode can be traced in Figure 1: with increasing field, the mode shifts upwards and eventually goes above 100 cm^{-1}, i.e., in the range, where the signal-to-noise ratio is worsened by the spectrometer noise and the phonons in the substrate (this prevents a meaningful spectra analysis in higher fields). Still, the shift of the mode in the applied magnetic field is apparent and can straightforwardly be interpreted as a magnetic-field-induced free-carrier localization or, in other words, a cyclotron-resonance absorption.

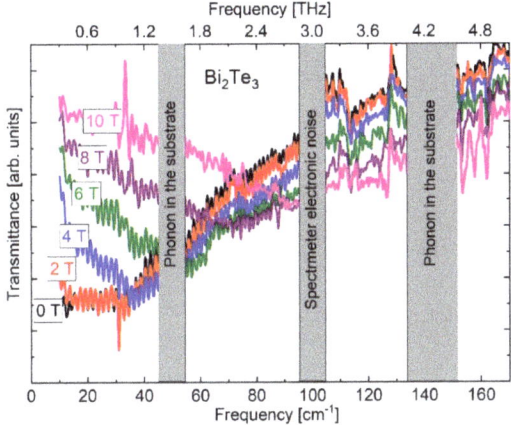

Figure 1. Raw transmission spectra of Bi$_2$Te$_3$ films on BaF$_2$ substrates as obtained in magnetic fields of up to 10 T. The areas with low signal due to either the substrate phonons or spectrometer electronic noise are shaded. The signal-to-noise ratio is best at around 80 cm^{-1} and becomes appreciably lower as frequency increases (see also Figure 2), preventing thus any meaningful measurements of the cyclotron resonance (CR) mode at the fields higher than 10 T.

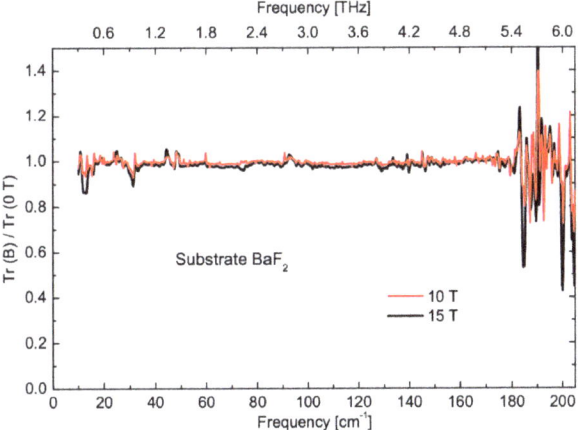

Figure 2. Frequency-dependent transmission of a bare BaF$_2$ substrate at 10 and 15 T normalized to its zero-field spectrum. The noise at high frequencies is due the experimental setup. The Figure is meant to demonstrate: (i) the absence of any field-induced changes in the optical spectra of BaF$_2$ and (ii) the frequency limits of the setup used.

The Lorentzian-fit results for this CR absorption mode in the fields from 0 to 10 T are shown in in Figure 4. One can see that the central frequency of the absorption line is linear in field (left panel). This immediately signals that the electronic band(s) responsible for the observed absorption have a quadratic dispersion relation. For linear electronic bands, the field dependence of the CR lines is supposed to have a square root dependence on applied field [21]. Thus, following the Occam's razor principle, we conclude that the mode is due to bulk (i.e., not linear, not topological) electronic bands. This conclusion is in full agreement, e.g., with ARPES [9] and quantum-oscillations [22] measurements, which show that the Fermi level in undoped Bi_2Te_3 crosses the bulk conduction band and hence there exists a large bulk Fermi surface.

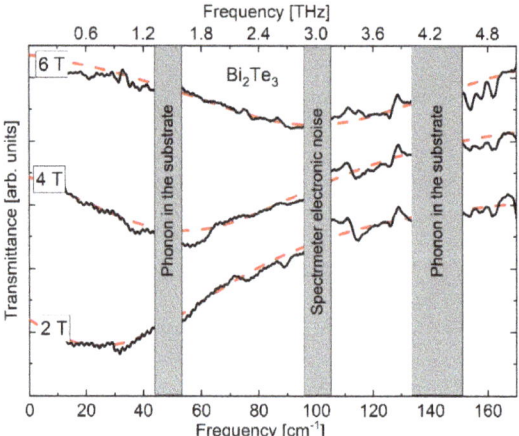

Figure 3. Examples of Lorentzian fits of the transmission spectra from Figure 1 for a few magnetic-field strengths as indicated. The raw experimental data are smoothed, using a Savitzki–Golay method [23]. Note that the spectra for 4 and 6 T are shifted upwards for clarity.

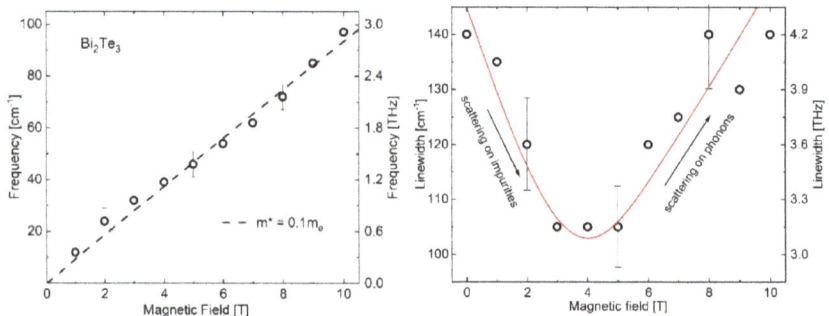

Figure 4. CR-line central frequency (left frame) and full width at half maximum (FWHM) (right frame) versus applied magnetic field. The dashed line is a fit with $m^* = 0.1 m_e$. The red solid line is a guide for the eye.

We note that weak modes due to the surface conduction channels may exist on top of the dominating bulk abortion, but within our accuracy they cannot be resolved.

The linear field dependence of the central CR frequency, ω_0, can be fitted with the standard parabolic-band expression, connecting the slope of $\omega_0(B)$ and the carrier cyclotron mass, m^*, $\omega_0 = eB/m^*c$ (CGS units are used, e is the elementary charge, c is the speed of light). This fit is shown in the left panel of Figure 4 as a straight line and provides $m^* = 0.1 m_e$ (m_e is the free-electron mass). This value is in very good agreement with the available literature data on the bulk effective mass in Bi_2Te_3 [24]: $m^* = 0.109 m_e$ for the response perpendicular to the c-axis, which we do probe in our transmission experiment with unpolarized light. This match provides another confirmation for the correctness of our interpretation. We would like to note here that the complete agreement between the calculated electronic band structure of Bi_2Te_3 and the entire body of the available experimental work is still to be achieved, as emphasized in a recent review [25].

Finally, we turn to the width of the absorption band. As one can see from the right panel of Figure 4, the full width at half maximum (FWHM) of the band demonstrates a non-monotonous field dependence: in low fields, it decreases with increasing B and then, starting at approximately 5 T, the FWHM starts growing with the applied field. The initial decrease of FWHM can be naturally explained by the decreasing cyclotron-orbit radius with increasing B and the consequent decrease of impurity scattering. The reason for the CR mode broadening in $B > 5$ T is not entirely clear. We propose that this could be due to the increased electron-phonon scattering. In higher fields, the CR mode approaches the frequencies, where phonon density grows (roughly, above 40 cm^{-1}; cf. the left panel of Figure 4 and [26], where the phonon density for Bi_2Te_3 was calculated) and hence the rate of the electron-phonon scattering starts to increase, leading to the observed total broadening of the CR line according to the Matthiessen rule.

4. Conclusions

We have investigated the magneto-optical response of undoped Bi_2Te_3 films at terahertz frequencies and in magnetic fields of up to 10 T. We observed an intense CR line, which can be fitted with a single Lorentz oscillator. The central frequency of the CR increases linearly with applied field, signaling the bulk origin of this resonance. In addition, we found the "in-plane" cyclotron mass, $m^* = 0.1 m_e$, which matches well the literature data for bulk Bi_2Te_3. The width of the CR mode demonstrates a behavior non-monotonous in field. We propose that the CR width is defined by two competing factors: impurity scattering, which rate decreases in increasing field, and electron-phonon scattering, which rate demonstrates the opposite behavior. We believe our findings can be exploited in future measurements of the surface-states CR in Bi_2Te_3 to disentangle the bulk and surface contributions.

Supplementary Materials: The following are available online at http://www.mdpi.com/2073-4352/10/9/722/s1.

Author Contributions: Far-infrared optical measurements and data analysis, D.L.K. and A.V.P.; ARPES measurements, H.M.B.; sample preparation and characterization, V.P.M., K.S.P., and Y.G.S.; writing—original draft preparation, D.L.K.; writing—review and editing, A.V.P. and Y.G.S.; funding acquisition, D.L.K., A.V.P., and Y.G.S. All authors have read and agreed to the published version of the manuscript.

Funding: This work was partially supported by the PRIME program of the German Academic Exchange Service (DAAD) with funds from the German Federal Ministry of Education and Research (BMBF) and by the Russian Foundation for Basic Research (grant No. 20-02-00989). H.M.B. acknowledges funding from the German Research Foundation (DFG) via Project No. BE 5190/1-1. We also acknowledge the support of HFML-RU/NWO, member of the European Magnetic Field Laboratory (EMFL).

Conflicts of Interest: The authors declare no conflict of interest. The funders had no role in the design of the study; in the collection, analyses, or interpretation of data; in the writing of the manuscript, or in the decision to publish the results.

References

1. Fu, L.; Kane, C.L.; Mele, E.J. Topological insulators in three dimensions. *Phys. Rev. Lett.* **2007**, *98*, 106803. [CrossRef] [PubMed]
2. Moore, J.E.; Balents, L. Topological invariants of time-reversal-invariant band structures. *Phys. Rev. B* **2007**, *75*, 121306. [CrossRef]
3. Hsieh, D.; Qian, D.; Wray, L.; Xia, Y.; Hor, Y.S.; Cava, R.J.; Hasan, M.Z. A topological Dirac insulator in a quantum spin Hall phase. *Nature* **2008**, *452*, 970–974. [CrossRef] [PubMed]

4. Hsieh, D.; Xia, Y.; Wray, L.; Qian, D.; Pal, A.; Dil, J.H.; Osterwalder, J.; Meier, F.; Bihlmayer, G.; Kane, C.L.; et al. Observation of unconventional quantum spin textures in topological insulators. *Science* **2009**, *323*, 919–922. [CrossRef]
5. Hasan, M.Z.; Kane, C.L. Colloquium: Topological insulators. *Rev. Mod. Phys.* **2010**, *82*, 3045–3067. [CrossRef]
6. Qi, X.-L.; Zhang, S.-C. Topological insulators and superconductors. *Rev. Mod. Phys.* **2011**, *83*, 1057–1110. [CrossRef]
7. Xia, Y.; Qian, D.; Hsieh, D.; Wray, L.; Pal, A.; Lin, H.; Bansil, A.; Grauer, D.; Hor, Y.S.; Cava, R.J.; et al. Observation of a large-gap topological-insulator class with a single Dirac cone on the surface. *Nat. Phys.* **2009**, *5*, 398–402. [CrossRef]
8. Zhang, H.; Liu, C.-X.; Qi, X.-L.; Dai, X.; Fang, Z.; Zhang, S.-C. Topological insulators in Bi_2Se_3, Bi_2Te_3 and Sb_2Te_3 with a single Dirac cone on the surface. *Nat. Phys.* **2009**, *5*, 438–442. [CrossRef]
9. Chen, Y.L.; Analytis, J.G.; Chu, J.-H.; Liu, Z.K.; Mo, S.-K.; Qi, X.L.; Zhang, H.J.; Lu, D.H.; Dai, X.; Fang, Z.; et al. Experimental realization of a three-dimensional topological insulator, Bi_2Te_3. *Science* **2009**, *325*, 178–181. [CrossRef]
10. Kulbachinskii, V.A.; Miura, N.; Arimoto, H.; Ikaida, T.; Lostak, P.; Horak, H.; Drasar, C. Cyclotron resonance in high magnetic fields in Bi_2Se_3, Bi_2Te_3 and Sb_2Te_3 based crystals. *J. Phys. Soc. Jpn.* **1999**, *68*, 3328–3333. [CrossRef]
11. Wolos, A.; Szyszko, S.; Drabinska, A.; Kaminska, M.; Strzelecka, S.G.; Hruban, A.; Materna, A.; Piersa, M. Landau-level spectroscopy of relativistic fermions with low Fermi velocity in the Bi_2Te_3 three-dimensional topological insulator. *Phys. Rev. Lett.* **2012**, *109*, 247604. [CrossRef] [PubMed]
12. Tung, L.-C.; Yu, W.; Cadden-Zimansky, P.; Miotkowski, I.; Chen, Y.P.; Smirnov, D.; Jiang, Z. Magnetoinfrared spectroscopic study of thin Bi_2Te_3 single crystals. *Phys. Rev. B* **2016**, *93*, 085140. [CrossRef]
13. Dordevic, S.V.; Lei, H.; Petrovic, C.; Ludwig, J.; Li, Z.Q.; Smirnov, D. Observation of cyclotron antiresonance in the topological insulator Bi_2Te_3. *Phys. Rev. B* **2018**, *98*, 115138. [CrossRef]
14. Kuntsevich, A.Y.; Gabdullin, A.A.; Prudkogliad, V.A.; Selivanov, Y.G.; Chizhevskii, E.G.; Pudalov, V.M. Low-temperature Hall effect in bismuth chalcogenides thin films. *Phys. Rev. B* **2016**, *94*, 235401. [CrossRef]
15. Volosheniuk, S.O.; Selivanov, Y.G.; Bryzgalov, M.A.; Martovitskii, V.P.; Kuntsevich, A.Y. Effect of Sr doping on structure, morphology, and transport properties of Bi_2Se_3 epitaxial thin films. *J. Appl. Phys.* **2019**, *125*, 095103. [CrossRef]
16. Melnikov, A.A.; Boldyrev, K.N.; Selivanov, Y.G.; Martovitskii, V.P.; Chekalin, S.V.; Ryabov, E.A. Coherent phonons in a Bi_2Se_3 film generated by an intense single-cycle THz pulse. *Phys. Rev. B* **2018**, *97*, 214304. [CrossRef]
17. Wiegers, S.A.J.; Christianen, P.C.M.; Engelkamp, H.; den Ouden, A.; Perenboom, J.A.A.J.; Zeitler, U.; Maan, J.C. The high field magnet laboratory at Radboud University Nijmegen. *J. Low Temp. Phys.* **2010**, *159*, 389–393. [CrossRef]
18. Tarelkin, S.A.; Bormashov, V.S.; Pavlov, S.G.; Kamenskyi, D.L.; Kuznetsov, M.S.; Terentiev, S.A.; Prikhodko, D.D.; Galkin, A.S.; Hübers, H.-W.; Blank, V.D. Evidence of linear Zeeman effect for infrared intracenter transitions in boron doped diamond in high magnetic fields. *Diam. Relat. Mater.* **2017**, *75*, 52–57. [CrossRef]
19. Palik, E.D.; Furdyna, J.K. Infrared and microwave magnetoplasma effects in semiconductors. *Rep. Prog. Phys.* **1970**, *33*, 1193–1322. [CrossRef]
20. Zhukova, E.S.; Aksenov, N.P.; Gorshunov, B.P.; Selivanov, Y.G.; Zasavitskiy, I.I.; Wu, D.; Dressel, M. Far infrared spectroscopy of $Pb_{1-x}Eu_xTe$ epitaxial layers. *Phys. Rev. B* **2010**, *82*, 205202. [CrossRef]
21. Wehling, T.O.; Black-Schaffer, A.M.; Balatsky, A.V. Dirac materials. *Adv. Phys.* **2014**, *63*, 1–76.
22. Qu, D.-X.; Hor, Y.S.; Xiong, J.; Cava, R.J.; Ong, N.P. Quantum oscillations and Hall anomaly of surface states in the topological insulator Bi_2Te_3. *Science* **2010**, *329*, 821–824. [CrossRef] [PubMed]
23. Savitzky, A.; Golay, M.J.E. Smoothing and differentiation of data by simplified least squares procedures. *Anal. Chem.* **1964**, *36*, 1627–1639. [CrossRef]
24. Stordeur, M.; Stolzer, M.; Sobotta, H.; Riede, V. Investigation of the valence band structure of thermoelectric $(Bi_{1-x}Sb_x)_2Te_3$ single crystals. *Phys. Status Solidi B* **1988**, *150*, 165–176. [CrossRef]

25. Fang, T.; Li, X.; Hu, C.; Zhang, Q.; Yang, J.; Zhang, W.; Zhao, X.; Singh, D.J.; Zhu, T. Complex band structures and lattice dynamics of Bi_2Te_3-based compounds and solid solutions. *Adv. Funct. Mater.* **2019**, *29*, 1900677. [CrossRef]
26. Cheng, W.; Ren, S.-F. Phonons of single quintuple Bi_2Te_3 and Bi_2Se_3 films and bulk materials. *Phys. Rev. B* **2011**, *83*, 094301. [CrossRef]

© 2020 by the authors. Licensee MDPI, Basel, Switzerland. This article is an open access article distributed under the terms and conditions of the Creative Commons Attribution (CC BY) license (http://creativecommons.org/licenses/by/4.0/).

Article

Crystal Growth by the Floating Zone Method of Ce-Substituted Crystals of the Topological Kondo Insulator SmB$_6$

Monica Ciomaga Hatnean *, Talha Ahmad, Marc Walker, Martin R. Lees and Geetha Balakrishnan

Department of Physics, University of Warwick, Coventry CV4 7AL, UK; S.T.S.Ahmad@warwick.ac.uk (T.A.); M.Walker@warwick.ac.uk (M.W.); m.r.lees@warwick.ac.uk (M.R.L.); G.Balakrishnan@warwick.ac.uk (G.B.)
* Correspondence: M.Ciomaga-Hatnean@warwick.ac.uk

Received: 19 August 2020; Accepted: 14 September 2020 ; Published: 17 September 2020

Abstract: SmB$_6$ is a mixed valence topological Kondo insulator. To investigate the effect of substituting Sm with magnetic Ce ions on the physical properties of samarium hexaboride, Ce-substituted SmB$_6$ crystals were grown by the floating zone method for the first time as large, good quality single crystal boules. The crystal growth conditions are reported. Structural, magnetic and transport properties of single crystals of Sm$_{1-x}$Ce$_x$B$_6$ ($x = 0.05$, 0.10 and 0.20) were investigated using X-ray diffraction techniques, electrical resistivity and magnetisation measurements. Phase composition analysis of the powder X-ray diffraction data collected on the as-grown boules revealed that the main phase was that of the parent compound, SmB$_6$. Substitution of Sm ions with magnetic Ce ions does not lead to long-range magnetic ordering in the Sm$_{1-x}$Ce$_x$B$_6$ crystals. The substitution with 5% Ce and above suppresses the cross-over from bulk conductivity at high temperatures to surface-only conductivity at low temperatures.

Keywords: crystal growth; optical floating zone method; SmB$_6$; Sm$_{1-x}$Ce$_x$B$_6$; topological insulator; kondo insulator

---

1. Introduction

Extensive investigations of the physical properties and excitations in the rare earth (RE) hexaboride compounds, REB$_6$, have been carried out over the past decades. These strongly correlated electron systems display an array of interesting magnetic and electrical properties, such as superconductivity (YB$_6$ [1–3]), intricate antiferromagnetic ordered phases owing to the displacement of rare earth ions within the rigid framework formed by the boron ions (GdB$_6$ [4–6]), complex antiferromagnetic phases with Kondo-like characteristics (CeB$_6$ [7–10]), semimetallic behaviour correlated with the transition to an unusual ferromagnetic state (EuB$_6$ [11–13]), typical metallic behaviour (LaB$_6$ [14–16]) or an exotic Kondo-like topological insulating state (SmB$_6$ [17–19]). Amongst the rare earth hexaboride compounds, cerium and samarium hexaborides have puzzled experimentalists and theoreticians alike, for a long time, in view of their intriguing physical properties. SmB$_6$ and CeB$_6$ are isostructural, crystallising in the same cubic CsCl-type structure ($Pm\bar{3}m$ space group) [20–22]. Sm and Ce ions replace the Cs ion, whilst the B$_6$ cubo-octohedral clusters take the place of the Cl ions at the corners of the cube. Nevertheless, the similarities between samarium and cerium hexaborides stop at the structural level, as they display very unusual, but different physical properties.

SmB$_6$ has long been known to be a Kondo insulator [23,24]; in recent times, new theoretical and experimental studies demonstrated that samarium hexaboride is a topological Kondo insulator (TKI) exhibiting topological surface properties [18,25–31], although this remains open to further investigation [32]. SmB$_6$ is one of the most investigated Kondo insulators, mainly due to its exciting low temperature transport behaviour. As the temperatures decreases, an energy gap arises due to the interaction of the strongly correlated f-electrons and the conducting d-electrons, leading to an exponential increase in the electrical resistance of SmB_6 [33–35]. Unexpectedly, upon further cooling, the resistance of SmB_6 does not continue rising, as would be the case for a conventional insulator, but instead the resistance saturates at a finite value, below 5 K. This plateau in the resistivity has been attributed to a transition from a bulk conductivity characteristic of the high temperature region to a surface-dominated conductivity with bulk insulation at low temperature [36]. SmB_6 is a mixed valence system that does not order magnetically, despite exhibiting antiferromagnetic correlations [33,37–40]. The Sm^{3+}:Sm^{2+} ratio was determined to be independent of the temperature, and equal to approximately 0.6∼0.7:0.4∼0.3 [37,41]. Nevertheless, recent studies have shown that, upon the application of an external pressure, the Sm^{3+} configuration can be stabilised for sufficient time to allow long-range magnetic ordering of the samarium ions [42,43].

CeB_6 is known to have a typical dense Kondo compound behaviour and a complex magnetic phase diagram [44–47]. Cerium hexaboride exhibits Kondo-like behaviour and has a Kondo temperature of $T_K = 19$ K. Upon cooling, CeB_6 undergoes two magnetic ordering transitions: the first to a state in which antiferroquadrupolar and field-induced octupolar order coexist, below $T_Q = 3.2$ K, and then to an antiferromagnetic ordering of the Ce dipoles, below $T_N = 2.3$ K. Moreover, a subsequent study reported a new transition, of unknown origin, at $T_2 = 1.6$ K [45].

Recent progress, e.g., the discovery of the coexistence of an unusual metallic surface state and an insulating bulk state in SmB_6 [19,48] and the observation of the long-range-ordered multipolar phases in CeB_6 [47], has generated new interest in these materials. One route towards the investigation of the exotic metallic surface state arising in SmB_6 and understanding of its topological nature, is through chemical substitution in this TKI with other rare earth ions. Recently, studies have been carried out on Eu, Gd, La, Y and Yb-substituted SmB_6 [18,21,49–54]. High levels of substitution of non-magnetic ions (above 30%), and substitutions with small amounts of magnetic ions, were found to destroy the saturation seen in the low temperature resistivity of pure SmB_6. It would therefore be interesting to investigate the effect that the substitution with a magnetic rare earth, such as Ce, in samarium hexaboride has on the robustness of the topological surface state of this TKI. Such an investigation is of course best carried out on high quality single crystals. In the present work, we investigated single crystals of $Sm_{1-x}Ce_xB_6$, with a focus on studying the effects that the substitution of the magnetic Ce ion have on the structural and physical properties of SmB_6. The physical properties of Ce-substituted SmB_6 samples have previously been investigated; however, this has only been done on polycrystalline samples and flux grown crystals [21,49,54]. Crystals of pure cerium and samarium hexaboride have previously been grown using the floating zone (FZ) technique [55–57]; however, Ce-substituted SmB_6 compounds have only been grown in crystal form using the flux method [54]. SmB_6 crystals grown using Al flux could suffer from contamination by the flux affecting some of the physical properties of the crystals, thereby making it difficult to study the intrinsic properties of pure samarium hexaboride [58]. We have successfully grown, for the first time, crystal boules of $Sm_{1-x}Ce_xB_6$ by the FZ method, which yields large, good quality crystals, free from flux or crucible contamination. The crystals obtained are especially suitable for the investigation of how the substitution with magnetic ions affects the surface and bulk behaviour of this interesting TKI.

2. Materials and Methods

Crystal boules of $Sm_{1-x}Ce_xB_6$ ($x = 0.05$, 0.10 and 0.20) were grown by the floating zone technique [57] using a CSI FZ-T-12000-X_VI-VP four-mirror xenon arc lamp (3 kW) optical image furnace (Crystal Systems Incorporated, Yamanashi, Japan). The crystal quality was checked using a backscattering X-ray Photonic-Science Laue camera system (Photonic-Science, St Leonards-on-Sea, UK). Single crystal samples were aligned for selected experiments, and rectangular prism-shaped samples with [001], [1-10] and [110] directions perpendicular to the faces of the prism were cut from the $Sm_{1-x}Ce_xB_6$ crystal boules.

Phase composition analysis was carried out using a Panalytical X-Pert Pro MPD diffractometer (Malvern Panalytical Ltd, Malvern, UK) with Cu Kα_1 radiation ($\lambda_{K\alpha 1} = 1.5406$ Å). The diffraction patterns were collected at room temperature over an angular range of 10 to 110° in 2θ with a step size in the scattering angle 2θ of 0.013° and at various scanning times. The analysis of the X-ray patterns was performed using the Fullprof software suite [59].

Chemical composition of the crystal boules was investigated by energy dispersive X-ray spectroscopy (EDX) using a Zeiss SUPRA 55-VP scanning electron microscope (Carl Zeiss GmbH, Jena, Germany). LaB$_6$ was used as a standard for the EDX measurements. X-ray photoelectron spectroscopy (XPS) analysis was also carried out in order to determine the elemental composition and the valence of the Sm ions. The samples were attached to electrically-conductive carbon tape, mounted on to a sample bar and loaded into a Kratos Axis Ultra DLD (Kratos Analytical Ltd, Manchester, UK) spectrometer (base vacuum of $\sim 2 \times 10^{-10}$ mbar). The measurements were performed using a monochromated Al Kα X-ray source, at room temperature and at a take-off angle of 90° with respect to the surface parallel. The data were analysed in the CasaXPS package (Casa Software Ltd, Teignmouth, UK), using Shirley backgrounds and mixed Gaussian-Lorentzian (Voigt) line-shapes and asymmetry parameters, where appropriate.

Magnetic susceptibility measurements were performed with a Quantum Design Magnetic Property Measurement System (Quantum Design Incorporated, San Diego, USA) on rectangular-prism-shaped Sm$_{1-x}$Ce$_x$B$_6$ samples with an applied field parallel to the [100] (tetragonal), [110] (rhombic) and [111] (trigonal) crystallographic directions. The samples were cooled to 1.8 K in zero field and then the susceptibility as a function of temperature up to 300 K was measured on warming and then cooling with an applied field of $H = 500$ Oe.

Alternating current (*ac*) resistivity measurements were performed using a Quantum Design Physical Property Measurement System on bar shaped samples of the Sm$_{1-x}$Ce$_x$B$_6$ single crystals using the standard four-probe technique. Silver wire contacts were attached with silver paint, in a linear configuration, to the surfaces of the samples. The resistivity measurements were made from 2 to 300 K on both cooling and warming in zero applied field with an ac current of 1 mA at a frequency of 113 Hz.

3. Results and Discussion

3.1. Crystal Growth

Stoichiometric ratios of high purity SmB$_6$ (99.9%, American Elements UK, Manchester, UK) and CeB$_6$ (99.5%, Cerac Incorporated, Milwaukee, USA) powders were mixed together by ball milling for over 15 h, to prepare 5%, 10% and 20% Ce-substituted SmB$_6$ polycrystalline samples. The resulting materials were then isostatically pressed into rods (typically 5–7 mm diameter and 40–50 mm long) and sintered in an alumina boat, at 1450 °C in a flow of argon gas for 12 h. Before the sintering process, the furnace was evacuated to give a vacuum of $\sim 10^{-5}$ mbar. The resulting polycrystalline feed rods were used for the crystal growth. A binder (polyvinyl alcohol or polyvinyl butyral) was mixed with the powders in some cases to facilitate the formation of the rods.

Crystals of Sm$_{1-x}$Ce$_x$B$_6$ ($x = 0.05$, 0.10 and 0.20) were successfully grown by the floating zone method. The growths were carried out in an argon atmosphere at a pressure of $\sim$3 bar, using a growth rate of 18 mm/h. The feed and the seed rods were counter-rotated at $\sim$15–25 rpm. Initially, a crystal boule of SmB$_6$ was used as a seed. Once good quality crystals were obtained, Sm$_{1-x}$Ce$_x$B$_6$ crystal seeds were used for subsequent growths. A dark grey coloured deposition on the quartz tube surrounding the feed and seed rods was observed for all the growths, indicating the evaporation of boron during the growth process.

The Sm$_{1-x}$Ce$_x$B$_6$ boules were typically 4–5 mm in diameter and measured approximately 45–50 mm in length. All the crystals obtained developed facets as they grew and two very strong facets were present on almost the entire lengths of most of the grown crystals. Figures 1a–c show photographs of $Sm_{1-x}Ce_xB_6$ crystals grown in argon atmosphere at a growth speed of 18 mm/h. The quality of the grown boules was investigated by X-ray Laue diffraction, and Laue photographs were taken along the length of the boule, on the faceted sides (see Figure 1). The Laue patterns were identical along the whole length of the crystal boules.

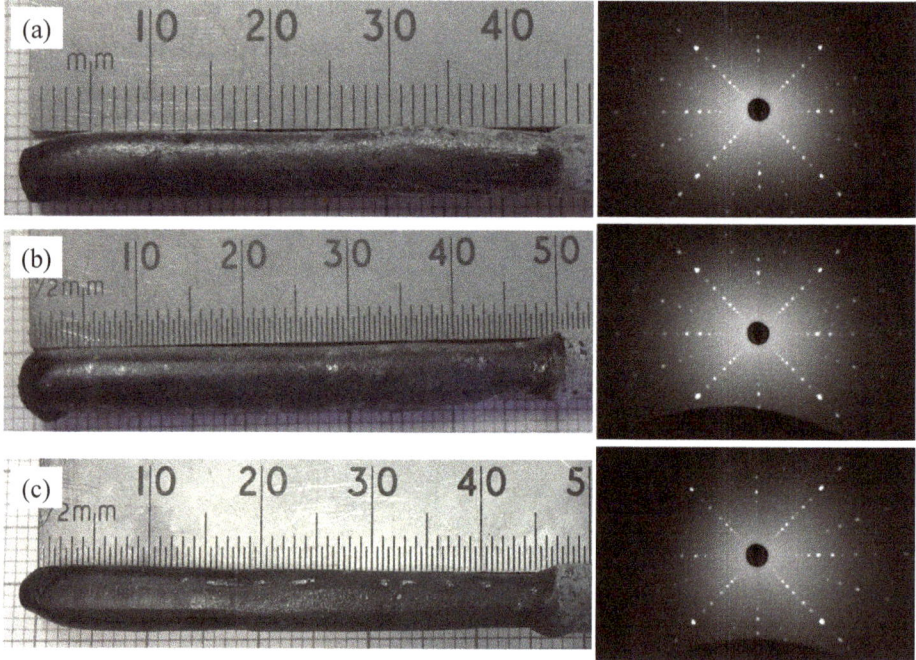

Figure 1. Crystal boules of (**a**) $Sm_{0.95}Ce_{0.05}B_6$, (**b**) $Sm_{0.90}Ce_{0.10}B_6$ and (**c**) $Sm_{0.80}Ce_{0.20}B_6$, prepared by the floating-zone method in argon atmosphere at a growth rate of 18 mm/h. X-ray Laue back reflection photographs show the [001] orientation of aligned $Sm_{1-x}Ce_xB_6$ samples used for the physical properties measurements.

3.2. Structural and Composition Analysis

Structural and phase purity analysis was carried out using powder X-ray diffraction measurements on small pieces of the $Sm_{1-x}Ce_xB_6$ crystals selected from close to the end of each crystal boule. Figures 2a–c show the patterns for $x = 0.05$, 0.10 and 0.20, and profile matching (goodness of fit, GOF = 1.35, 1.51 and 1.92, respectively) to the cubic $Pm\overline{3}m$ space group [20] indicates that in each case the main phase is $Sm_{1-x}Ce_xB_6$, with no significant impurity phases present. One peak that does not belong to the $Pm\overline{3}m$ cubic structure can be observed at $\sim26.6°$ in the powder X-ray profiles of each of the $Sm_{1-x}Ce_xB_6$ crystals grown. The impurity was identified to be a hexagonal ($P6_3/mmc$) $SmBO_3$ phase [60]. Lattice parameters calculated from the profile matching were determined to be 4.1351(2) Å, 4.1384(2) Å and 4.1393(2) Å, respectively, for $Sm_{0.95}Ce_{0.05}B_6$, $Sm_{0.90}Ce_{0.10}B_6$ and $Sm_{0.80}Ce_{0.20}B_6$ (see Table 1). The values are in agreement with those reported in previous studies on $Sm_{1-x}Ce_xB_6$ polycrystalline samples [21].

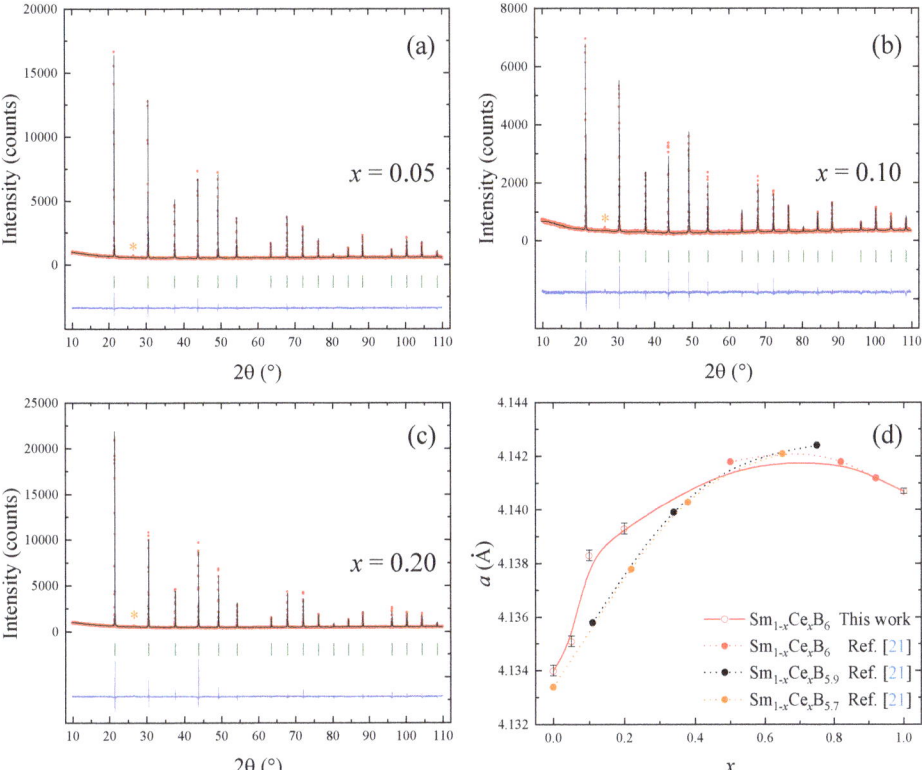

Figure 2. Powder X-ray diffraction patterns of $Sm_{1-x}Ce_xB_6$ with (**a**) $x = 0.05$, (**b**) $x = 0.10$ and (**c**) $x = 0.20$) for samples taken from the crystal boules. The experimental profile (red closed circles) and a full profile matching refinement (black solid line) made using the $Pm\bar{3}m$ cubic structure are shown, with the difference given by the blue solid line. The orange coloured symbols * indicate the impurity peaks belonging to $SmBO_3$ impurity phases. (**d**) Evolution of the lattice parameter, a, as a function of the concentration, x, of the Ce-substituent for $Sm_{1-x}Ce_xB_6$. The experimental values obtained in the present work (red open circles) are also given in Table 1. The previously reported values (red, black and orange closed circles) of the crystallographic parameters for the $Sm_{1-x}Ce_xB_{6-y}$ series [21] are given for completeness.

Figure 2d shows the dependence of the lattice constant on the concentration of Ce for the $Sm_{1-x}Ce_xB_6$ samples. The composition dependence of the cubic parameter, a, does not obey Vegard's law [61], for the $Sm_{1-x}Ce_xB_6$ series. The anomalously large positive deviation observed in Figure 2d can be attributed to the mixed valence of samarium ions [37,38,62]. As the concentration of the Ce-substituent changes from $x = 0$ to 1, the Ce^{3+} ions replace the Sm^{3+} ions preferentially, whereas the concentration of Sm^{2+} ions remains constant [21,38,50]. The effective ionic radius [63,64] of Ce^{3+} (1.01 Å) is larger than the ionic radius of Sm^{3+} (0.958 Å); thus, the substitution of samarium with cerium ions results initially in a lattice expansion (up to $x \sim 0.6$). Further substitution of samarium with cerium is followed by a subtle lattice contraction, which is attributed to the replacement of the larger Sm^{2+} ions (1.15 Å) with Ce^{3+}. A similar effect on the lattice constant has been observed in the case of Gd and La-substituted SmB_6 [38,50,65].

Table 1. Lattice parameters calculated from profile matching the powder X-ray diffraction patterns of the $Sm_{1-x}Ce_xB_6$ ($x = 0.05, 0.10$ and 0.20) crystals to the $Pm\bar{3}m$ cubic structure. The previously reported structural parameters quoted for other members of the $Sm_{1-x}Ce_xB_{6-y}$ series [21] are included for completeness.

$Sm_{1-x}Ce_xB_{6-y}$	Chemical Composition		a (Å)	Study
	x	y		
SmB_6	0	0	4.1340(2)	Present work
$Sm_{0.95}Ce_{0.05}B_6$	0.05	0	4.1351(2)	Present work
$Sm_{0.90}Ce_{0.10}B_6$	0.10	0	4.1384(2)	Present work
$Sm_{0.89}Ce_{0.11}B_{5.9}$	0.11	0.1	4.1358	Ref. [21]
$Sm_{0.80}Ce_{0.20}B_6$	0.20	0	4.1393(2)	Present work
$Sm_{0.78}Ce_{0.22}B_{5.7}$	0.22	0.3	4.1378	Ref. [21]
$Sm_{0.66}Ce_{0.34}B_{5.9}$	0.34	0.1	4.1399	Ref. [21]
$Sm_{0.62}Ce_{0.38}B_{5.7}$	0.38	0.3	4.1403	Ref. [21]
$Sm_{0.50}Ce_{0.50}B_6$	0.50	0	4.1418	Ref. [21]
$Sm_{0.35}Ce_{0.65}B_{5.7}$	0.65	0.3	4.1421	Ref. [21]
$Sm_{0.25}Ce_{0.75}B_{5.9}$	0.75	0.1	4.1424	Ref. [21]
$Sm_{0.18}Ce_{0.82}B_6$	0.82	0	4.1418	Ref. [21]
$Sm_{0.08}Ce_{0.92}B_6$	0.92	0	4.1412	Ref. [21]
CeB_6	1.00	0	4.1407(1)	Present work

Composition analysis of the crystals of $Sm_{1-x}Ce_xB_6$ was carried out by EDX to determine the concentrations of Ce in each crystal. The results, given in Table 2, show that the ratios for Sm:Ce are similar to the expected chemical compositions for the crystals, relative to the starting compositions of the polycrystalline materials (5%, 10% and 20% Ce-substituted SmB_6 samples).

Table 2. Chemical composition and valence of the Sm ions determined by EDX and XPS for the $Sm_{1-x}Ce_xB_6$ crystal boules grown. The data collected on a pure SmB_6 crystal are included for completeness. The XPS measurements were carried out on a piece of an as-grown SmB_6 crystal boule and on a sample cleaved (in-situ) from the as-grown SmB_6 crystal fragment.

Chemical Composition	Sm:B Ratio (EDX)	Sm:B Ratio (XPS)	Sm Valence Present Work (XPS)	Literature (Refs. [37,41])
SmB_6	1.00(2):5.50(2)	1.00(3):6.4(3)	+2.80(2)	~2.6–2.7
SmB_6 cleaved	-	1:00(3):7.30(3)	+2.72(2)	
$Sm_{1-x}Ce_xB_6$	x (EDX)	x (XPS)	Sm valence (XPS)	
$Sm_{0.95}Ce_{0.05}B_6$	0.07(2)	0.09(3)	+2.86(2)	
$Sm_{0.90}Ce_{0.10}B_6$	0.11(2)	0.14(3)	+2.86(2)	
$Sm_{0.80}Ce_{0.20}B_6$	0.21(2)	0.23(3)	+2.85(2)	

Core level XPS spectra were recorded using a pass energy of 20 eV (resolution ~0.4 eV) on an area of 300 µm × 700 µm of the $Sm_{1-x}Ce_xB_6$ crystals and used to study the electronic states of Sm $4d$, Ce $3d_{3/2}$ and Ce $3d_{5/2}$ levels, shown in Figure 3. The Sm $4d$ XPS spectrum (see Figure 3a) is composed of one singlet, at 123.5 eV, and one multiplet, at 134.1 eV, separated by approximately 10.6 eV. The Sm^{2+} ($4f^6$ ground-state) feature appears near 129 eV (Sm $4d$ photoelectron line position), which is in agreement with previously published XPS studies on pure SmB_6 [66,67]. The Sm^{3+} ($4f^5$) multiplet appears at a higher binding energy, well separated from the 2+ peak. The contributions of the two features to the XPS spectra were used to determine the valence of the Sm ions. The results, given in Table 2, reveal that $Sm_{1-x}Ce_xB_6$ are mixed valence systems, similar to the parent compound SmB_6 [37,38]. The average Sm valence values of the $Sm_{1-x}Ce_xB_6$ boules are slightly larger than the values determined previously for pure SmB_6 [67–70], due to surface oxidation effects (an increased concentration of Sm^{3+} to the detriment of the Sm^{2+} ions). Previous XPS results reported an increased average Sm valence and a B/Sm ratio lower than the nominal stoichiometric value of 6:1 when the SmB_6 crystals were exposed to ambient conditions [67]. To confirm this hypothesis, XPS spectra were collected on two SmB_6 crystal samples, an as-grown and a cleaved crystal fragment. The average samarium valence is ~2.8 for the as-grown crystal fragment of SmB_6. In the case of SmB_6 cleaved in-situ from the as-grown crystal, the Sm valence is 2.7, corresponding to a Sm^{3+}:Sm^{2+} ratio of approximately ~0.7:~0.3, which is in agreement with previous results [37,41].

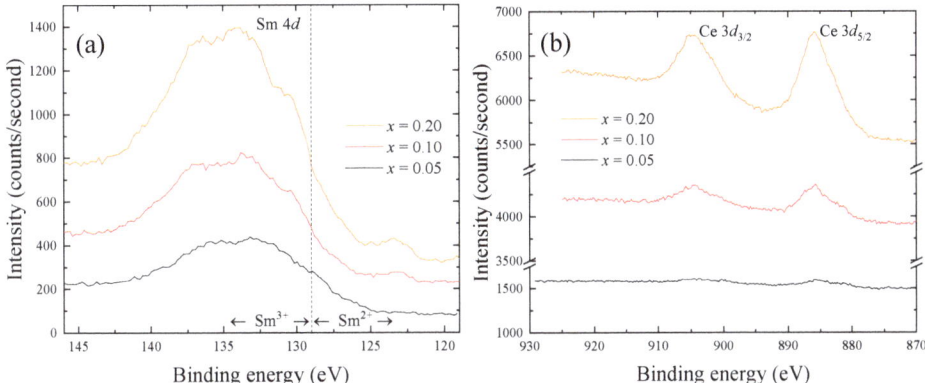

Figure 3. (a) Sm 4d XPS spectrum and (b) Ce 3$d_{3/2,5/2}$ XPS spectra collected for the $Sm_{1-x}Ce_xB_6$ (x = 0.05, 0.10, and 0.20) crystal boules.

The Ce 3d spectrum, shown in Figure 3b, is comprised of two multiplets, at 885.8 eV and 904.8 eV, corresponding to the spin-orbit split 3$d_{5/2}$ and 3$d_{3/2}$ core levels. The spin-orbit splitting is approximately 19 eV, with the complex electronic structure of different Ce oxidation states yielding useful spectral features which can be used to distinguish Ce^{3+} and Ce^{4+}. In our data, each component of the Ce 3d XPS spectrum is dominated by two features. The absence of a third component at 916 eV, characteristic of the Ce^{4+} (4f^0) [71,72], indicates that the Ce ion is in the 3+ state in the $Sm_{1-x}Ce_xB_6$ samples. The analysis of the XPS results, given in Table 2, allowed us to estimate the amount of Ce-substituent in the $Sm_{1-x}Ce_xB_6$ crystal boules. A comparison of the Ce concentrations determined from the XPS spectra and those estimated from the EDX compositional analysis is provided in Table 2.

3.3. Magnetisation

Zero-field-cooled warming (ZFCW) and field-cooled cooling (FCC) magnetisation versus temperature curves were collected on pieces of the $Sm_{1-x}Ce_xB_6$ (x = 0.05, 0.10 and 0.20) single crystals with an applied field of 500 Oe along three different crystallographic directions ([001], [110] and [111]). The temperature dependence of the dc magnetic susceptibility, $\chi(T)$, is shown in Figure 4a. The magnetic susceptibility measured along the different crystallographic directions for all three $Sm_{1-x}Ce_xB_6$ crystals decreased on warming from 1.8 K to room temperature. In addition, for each $Sm_{1-x}Ce_xB_6$ composition, the magnetic susceptibilities collected with field applied along the three different high-symmetry directions all overlap to within experimental error across the whole temperature range.

The temperature dependent magnetic susceptibility of the $Sm_{1-x}Ce_xB_6$ crystals was compared with data collected on a pure SmB_6 crystal grown by the floating zone method [57]. In the temperature range 300 to 60 K, the magnetic susceptibility of Ce-substituted and pure SmB_6 crystals show a similar behaviour, i.e., a gradual increase of $\chi(T)$ with decreasing temperature. Below 60 K, the $Sm_{1-x}Ce_xB_6$ crystals exhibit a more rapid increase in susceptibility, down to 1.8 K. In contrast, the susceptibility data of pure SmB_6 crystals contain a broad maximum centred around 50–60 K, characteristic of a

Kondo insulator, before a more gradual upturn at lower temperatures. Moreover, in the temperature range 1.8–60 K, the magnetic susceptibility of $Sm_{1-x}Ce_xB_6$ crystals increases sharply with increasing Ce content. The change in the magnetic response of both Ce-substituted and pure SmB_6 crystals below 60 K coincides with the increase observed in the resistivity (see Figure 5).

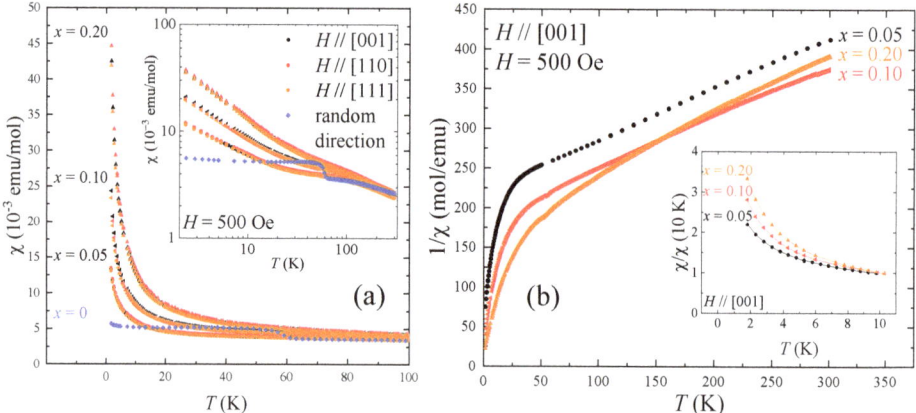

Figure 4. (**a**) Temperature dependence of the *dc* magnetic susceptibility, χ versus *T*, in the temperature range 1.8–100 K for the $Sm_{1-x}Ce_xB_6$ (x = 0, 0.05, 0.10 and 0.20) crystals, with a magnetic field applied along the [001] (black), [110] (red) and [111] (orange) crystallographic directions. The previously reported susceptibility data for a SmB_6 crystal [57] are given for comparison. The inset shows χ versus *T*, on a logarithmic scale, in the temperature range 1.8–300 K. (**b**) Temperature dependence of the reciprocal of the *dc* susceptibility, χ^{-1} versus *T*, of $Sm_{1-x}Ce_xB_6$ for a field applied along the [001] direction. The inset shows the normalised magnetic susceptibilities of $Sm_{1-x}Ce_xB_6$ samples, with a magnetic field applied along the [001] direction. The χ/χ (10 K) versus *T* data increase rapidly at low temperatures, but with no signature of long-range magnetic order, for all Ce concentrations.

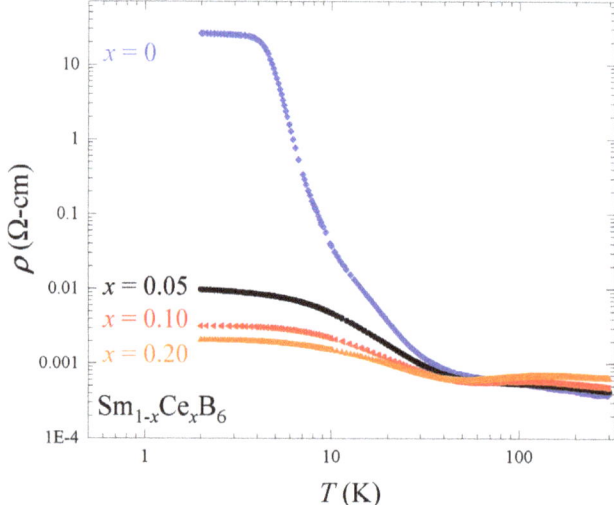

Figure 5. Temperature dependence of the bulk *ac* resistivity, ρ versus *T*, in the temperature range 1.8–300 K for the $Sm_{1-x}Ce_xB_6$ (x = 0, 0.05, 0.10 and 0.20) crystals. The previously reported resistivity data for a SmB_6 crystal [57] are given for comparison.

Attempts to fit the temperature-dependent reciprocal magnetic susceptibilities, $\chi^{-1}(T)$ (see Figure 4b), in the temperature range 100–300 K reveal that pure SmB_6 and the $Sm_{1-x}Ce_xB_6$ materials all appear to follow a Curie–Weiss law. The effective moment, μ_{eff}, per formula unit at 300 K varies from $2.4(1)\mu_B$ for $x = 0.00$ to $2.5(1)\mu_B$ for $x = 0.20$. The form of $\chi(T)$ for the $Sm_{1-x}Ce_xB_6$ crystals is qualitatively similar than data reported for aluminium flux grown Ce-substituted SmB_6 single crystals, although the effective moments in our samples are substantially lower, especially for lower Ce concentrations [54]. The $\chi(T)$ data are consistent with magnetic response expected for a mixture of $4f^1$ Ce^{3+} ions $(2.54\mu_B/Ce^{3+})$ and divalent and trivalent Sm ions in a variety of magnetic and nonmagnetic electronic configurations, $(4f^6)$, $(4f^5d^1)$, and $(4f^5)$ [68,73,74].

A previous study reported that substituting Sm with another magnetic rare earth ion, such as Gd^{3+}, in large concentrations ($\geq 40\%$), leads to antiferromagnetic ordering at low temperature due to coupling between the Gd sites [18]. This is predicted by the existence of a saturation plateau in the normalised magnetic susceptibility data of 40% Gd-substituted SmB_6. In contrast, the magnetisation curves for our $Sm_{1-x}Ce_xB_6$ crystals exhibit a rapid increase at low temperatures, but with no evidence for the onset of long-range magnetic order down to 2 K, as shown in the inset of Figure 4b. For the Ce^{3+} concentrations used in our work, the magnetic data suggest that the Ce ions are distributed randomly in the lattice.

3.4. Resistivity

Alternating current resistivity versus temperature, $\rho(T)$, measurements were made on bar shaped samples cut from the $Sm_{1-x}Ce_xB_6$ ($x = 0.05, 0.10$ and 0.20) single crystals. The ac resistivity data are shown in Figure 5 for temperatures between 1.8 and 300 K. These resistivity data are compared with data for a pure SmB_6 crystal grown by the FZ method and reported in our previous work [57]. At 300 K, the $Sm_{1-x}Ce_xB_6$ samples all have resistivity values similar to SmB_6 and $\rho(300\ K)$ increases with x. Below 300 K, SmB_6 exhibits a continuous increase in the bulk electrical resistivity. In contrast, the $\rho(T)$ data for the Ce-substituted samples exhibit a broad maximum centred around 150 K, followed by an increasingly prominent minimum at ~ 50 K. On further cooling below 50 K, the resistivity of SmB_6 increases by four orders of magnitude, whereas the resistivity of the Ce-substituted samples increases by only a single order of magnitude or less. Nevertheless, the $Sm_{1-x}Ce_xB_6$ samples still have resistivities larger than pure CeB_6, over the entire temperature range studied. The resistivity of CeB_6 is approximately 10^{-5} Ω-cm from 2 to 300 K [75], whereas for the $Sm_{1-x}Ce_xB_6$ samples it is 10^{-3} Ω-cm or higher over the same temperature range, for the $x = 0.20$ sample.

In contrast to the saturation plateau seen in the resistivity of SmB_6 at lowest temperatures, $\rho(T)$ for the $Sm_{1-x}Ce_xB_6$ samples increases monotonically with decreasing temperature below 10 K. These results are in agreement with the transport measurements performed on aluminium flux grown Ce-substituted SmB_6 single crystals [54]. There is an evolution from the TKI behaviour of pure SmB_6 to a dense Kondo system with low temperature spin ordering of CeB_6 [7,8,75]. The data suggest that it is bulk conductivity, modified by crystalline electric field and Kondo effects alongside phonon scattering, that determines the form of the $\rho(T)$ curves for these $Sm_{1-x}Ce_xB_6$ samples over the entire temperature range studied. A more quantitative description of the transport properties of the $Sm_{1-x}Ce_xB_6$ crystals, including extensive measurements in a magnetic field, will be presented elsewhere [76].

4. Conclusions

Crystal boules of $Sm_{1-x}Ce_xB_6$ ($x = 0.05, 0.10$, and 0.20) compounds were grown, for the first time, by the FZ technique. Investigation of the crystals using X-ray diffraction techniques revealed that the Ce-substituent is successfully incorporated in the SmB_6 structure and that the structural distortions due to the substitution of Sm with Ce follow a similar trend to the one reported for polycrystalline samples of Ce-substituted SmB_6. EDX and XPS results confirm that the Ce concentration is close to the nominal stoichiometric values of $x = 0.05, 0.10$ and 0.20. Analysis of the average Sm valence data determined by XPS on $Sm_{1-x}Ce_xB_6$ and pure SmB_6 samples showed that the results are extremely dependent on the quality of the surface studied; i.e., an increase in the Sm valence is observed when the surface is exposed to ambient conditions. Magnetic property measurements show that our $Sm_{1-x}Ce_xB_6$ crystals exhibit no sign of long-range magnetic ordering, at substitution concentrations below 20%. Temperature dependent resistivity measurements revealed that a 5% (and above) substitution with Ce suppresses the crossover from bulk to surface conductivity seen in pure SmB_6 as the temperature is reduced. Detailed low temperature magneto-transport measurements are now being carried out to investigate the bulk and surface properties of the $Sm_{1-x}Ce_xB_6$ crystals.

Author Contributions: M.C.H. and T.A. performed the crystal growths; characterisation measurements were carried out by M.C.H. and T.A. with M.W. and M.R.L.; M.C.H., T.A., M.W., M.R.L. and G.B. analysed the data; M.C.H. and T.A. drafted the paper; M.R.L. and G.B. reviewed the manuscript; G.B. secured the funding and managed the project. All authors have read and agreed to the published version of the manuscript.

Funding: Financial support was provided by EPSRC, UK, through grant EP/T005963/1.

Acknowledgments: The authors thank S. York for the EDX compositional analysis, and A. Julian and T. E. Orton for valuable technical support.

Conflicts of Interest: The authors declare no conflict of interest.

Abbreviations

The following abbreviations are used in this manuscript:

RE	Rare earth
TKI	Topological Kondo insulator
FZ	Floating zone
EDX	Energy dispersive X-ray spectroscopy
XPS	X-ray photoelectron spectroscopy
ac	Alternating current
ZFCW	Zero-field-cooled warming
FCC	Field-cooled cooling

References

1. Matthias, B.T.; Geballe, T.H.; Andres, K.; Corenzwit, E.; Hull, G.W.; Maita, J.P. Superconductivity and Antiferromagnetism in Boron-Rich Lattices. *Science* **1968**, *159*, 530. [CrossRef]
2. Lortz, R.; Wang, Y.; Tutsch, U.; Abe, S.; Meingast, C.; Popovich, P.; Knafo, W.; Shitsevalova, N.; Paderno, Y.B.; Junod, A. Superconductivity mediated by a soft phonon mode: Specific heat, resistivity, thermal expansion, and magnetization of YB_6. *Phys. Rev. B* **2006**, *73*, 024512. [CrossRef]
3. Flachbart, K.; Gabáni, S.; Kačmarčik, J.; Mori, T.; Otani, S.; Pavlík, V. Low Temperature Properties and Superconductivity of YB_6 and YB_4. *AIP Conf. Proc.* **2006**, *850*, 635.
4. Coles, B.R.; Griffiths, D. Antiferromagnetic behaviour of GdB_6. *Proc. Phys. Soc. (1958–1967)* **1961**, *77*, 213–215. [CrossRef]
5. Nozaki, H.; Tanaka, T.; Ishizawa, Y. Magnetic behaviour and structure change of GdB_6 single crystals at low temperatures. *J. Phys. C Solid State Phys.* **1980**, *13*, 2751. [CrossRef]
6. Semeno, A.V.; Gil'manov, M.I.; Sluchanko, N.E.; Shitsevalova, N.Y.; Filipov, V.B.; Demishev, S.V. Antiferromagnetic Resonance in GdB_6. *JETP Lett.* **2018**, *108*, 237–242. [CrossRef]
7. Fujita, T.; Suzuki, M.; Komatsubara, T.; Kunii, S.; Kasuya, T.; Ohtsuka, T. Anomalous specific heat of CeB_6. *Solid State Commun.* **1980**, *35*, 569–572. [CrossRef]
8. Takase, A.; Kojima, K.; Komatsubara, T.; Kasuya, T. Electrical resistivity and magnetoresistance of CeB_6 single crystal. *Solid State Commun.* **1980**, *36*, 461–464. [CrossRef]
9. Friemel, G.; Li, Y.; Dukhnenko, A.; Shitsevalova, N.Y.; Sluchanko, N.E.; Ivanov, A.; Filipov, V.B.; Keimer, B.; Inosov, D.S. Resonant magnetic exciton mode in the heavy-fermion antiferromagnet CeB_6. *Nat. Commun.* **2012**, *3*, 830. [CrossRef]
10. Koitzsch, A.; Heming, N.; Knupfer, M.; Büchner, B.; Portnichenko, P.Y.; Dukhnenko, A.V.; Shitsevalova, N.Y.; Filipov, V.B.; Lev, L.L.; Strocov, V.N.; et al. Nesting-driven multipolar order in CeB_6 from photoemission tomography. *Nat. Commun.* **2016**, *7*, 10876. [CrossRef]

11. Guy, C.N.; von Molnar, S.; Etourneau, J.; Fisk, Z. Charge transport and pressure dependence of T_c of single crystal, ferromagnetic EuB$_6$. *Solid State Commun.* **1980**, *33*, 1055–1058. [CrossRef]
12. Goodrich, R.G.; Harrison, N.; Vuillemin, J.J.; Teklu, A.; Hall, D.W.; Fisk, Z.; Young, D.; Sarrao, J. Fermi surface of ferromagnetic EuB$_6$. *Phys. Rev. B* **1998**, *58*, 14896–14902. [CrossRef]
13. Nie, S.; Sun, Y.; Prinz, F.B.; Wang, Z.; Weng, H.; Fang, Z.; Dai, X. Magnetic semimetals and quantized anomalous Hall effect in EuB$_6$. *Phys. Rev. Lett.* **2020**, *124*, 076403. [CrossRef] [PubMed]
14. Arko, A.J.; Crabtree, G.; Karim, D.; Mueller, F.M.; Windmiller, L.R.; Ketterson, J.B.; Fisk, Z. de Haas-van Alphen effect and the Fermi surface of LaB$_6$. *Phys. Rev. B* **1977**, *13*, 5240–5247. [CrossRef]
15. Bai, L.; Ma, N.; Liu, F. Structure and chemical bond characteristics of LaB$_6$. *Phys. B Condens. Matter* **2009**, *404*, 4086–4089. [CrossRef]
16. Kasai, H.; Nishibori, E. Spatial distribution of electrons near the Fermi level in the metallic LaB$_6$ through accurate X-ray charge density study. *Sci. Rep.* **2017**, *7*, 41375. [CrossRef] [PubMed]
17. Wolgast, S.; Kurdak, Ç.; Sun, K.; Allen, J.W.; Kim, D.J.; Fisk, Z. Low-temperature surface conduction in the Kondo insulator SmB$_6$. *Phys. Rev. B* **2013**, *88*, 180405(R). [CrossRef]
18. Kim, D.J.; Xia, J.; Fisk, Z. Topological surface state in the Kondo insulator samarium hexaboride. *Nat. Mater.* **2014**, *13*, 466–470. [CrossRef]
19. Tan, B.S.; Hsu, Y.T.; Zeng, B.; Ciomaga Hatnean, M.; Harrison, N.; Zhu, Z.; Hartstein, M.; Kiourlappou, M.; Srivastava, A.; Johannes, M.D.; et al. Unconventional Fermi surface in an insulating state. *Science* **2015**, *349*, 287–290. [CrossRef] [PubMed]
20. Stackelberg, M.; Neumann, F. Die kristallstruktur der boride der zusammensetzung MeB$_6$. *Zeitschrift für Physikalische Chemie* **1932**, *B19*, 314.
21. Aivazov, M.I.; Aleksandrovich, S.V.; Mkrtchyan, V.S. Magnetic susceptibility of Ce$_x$La$_{1-x}$B$_6$, Ce$_x$Eu$_{1-x}$B$_6$, Sm$_x$La$_{1-x}$B$_6$, and Sm$_x$Ce$_{1-x}$B$_6$ solid solutions. *Phys. Status Solidi* **1980**, *62*, 109–114. [CrossRef]
22. Funahashi, S.; Tanaka, K.; Iga, F. X-ray atomic orbital analysis of 4f and 5d electron configuration of SmB6 at 100, 165, 230 and 298 K. *Acta Crystallogr. Sect. B Struct. Sci.* **2010**, *66*, 292–306. [CrossRef] [PubMed]
23. Aeppli, G.; Fisk, Z. Kondo insulators. *Comments Condens. Matter Phys.* **1992**, *16*, 155–165.
24. Riseborough, P.S. Heavy fermion semiconductors. *Adv. Phys.* **2000**, *49*, 257–320. [CrossRef]
25. Fu, L.; Kane, C.L.; Mele, E.J. Topological insulators in three dimensions. *Phys. Rev. Lett.* **2007**, *98*, 106803. [CrossRef] [PubMed]
26. Moore, J.E.; Balents, L. Topological invariants of time-reversal-invariant band structures. *Phys. Rev. B* **2007**, *75*, 121306(R). [CrossRef]
27. Roy, R. Topological phases and the quantum spin Hall effect in three dimensions. *Phys. Rev. B* **2009**, *79*, 195322. [CrossRef]
28. Dzero, M.; Sun, K.; Galitski, V.; Coleman, P. Topological Kondo insulators. *Phys. Rev. Lett.* **2010**, *104*, 106408. [CrossRef]
29. Takimoto, T. SmB$_6$: A promising candidate for a topological insulator. *J. Phys. Soc. Jpn.* **2011**, *80*, 123710. [CrossRef]
30. Dzero, M.; Sun, K.; Coleman, P.; Galitski, V. Theory of topological Kondo insulators. *Phys. Rev. B* **2012**, *85*, 045130. [CrossRef]
31. Neupane, M.; Alidoust, N.; Xu, S.Y.; Kondo, T.; Ishida, Y.; Kim, D.J.; Liu, C.; Belopolski, I.; Jo, Y.J.; Chang, T.R.; et al. Surface electronic structure of the topological Kondo-insulator candidate correlated electron system SmB$_6$. *Nat. Commun.* **2013**, *4*, 2991. [CrossRef] [PubMed]
32. Hlawenka, P.; Siemensmeyer, K.; Weschke, E.; Varykhalov, A.; Sánchez-Barriga, J.; Shitsevalova, N.Y.; Dukhnenko, A.V.; Filipov, V.B.; Gabáni, S.; Flachbart, K.; et al. Samarium hexaboride is a trivial surface conductor. *Nat. Commun.* **2018**, *9*, 517. [CrossRef] [PubMed]
33. Menth, A.; Buehler, E.; Geballe, T.H. Magnetic and semiconducting properties of SmB$_6$. *Phys. Rev. Lett.* **1969**, *22*, 295–297. [CrossRef]
34. Allen, J.W.; Batlogg, B.; Wachter, P. Large low-temperature Hall effect and resistivity in mixed-valent SmB$_6$. *Phys. Rev. B* **1979**, *20*, 4807–4813. [CrossRef]
35. Cooley, J.C.; Aronson, M.C.; Fisk, Z.; Canfield, P.C. SmB$_6$: Kondo insulator or exotic metal? *Phys. Rev. Lett.* **1995**, *74*, 1629–1632. [CrossRef] [PubMed]

36. Phelan, W.; Koohpayeh, S.; Cottingham, P.; Freeland, J.; Leiner, J.; Broholm, C.; McQueen, T. Correlation between bulk thermodynamic measurements and the low-temperature-resistance plateau in SmB_6. *Phys. Rev. X* **2014**, *4*, 031012.
37. Kasuya, T.; Takegahara, K.; Fujita, T.; Tanaka, T.; Bannai, E. Valence fluctuating state in SmB_6. *J. Phys. Colloq.* **1979**, *40*, 308–313. [CrossRef]
38. Kasuya, T. Mixed-salence state in SmB_6. *Europhys. Lett. (EPL)* **1994**, *26*, 283–287. [CrossRef]
39. Flachbart, K.; Gabáni, S.; Herrmannsdörfer, T.; Konovalova, E.; Paderno, Y.; Pavlík, V. Low-temperature magnetic properties of SmB_6. *Phys. B Condens. Matter* **2000**, *284–288*, 1353–1354. [CrossRef]
40. Gheidi, S.; Akintola, K.; Akella, K.S.; Côté, A.M.; Dunsiger, S.R.; Broholm, C.; Fuhrman, W.T.; Saha, S.R.; Paglione, J.; Sonier, J.E. Intrinsic Low-Temperature Magnetism in SmB_6. *Phys. Rev. Lett.* **2019**, *123*, 197203. [CrossRef]
41. Chazalviel, J.N.; Campagna, M.; Wertheim, G.K.; Schmidt, P.H.; Longinotti, L.D. Electronic structure of SmB_6 and related rare-earth borides by x-ray photoelectron spectroscopy. *Physica B+C* **1977**, *86–88*, 237–238. [CrossRef]
42. Barla, A.; Derr, J.; Sanchez, J.P.; Salce, B.; Lapertot, G.; Doyle, B.P.; Rüffer, R.; Lengsdorf, R.; Abd-Elmeguid, M.M.; Flouquet, J. High-Pressure Ground State of SmB_6: Electronic Conduction and Long Range Magnetic Order. *Phys. Rev. Lett.* **2005**, *94*, 166401. [CrossRef] [PubMed]
43. Miyazaki, H.; Hajiri, T.; Ito, T.; Kunii, S.; Kimura, S.I. Momentum-dependent hybridization gap and dispersive in-gap state of the Kondo semiconductor SmB_6. *Phys. Rev. B* **2012**, *86*, 075105. [CrossRef]
44. Hall, D.; Fisk, Z.; Goodrich, R.G. Magnetic-field dependence of the paramagnetic to the high-temperature magnetically ordered phase transition in CeB_6. *Phys. Rev. B* **2000**, *62*, 84–86. [CrossRef]
45. Goodrich, R.G.; Young, D.P.; Hall, D.; Balicas, L.; Fisk, Z.; Harrison, N.; Betts, J.; Migliori, A.; Woodward, F.M.; Lynn, J.W. Extension of the temperature-magnetic field phase diagram of CeB_6. *Phys. Rev. B* **2004**, *69*, 054415. [CrossRef]
46. Terzioglu, C.; Ozturk, O.; Kilic, A.; Goodrich, R.; Fisk, Z. Magnetic and electronic measurements in CeB_6. *J. Magn. Magn. Mater.* **2006**, *298*, 33–37. [CrossRef]
47. Portnichenko, P.; Akbari, A.; Nikitin, S.; Cameron, A.; Dukhnenko, A.; Filipov, V.; Shitsevalova, N.; Čermák, P.; Radelytskyi, I.; Schneidewind, A.; et al. Field-Angle-Resolved Magnetic Excitations as a Probe of Hidden-Order Symmetry in CeB_6. *Phys. Rev. X* **2020**, *10*, 021010. [CrossRef]
48. Hartstein, M.; Toews, W.H.; Hsu, Y.T.; Zeng, B.; Chen, X.; Ciomaga Hatnean, M.; Zhang, Q.R.; Nakamura, S.; Padgett, A.S.; Rodway-Gant, G.; et al. Fermi surface in the absence of a Fermi liquid in the Kondo insulator SmB_6. *Nat. Phys.* **2018**, *14*, 166–172. [CrossRef]
49. Aivazov, M.I.; Aleksandrovich, S.V.; Evseev, B. Physical properties of solid solutions $Sm_xCe_{1-x}B_6$. *Inorg. Mater.* **1980**, *16*, 300–303.
50. Kasaya, M.; Tarascon, J.M.; Etourneau, J. Study of the valence transition in La- and Yb-substituted SmB_6. *Solid State Commun.* **1980**, *33*, 1005–1007. [CrossRef]
51. Liu, B.; Kasaya, M.; Iga, F.; Kasuya, T. Kondo effect in $Sm_{1-y}Yb_yB_6$ and $Tm_{1/2}Yb_{1/2}B_6$. *J. Magn. Magn. Mater.* **1985**, *47-48*, 472–474. [CrossRef]
52. Yeo, S.; Song, K.; Hur, N.; Fisk, Z.; Schlottmann, P. Effects of Eu doping on SmB_6 single crystals. *Phys. Rev. B* **2012**, *85*, 115125. [CrossRef]
53. Gabáni, S.; Flachbart, K.; Bednarčík, J.; Welter, E.; Filipov, V.; Shitsevalova, N. Investigation of Mixed Valence State of $Sm_{1-x}B_6$ and $Sm_{1-x}La_xB_6$ by XANES. *Acta Phys. Pol. A* **2014**, *126*, 292–306. [CrossRef]
54. Miao, L.; Min, C.H.; Xu, Y.; Huang, Z.; Kotta, E.C.; Basak, R.; Song, M.S.; Kang, B.Y.; Cho, B.K.; Kißner, K.; et al. Robust surface states and coherence phenomena in magnetically alloyed SmB_6. *arXiv* **2020**, arXiv:1907.07074v2.
55. Otani, S.; Nakagawa, H.; Nishi, Y.; Kieda, N. Floating zone growth and high temperature hardness of rare-earth hexaboride crystals: LaB_6, CeB_6, PrB_6, NdB_6, and SmB_6. *J. Solid State Chem.* **2000**, *154*, 238–241. [CrossRef]
56. Balakrishnan, G.; Lees, M.R.; Paul, D.M. Growth of large single crystals of rare earth hexaborides. *J. Cryst. Growth* **2003**, *256*, 206–209. [CrossRef]
57. Ciomaga Hatnean, M.; Lees, M.R.; Paul, D.M.; Balakrishnan, G. Large, high quality single-crystals of the new Topological Kondo Insulator, SmB_6. *Sci. Rep.* **2013**, *3*, 3071. [CrossRef]

58. Thomas, S.M.; Ding, X.; Ronning, F.; Zapf, V.; Thompson, J.D.; Fisk, Z.; Xia, J.; Rosa, P.F.S. Quantum oscillations in flux-grown SmB$_6$ with embedded aluminum. *Phys. Rev. Lett.* **2019**, *122*, 166401. [CrossRef]
59. Rodríguez-Carvajal, J. Recent advances in magnetic structure determination by neutron powder diffraction. *Physica B* **1993**, *192*, 55–69. [CrossRef]
60. Newnham, R.E.; Redman, M.J.; Santoro, R.P. Crystal Structure of yttrium and other rare-earth borates. *J. Am. Ceram. Soc.* **1963**, *46*, 253–256. [CrossRef]
61. Vegard, L. Die konstitution der mischkristalle und die raumfüllung der atome. *Z. Phys.* **1921**, *5*, 17–26. [CrossRef]
62. Tarascon, J.; Isikawa, Y.; Chevalier, B.; Etourneau, J.; Hagenmuller, P.; Kasaya, M. Valence transition of samarium in hexaboride solid solutions $Sm_{1-x}M_xB_6$ (M = Yb^{2+}, Sr^{2+}, La^{3+}, Y^{3+}, Th^{4+}). *J. Phys.* **1980**, *41*, 1135–1140. [CrossRef]
63. Shannon, R.D. Revised effective ionic radii and systematic studies of interatomic distances in halides and chalcogenides. *Acta Crystallogr. Sect. A* **1976**, *32*, 751–767. [CrossRef]
64. Jia, Y.Q. Crystal radii and effective ionic radii of the rare earth ions. *J. Solid State Chem.* **1991**, *95*, 184–187. [CrossRef]
65. Konovalova, E.S.; Paderno, Y.B.; Lundstrem, T.; Finkel'shtein, L.D.; Efremova, N.N.; Dudnik, E.M. Effect of vacancies and foreign metal ions on the valent state of samarium in SmB$_6$. *Sov. Powder Metall. Met. Ceram.* **1982**, *21*, 820–823. [CrossRef]
66. Chazalviel, J.N.; Campagna, M.; Wertheim, G.K.; Schmidt, P.H. Study of valence mixing in SmB$_6$ by x-ray photoelectron spectroscopy. *Phys. Rev. B* **1976**, *14*, 4586–4592. [CrossRef]
67. Heming, N.; Treske, U.; Knupfer, M.; Büchner, B.; Inosov, D.S.; Shitsevalova, N.Y.; Filipov, V.B.; Krause, S.; Koitzsch, A. Surface properties of SmB$_6$ from x-ray photoelectron spectroscopy. *Phys. Rev. B* **2014**, *90*, 195128. [CrossRef]
68. Mizumaki, M.; Tsutsui, S.; Iga, F. Temperature dependence of Sm valence in SmB$_6$ studied by X-ray absorption spectroscopy. *J. Phys. Conf. Ser.* **2009**, *176*, 012034. [CrossRef]
69. Emi, N.; Mito, T.; Kawamura, N.; Mizumaki, M.; Ishimatsu, N.; Pristáš, G.; Kagayama, T.; Shimizu, K.; Osanai, Y.; Iga, F. Temperature and pressure dependences of Sm valence in intermediate valence compound SmB$_6$. *Phys. B Condens. Matter* **2018**, *536*, 197–199. [CrossRef]
70. Savchenkov, P.S.; Alekseev, P.A.; Podlesnyak, A.; Kolesnikov, A.I.; Nemkovski, K.S. Intermediate-valence state of the Sm and Eu in SmB$_6$ and EuCu$_2$Si$_2$: Neutron spectroscopy data and analysis. *J. Phys. Condens. Matter* **2018**, *30*, 055801. [CrossRef]
71. Paparazzo, E. On the curve-fitting of XPS Ce(3d) spectra of cerium oxides. *Mater. Res. Bull.* **2011**, *46*, 323–326. [CrossRef]
72. Revoy, M.N.; Scott, R.W.J.; Grosvenor, A.P. Ceria nanocubes: Dependence of the electronic structure on synthetic and experimental conditions. *J. Phys. Chem. C* **2013**, *117*, 10095–10105. [CrossRef]
73. Gabáni, S.; Flachbart, K.; Pavlík, V.; Herrmannsdorfer, T.; Konovalova, E.; Paderno, Y.; Briančin, J.; Trpčevská, J. Magnetic properties of $Sm_{1-x}B_6$ and $Sm_{1-x}La_xB_6$ solid solutions. *Czechoslov. J. Phys.* **2002**, *52*, A225–A228. [CrossRef]
74. Nickerson, J.C.; White, R.M.; Lee, K.N.; Bachmann, R.; Geballe, T.H.; Hull, G.W. Physical properties of SmB$_6$. *Phys. Rev. B* **1971**, *3*, 2030–2042. [CrossRef]
75. Tanaka, T.; Nishitani, R.; Oshima, C.; Bannai, E.; Kawai, S. The preparation and properties of CeB$_6$, SmB$_6$, and GdB$_6$. *J. Appl. Phys.* **1980**, *51*, 3877. [CrossRef]
76. Ciomaga Hatnean, M.; Lees, M.R.; Ahmad, T.; Balakrishnan, G. University of Warwick, Coventry. 2020, in preparation.

© 2020 by the authors. Licensee MDPI, Basel, Switzerland. This article is an open access article distributed under the terms and conditions of the Creative Commons Attribution (CC BY) license (http://creativecommons.org/licenses/by/4.0/).

Article

Optical Response of Chiral Multifold Semimetal PdGa

Sascha Polatkan * and Ece Uykur

Physikalisches Institut, Universität Stuttgart, Pfaffenwaldring 57, 70569 Stuttgart, Germany; ece.uykur@pi1.physik.uni-stuttgart.de
* Correspondence: sascha.polatkan@pi1.uni-stuttgart.de

Abstract: We present a theoretical study of the band structure and optical conductivity for the chiral multifold semimetal PdGa. We identify several characteristic features in the optical conductivity and provide their origins within the band structure. As experimental optical studies for the mentioned compound have not been reported, we contrast our results with the related compounds, RhSi and CoSi. We believe that the presented hallmarks will provide guidance to future experimental works.

Keywords: topology; chirality; multifold semimetal; optics; DFT

1. Introduction

First hints of topological characters of materials were found in crystals, where avoided band crossings caused a separation of band energies accompanied by a mixture of band characters. Brought into contact with a different material, that hosts a regular order of bands, without band mixing, this enforces surface states at the interface, which would host linear, intersecting bands with opposite spin characters. Later, it was found that this can be extended to be a bulk property, when the Weyl semimetal was born [1], hosting a three-dimensional bulk realization of linear, spin non-degenerate bands. Their equivalency to the surface states of topological insulators is immediatelly obvious, but can further be quantized by the Chern number χ, for which the Weyl semimetal is the lowest integer realization with $\chi = \pm 1$ [2–4]. Weyl semimetals were promising for applications in spintronics [5–7], in optoelectronics [8–11], or even in chemistry [12–16]. Of essence, here, was either the breaking of the time-reversal symmetry, or the inversion symmetry in combination with sufficiently strong spin-orbit coupling (SOC). The first confirmed Weyl-semimetal is TaAs [17–19], which lacks inversion symmetry.

This can be extended to crystals, which host, besides broken inversion symmetry, also a lack of mirror symmetries. Among the 230 space groups, the 65 Sohncke groups fall under this condition and can provide a *chiral* crystal structure. Note that the 65 Sohnke groups are not necessarily chiral space groups, but can provide chiral crystal structures. In total, there are only 22 chiral space groups (11 enantiomorphic pairs). These 22 chiral space groups are contained within the 65 Sohnke groups. The group of PdGa, $P2_13$ is not a chiral space group, but a Sohnke group [20,21].

It has recently been suggested, that in chiral crystals a new type of fermionic state can be realized, extending the pool of topological quasiparticles by the so called multifold fermion [22]. They differ from the Weyl fermion in that they are hosted by conical band intersection with Chern numbers $|\chi| > 1$. To this end, chiral crystal structures belonging to the RhSi family, space group $P2_13$, number 198, have garnered attention as angle resolved photoemission spectroscopy (ARPES) measurements provided strong indications that these materials host surface states, which are maximally extended in k-space [23–28]. The lack of inversion and mirror symmetries, in combination with SOC, leads to the splitting of bands around the high symmetry points Γ and R, giving rise to a non-collinear spin arrangement with Chern numbers $\chi = \pm 4$ [29] with maximally extended surface states, ranging from the center to the edge of the Brillouin zone [25,27,30]. In such semimetals, the

Citation: Polatkan, S.; Uykur, E. Optical Response of Chiral Multifold Semi-metal PdGa. *Crystals* **2021**, *11*, 80. https://doi.org/10.3390/cryst11020080

Academic Editor: Yuri Kivshar
Received: 16 December 2020
Accepted: 18 January 2021
Published: 21 January 2021

Publisher's Note: MDPI stays neutral with regard to jurisdictional clai-ms in published maps and institutio-nal affiliations.

Copyright: © 2021 by the authors. Licensee MDPI, Basel, Switzerland. This article is an open access article distributed under the terms and conditions of the Creative Commons Attribution (CC BY) license (https://creativecommons.org/licenses/by/4.0/).

quantized circular photogalvanic effect has been predicted, which, by effect of topological states, constitutes a photocurrent, quantized in units of material-independent fundamental constants [31–34].

In this paper, we theoretically investigated the material PdGa, which belongs to the same family. So far, PdGa has not been as extensively investigated as its silicon-based counterparts. In contrast to CoSi and RhSi, the Fermi surface of PdGa is considerably larger and is expected to host a larger number of free carriers, perhaps making the experimental observation of the low energy dynamics challenging, as in the case of RhSi [35]. Hence, the theoretical approach would be beneficiary for comparison and provide some guide for the interpretation of the high energy part of the measured spectra.

Furthermore, the optical conductivity provides a useful tool to identify fingerprints of Dirac fermions [36–40], which should express themselves as linear signatures $\sigma(\omega)_1 \propto \omega$ [41,42]. In the silicides, they are thought to occur as low energy excitations near the Γ-point, as the Fermi level almost coincides with the multifold chiral intersection. Even though the Fermi level in PdGa is much higher, we nonetheless find a nearly linear ridge in the optical spectrum and identify its origin, as discussed in the results.

The combination with external stimuli, such as magnetic fields [43–45] or external pressure [46,47], which provide clean, non-invasive tuning mechanisms, makes the optical conductivity especially desirable in the search for topological materials.

We provide theoretical estimates for intra- and interband optical conductivities, which we contrast to and interpret along with the published experimental results of PdGa's sister compounds CoSi [48] and RhSi [35], as no experimental data for PdGa are available.

2. Results and Discussion

We performed DFT calculations using Wien2k's full-potential linearized augmented plane wave (LAPW) methods with the Perdew–Burke–Ernzerhof (PBE) exchange correlation, accounting for the semimetallic nature of the chiral multifold compound PdGa [49,50]. The lattice parameters were adopted from Ref. [29]. Figure 1 shows the chiral atomic structure and the Fermi surface of PdGa. The Fermi surface is comparatively large, with reference to RhSi and CoSi, indicating a much stronger intraband response. In Figure 1d the Fermi surfaces of the separate contributing bands are shown, sorted by energy from left to right. Within the cube-like structure, a set of eight droplet-shaped Fermi surfaces are hidden, positioned within the corners of the cube.

The band structures of PdGa were calculated on an $18 \times 18 \times 18$ k-mesh with and without SOC, as shown in Figure 2a–c. The calculations were converged within 14 cycles down to the charge 10^{-5} e, with e being the electron charge. Core leakage was well within acceptable levels: the core charges for Pd and Ga integrated to 29.998 e and 17.999 e, respectively. These core electrons arise from choosing a generous energy interval of -9.0 Ry for outer electrons. We chose the parameter $RK_{\text{Max}} = 7.0$ and excluded relativistic linear orbitals (RLOs). Due to SOC in combination with the lack of inversion symmetry, bands with opposite spin split throughout the Brillouin zone (BZ) under the action of the Dresselhaus effect. Exempt from the splitting is the Γ-point, at the BZ center, and points or paths on the BZ boundaries. The Γ-point hosts a four-fold degenerate spin 3/2 fermion, also known as the Rarita–Schwinger fermion [51], and the R-point two three-fold degenerate spin 1 fermions, each with the maximum possible Chern number of $|\chi| = 4$ [29,30]. A detailed view of bandstructures around the Γ-point is given in Figure 2b,c without and with SOC, respectively.

The calculations summarized in Figures 3 and 4 were performed on a denser $32 \times 32 \times 32$ k-mesh with SOC, using the `optic` module [52]. Figure 3 shows the density of states (DOS) of PdGa, as well as the atomic densities of Pd and Ga separately. It can be clearly seen that the majority of carriers at the Fermi surface, as well as electrons involved in optical transitions far beyond the visible spectrum, are entirely contributed by Pd. Significant contributions to the DOS from Ga arise at energies only as low as -15 eV, and beyond.

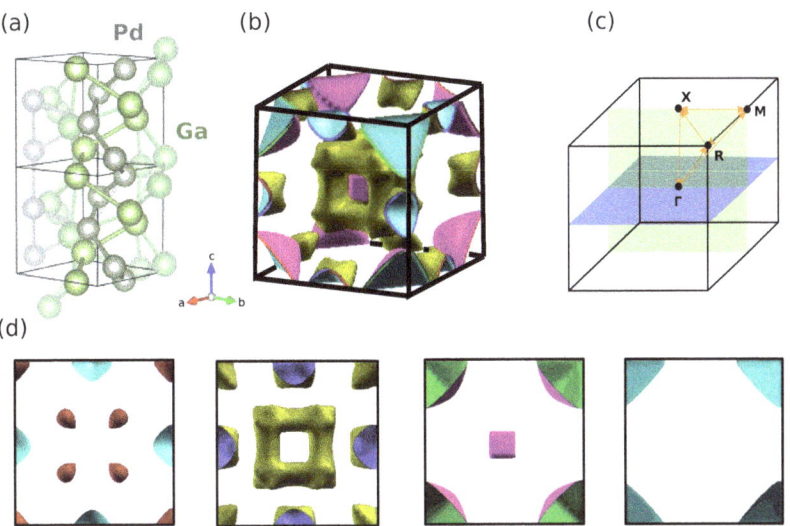

Figure 1. (**a**) The crystal structure of PdGa. The Pd and Ga atoms are arranged chirally along the c-axis, with a distinct handedness, giving rise to chiral properties in the band structure and optical interactions. (**b**) Fermi surface of PdGa. (**c**) Brillouin zone of PdGa representing the high symmetry points used in the band structure plots. (**d**) Contributions of the different bands to the Fermi surface, sorted from lowest to highest energy going from left to right.

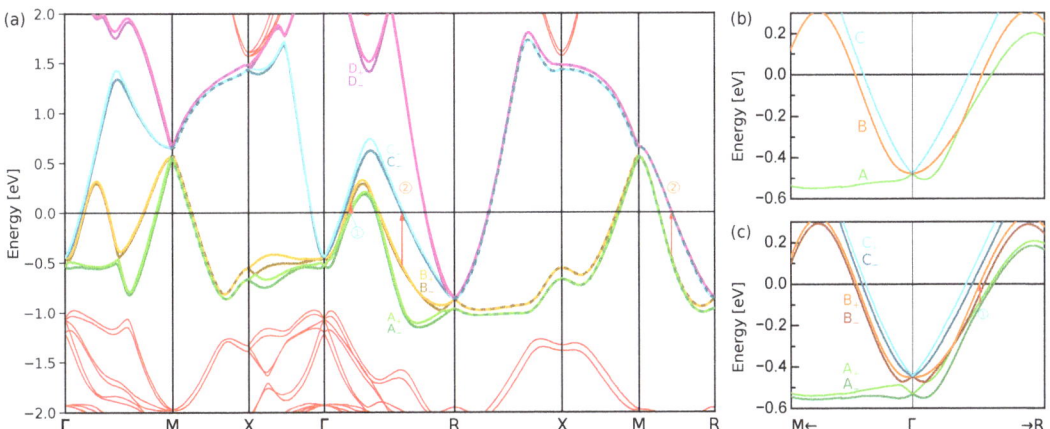

Figure 2. Band structure of PdGa (**a**) with spin-orbit coupling (SOC). Bands that cross the Fermi surface are labeled in pairs $A_\pm$ to $D_\pm$, with respect to their energy. The Fermi energy is positioned at $E_F = 0$ eV. The label $\pm$ refer to spin pairs, which split away from high symmetry points. This splitting, due to lack of inversion and mirror symmetries, gives rise to a 4-fold intersection at Γ and 6-fold intersection at R, both with Chern numbers of magnitude $|\chi| = 4$. (**b**) Magnified view of the band structure around the Γ-point without SOC. (**c**) Magnified view around Γ with SOC.

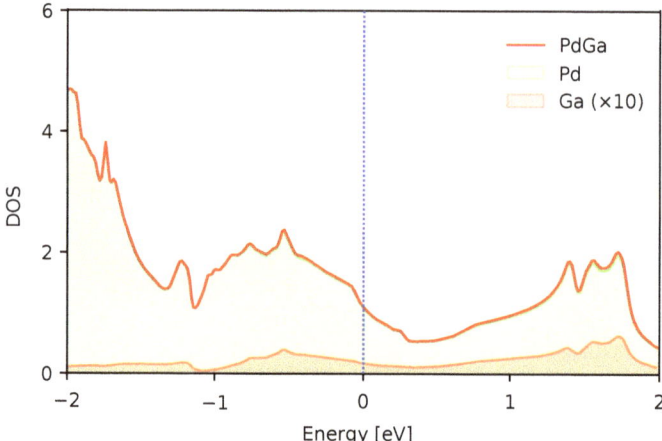

Figure 3. Density of states of PdGa and the atoms Pd and Ga separately. The Gd contribution is negligible, and has been magnified by a factor of 10. Most bands around the Fermi energy are thus contributed by the Pd atoms, underlining the relevance of chirality among carriers and optical transition. The Fermi level is positioned at $E_F = 0$ eV as indicated by the blue dotted line.

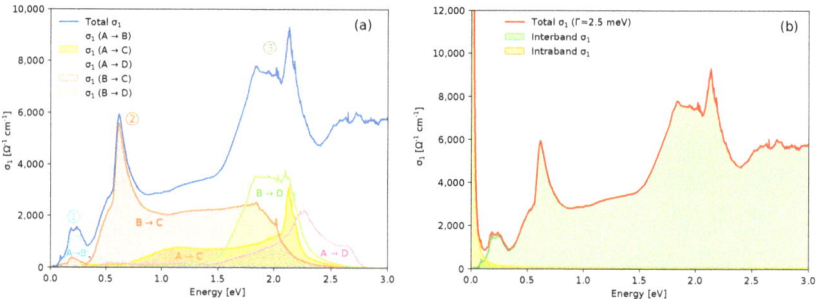

Figure 4. (a) The calculated real part of the interband optical conductivity $\sigma_1(\omega)$ with weight analysis. The features were sorted according to the labelling in Figure 2a. (b) Intra-, interband, and total optical conductivity $\sigma_1(\omega)$ of PdGa for parameters $\Gamma = 2.5$ meV and $\omega_p = 4.43$ eV.

The interband contribution to the optical conductivity of PdGa, without scattering, is shown in Figure 4a. It can be obtained from the imaginary part of the relative permittivity ε_2, which is the standard output of Wien2k, via the convention (CGS units)

$$\sigma_1 = \frac{\omega \varepsilon_2}{4\pi}. \tag{1}$$

Several distinct features can be seen. Two features of special interest have been marked ①, at around 150–300 meV, and ②, which shows a distinct peak at around 600 meV. The former originates from bands near the Γ-point, see again Figure 2c, corresponding to transitions from the Fermi surface droplets in Figure 1d to the corners of the cube-shaped Fermi surface. The latter is of particular interest as it seems to reproduce a known feature in CoSi around 560 meV [48] very well and is also in the energy range of a broader feature, likely of similar origin, in RhSi, around 750 meV [35], both measured at $T = 10$ K. The sharp peak at 600 meV can be attributed to transitions between the parallel bands dispersing from Γ to R and similar transitions between M and R. Since for CoSi and RhSi the corresponding bands between Γ and R are not as parallel, we predict that the optical transition for PdGa will be distinctly sharper. Note that the interband conductivities were not broadened in our calculations. In the case of RhSi, the mentioned feature merges with a rising edge the in optical conductivity around 1 eV [35], which may indicate what could be identified with the lower edge of feature ③ in our calculations, which arises from a combination of transitions $A \to C, D$ and $B \to D$.

As mentioned earlier, another interesting aspect of the the calculated $\sigma_1(\omega)$, is the nearly linear ridge extending over a rather large energy range, from roughly 0.9 eV to 1.5 eV. Linear features in the optical conductivity are readily identified as signatures of Dirac fermions [36–40]. We can assign it to the transition $B \to C$. In an experimental setting, this feature may mistakenly be interpreted as transitions between bands extending from the lower lying multifold point, intersecting Γ at around -1.0 eV, to bands above, which we can safely exclude. Note further that the contributing bands contain accidental near-degeneracies, akin to gapped Dirac points, between $\Gamma - X$ and $\Gamma - R$. Away from the high-symmetry lines, these features may develop into real conical intersections, implying that the discussed transition may very well contain character of Dirac fermions. This warrants closer inspection in future works and may motivate experimental investigations.

In Figure 4b the intra- and interband contributions are plotted alongside the total optical conductivity, $\sigma_1(\omega)$. For the intraband contribution we make the reasonable assumption for the dc conductivity, $\sigma_0 = 1 \cdot 10^6 \, \Omega^{-1} \text{cm}^{-1}$ supported by on-site dc measurements, and use the theoretically obtained value for the plasma frequency, $\omega_p = 4.43$ eV (note that this is the unscreened plasma frequency). Both values are significantly larger than the experimentally obtained parameters for CoSi and RhSi [35,48], which is consistent with the much larger Fermi surface of PdGa. These values, under assumption of a single Drude contribution for the intraband transitions, yield a scattering rate of $\Gamma = 2.5$ meV, which is expressed by a very sharp Drude peak, seen in Figure 4b. All discussed interband features remain clearly visible after inclusion of the intraband contribution. Whether such a sharp Drude peak is experimentally reproducible remains to be seen. Accounting for interband broadening, the feature ② might be brought to closer coincidence with the CoSi peak, as well as the much broader RhSi feature. Note that the low energy feature ① is inherent only to PdGa. This is, again, due to fact that bands, originating from the Γ-point in PdGa, disperse in parallel towards R, while in CoSi and RhSi these bands take the form of a double flat band overlaid with a Dirac cone, contributing an energetically much broader joint DOS, smearing out the transition.

3. Conclusions

In summary, we performed DFT calculations on one of the chiral multifold semimetals, PdGa, and estimated the optical conductivity in a broad frequency range, providing a detailed picture the band structure and a guide for interpretation of future optical experiments on this currently popular compound. A plethora of tuning mechanisms, such as application of pressure, magnetic fields, gating or doping may be applied to effectively alter the band structure, which our work should provide a helpful reference to. Optical transitions were assigned to the specific bands based on the band structure of the compound. Several common features were found in the related compounds, CoSi and RhSi, based on the experimental reports: A sharp, prominent mid-infrared absorption, which originates from the parallel bands between the Γ and R-points and the successive linear-in-frequency increase. In addition, PdGa seems to possess a low lying optical transition at around 150–300 meV that is predicted to be absent in the sister compounds. Indeed, it has not been reported for either CoSi or for RhSi in previous experimental studies [35,48].

Furthermore, a linear-in-frequency section of the optical conductivity, often taken as a hint towards the presence of Dirac or Weyl fermions, around 0.9 eV to 1.5 eV has been identified, excluding the origin as transitions between the multifold chiral points intersecting Γ at around 0.5 eV and 1.0 eV. Nearly degenerate bands between $\Gamma - X$ and $\Gamma - M$ may hint at accidental Dirac-like degeneracies near the high-symmetry lines, warranting further investigation.

Author Contributions: All authors contributed to the calculations and the writing of the manuscript. All authors have read and agreed to the published version of the manuscript.

Funding: The work was supported by the Deutsche Forschungsgesellschaft (DFG) via DR228/51-3. E.U. acknowledges the European Social Fund and the Baden-Württemberg Stiftung for the financial support of this research project by the Eliteprogramme.

Acknowledgments: We thank Alexander A. Tsirlin for insightful discussions.

Conflicts of Interest: The authors declare no conflict of interest.

References

1. Yan, B.; Felser, C. Topological Materials: Weyl Semimetals. *Annu. Rev. Condens. Matter Phys.* **2017**, *8*, 337–354. [CrossRef]
2. Murakami, S. Phase transition between the quantum spin Hall and insulator phases in 3D: Emergence of a topological gapless phase. *New J. Phys.* **2007**, *9*, 356. [CrossRef]
3. Wan, X.; Turner, A.M.; Vishwanath, A.; Savrasov, S.Y. Topological semimetal and Fermi-arc surface states in the electronic structure of pyrochlore iridates. *Phys. Rev. B* **2011**, *83*, 205101. [CrossRef]
4. Burkov, A.A.; Balents, L. Weyl Semimetal in a Topological Insulator Multilayer. *Phys. Rev. Lett.* **2011**, *107*, 127205. [CrossRef] [PubMed]
5. Šmejkal, L.; Jungwirth, T.; Sinova, J. Route towards Dirac and Weyl antiferromagnetic spintronics. *Phys. Status Solidi RRL* **2017**, *11*, 1700044. [CrossRef]
6. Šmejkal, L.; Mokrousov, Y.; Yan, B.; MacDonald, A.H. Topological antiferromagnetic spintronics. *Nat. Phys.* **2018**, *14*, 242–251. [CrossRef]
7. Shi, Z.; Wang, M.; Wu, J. A spin filter transistor made of topological Weyl semimetal. *Appl. Phys. Lett.* **2015**, *107*, 102403. [CrossRef]
8. Grushin, A.G.; Bardarson, J.H. How to Make Devices with Weyl Materials. *Physics* **2017**, *10*, 63. [CrossRef]
9. Hills, R.D.Y.; Kusmartseva, A.; Kusmartsev, F.V. Current-voltage characteristics of Weyl semimetal semiconducting devices, Veselago lenses, and hyperbolic Dirac phase. *Phys. Rev. B* **2017**, *95*, 214103. [CrossRef]
10. Zhu, C.; Wang, F.; Meng, Y.; Yuan, X.; Xiu, F.; Luo, H.; Wang, Y.; Li, J.; Lv, X.; He, L.; et al. A robust and tuneable mid-infrared optical switch enabled by bulk Dirac fermions. *Nat. Commun.* **2017**, *8*, 1–7. [CrossRef]
11. Sun, Y.; Meng, Y.; Jiang, H.; Qin, S.; Yang, Y.; Xiu, F.; Shi, Y.; Zhu, S.; Wang, F. Dirac semimetal saturable absorber with actively tunable modulation depth. *Opt. Lett.* **2019**, *44*, 582–585. [CrossRef] [PubMed]
12. Müchler, L.; Zhang, H.; Chadov, S.; Yan, B.; Casper, F.; Kübler, J.; Zhang, S.C.; Felser, C. Topological Insulators from a Chemist's Perspective. *Angew. Chem. Int. Ed.* **2012**, *51*, 7221–7225. [CrossRef] [PubMed]
13. Kong, D.; Cui, Y. Opportunities in chemistry and materials science for topological insulators and their nanostructures. *Nat. Chem.* **2011**, *3*, 845–849. [CrossRef] [PubMed]
14. Chen, H.; Zhu, W.; Xiao, D.; Zhang, Z. CO Oxidation Facilitated by Robust Surface States on Au-Covered Topological Insulators. *Phys. Rev. Lett.* **2011**, *107*, 056804. [CrossRef]
15. Yan, B.; Stadtmüller, B.; Haag, N.; Jakobs, S.; Seidel, J.; Jungkenn, D.; Mathias, S.; Cinchetti, M.; Aeschlimann, M.; Felser, C. Topological states on the gold surface. *Nat. Commun.* **2015**, *6*, 1–6. [CrossRef]
16. Xiao, J.; Kou, L.; Yam, C.Y.; Frauenheim, T.; Yan, B. Toward Rational Design of Catalysts Supported on a Topological Insulator Substrate. *ACS Catal.* **2015**, *5*, 7063–7067. [CrossRef]
17. Lv, B.Q.; Weng, H.M.; Fu, B.B.; Wang, X.P.; Miao, H.; Ma, J.; Richard, P.; Huang, X.C.; Zhao, L.X.; Chen, G.F.; et al. Experimental Discovery of Weyl Semimetal TaAs. *Phys. Rev. X* **2015**, *5*, 031013. [CrossRef]
18. Weng, H.; Fang, C.; Fang, Z.; Bernevig, B.A.; Dai, X. Weyl Semimetal Phase in Noncentrosymmetric Transition-Metal Monophosphides. *Phys. Rev. X* **2015**, *5*, 011029. [CrossRef]
19. Sun, Y.; Zhang, Y.; Felser, C.; Yan, B. Strong Intrinsic Spin Hall Effect in the TaAs Family of Weyl Semimetals. *Phys. Rev. Lett.* **2016**, *117*, 146403. [CrossRef]
20. Aroyo, M.I. *International Tables for Crystallography, Volume A*, 6th ed.; Wiley: Hoboken, NJ, USA, 2013.
21. Sohncke, L. *Entwicklung einer Theorie der Kristallstruktur*; B. G. Teubner: Leipzig, Germany, 1879.
22. Bradlyn, B.; Cano, J.; Wang, Z.; Vergniory, M.G.; Felser, C.; Cava, R.J.; Bernevig, B.A. Beyond Dirac and Weyl fermions: Unconventional quasiparticles in conventional crystals. *Science* **2016**, *353*. [CrossRef]
23. Sanchez, D.S.; Belopolski, I.; Cochran, T.A.; Xu, X.; Yin, J.X.; Chang, G.; Xie, W.; Manna, K.; Süß, V.; Huang, C.Y.; et al. Topological chiral crystals with helicoid-arc quantum states. *Nature* **2019**, *567*, 500–505. [CrossRef] [PubMed]
24. Schröter, N.B.M.; Pei, D.; Vergniory, M.G.; Sun, Y.; Manna, K.; de Juan, F.; Krieger, J.A.; Süss, V.; Schmidt, M.; Dudin, P.; et al. Chiral topological semimetal with multifold band crossings and long Fermi arcs. *Nat. Phys.* **2019**, *15*, 759–765. [CrossRef]
25. Chang, G.; Xu, S.Y.; Wieder, B.J.; Sanchez, D.S.; Huang, S.M.; Belopolski, I.; Chang, T.R.; Zhang, S.; Bansil, A.; Lin, H.; et al. Unconventional Chiral Fermions and Large Topological Fermi Arcs in RhSi. *Phys. Rev. Lett.* **2017**, *119*, 206401. [CrossRef] [PubMed]
26. Rao, Z.; Li, H.; Zhang, T.; Tian, S.; Li, C.; Fu, B.; Tang, C.; Wang, L.; Li, Z.; Fan, W.; et al. Observation of unconventional chiral fermions with long Fermi arcs in CoSi. *Nature* **2019**, *567*, 496–499. [CrossRef] [PubMed]

27. Tang, P.; Zhou, Q.; Zhang, S.C. Multiple Types of Topological Fermions in Transition Metal Silicides. *Phys. Rev. Lett.* **2017**, *119*, 206402. [CrossRef]
28. Takane, D.; Wang, Z.; Souma, S.; Nakayama, K.; Nakamura, T.; Oinuma, H.; Nakata, Y.; Iwasawa, H.; Cacho, C.; Kim, T.; et al. Observation of Chiral Fermions with a Large Topological Charge and Associated Fermi-Arc Surface States in CoSi. *Phys Rev. Lett.* **2019**, *122*, 076402. [CrossRef]
29. Sessi, P.; Fan, F.R.; Küster, F.; Manna, K.; Schröter, N.B.M.; Ji, J.R.; Stolz, S.; Krieger, J.A.; Pei, D.; Kim, T.K.; et al. Handedness-dependent quasiparticle interference in the two enantiomers of the topological chiral semimetal PdGa. *Nat. Commun.* **2020**, *11*, 3507. [CrossRef]
30. Schröter, N.B.M.; Stolz, S.; Manna, K.; de Juan, F.; Vergniory, M.G.; Krieger, J.A.; Pei, D.; Schmitt, T.; Dudin, P.; Kim, T.K.; et al. Observation and control of maximal Chern numbers in a chiral topological semimetal. *Science* **2020**, *369*, 179. [CrossRef]
31. De Juan, F.; Grushin, A.G.; Morimoto, T.; Moore, J.E. Quantized circular photogalvanic effect in Weyl semimetals. *Nat. Commun.* **2017**, *8*. [CrossRef]
32. Le, C.; Zhang, Y.; Felser, C.; Sun, Y. Ab initio study of quantized circular photogalvanic effect in chiral multifold semimetals. *Phys. Rev. B* **2020**, *102*, 121111. [CrossRef]
33. Rees, D.; Manna, K.; Lu, B.; Morimoto, T.; Borrmann, H.; Felser, C.; Moore, J.E.; Torchinsky, D.H.; Orenstein, J. Helicity-dependent photocurrents in the chiral Weyl semimetal RhSi. *Sci. Adv.* **2020**, *6*, eaba0509. [CrossRef] [PubMed]
34. Ni, Z.; Wang, K.; Zhang, Y.; Pozo, O.; Xu, B.; Han, X.; Manna, K.; Paglione, J.; Felser, C.; Grushin, A.G.; et al. Giant topological longitudinal circular photo-galvanic effect in the chiral multifold semimetal CoSi. *Nat. Commun.* **2021**, *12*, 1–8. [CrossRef] [PubMed]
35. Maulana, L.Z.; Manna, K.; Uykur, E.; Felser, C.; Dressel, M.; Pronin, A.V. Optical conductivity of multifold fermions: The case of RhSi. *Phys. Rev. Res.* **2020**, *2*, 023018. [CrossRef]
36. Neubauer, D.; Carbotte, J.P.; Nateprov, A.A.; Löhle, A.; Dressel, M.; Pronin, A.V. Interband optical conductivity of the [001]-oriented Dirac semimetal Cd_3As_2. *Phys. Rev. B* **2016**, *93*, 121202. [CrossRef]
37. Schilling, M.B.; Schoop, L.M.; Lotsch, B.V.; Dressel, M.; Pronin, A.V. Flat Optical Conductivity in ZrSiS due to Two-Dimensional Dirac Bands. *Phys. Rev. Lett.* **2017**, *119*, 187401. [CrossRef]
38. Hütt, F.; Yaresko, A.; Schilling, M.B.; Shekhar, C.; Felser, C.; Dressel, M.; Pronin, A.V. Linear-in-Frequency Optical Conductivity in GdPtBi due to Transitions near the Triple Points. *Phys. Rev. Lett.* **2018**, *121*, 176601. [CrossRef]
39. Biswas, A.; Iakutkina, O.; Wang, Q.; Lei, H.C.; Dressel, M.; Uykur, E. Spin-Reorientation-Induced Band Gap in Fe_3Sn_2: Optical Signatures of Weyl Nodes. *Phys. Rev. Lett.* **2020**, *125*, 076403. [CrossRef]
40. Shao, Y.; Sun, Z.; Wang, Y.; Xu, C.; Sankar, R.; Breindel, A.J.; Cao, C.; Fogler, M.M.; Millis, A.J.; Chou, F.; et al. Optical signatures of Dirac nodal lines in $NbAs_2$. *Proc. Natl. Acad. Sci. USA* **2019**, *116*, 1168–1173. [CrossRef]
41. Hosur, P.; Parameswaran, S.A.; Vishwanath, A. Charge Transport in Weyl Semimetals. *Phys. Rev. Lett.* **2012**, *108*, 046602. [CrossRef]
42. Bácsi, Á.; Virosztek, A. Low-frequency optical conductivity in graphene and in other scale-invariant two-band systems. *Phys. Rev. B* **2013**, *87*, 125425. [CrossRef]
43. Polatkan, S.; Goerbig, M.O.; Wyzula, J.; Kemmler, R.; Maulana, L.Z.; Piot, B.A.; Crassee, I.; Akrap, A.; Shekhar, C.; Felser, C.; et al. Magneto-Optics of a Weyl Semimetal beyond the Conical Band Approximation: Case Study of TaP. *Phys. Rev. Lett.* **2020**, *124*, 176402. [CrossRef] [PubMed]
44. Mohelský, I.; Dubroka, A.; Wyzula, J.; Slobodeniuk, A.; Martinez, G.; Krupko, Y.; Piot, B.A.; Caha, O.; Humlíček, J.; Bauer, G.; et al. Landau level spectroscopy of Bi2Te3. *Phys. Rev. B* **2020**, *102*. [CrossRef]
45. Akrap, A.; Hakl, M.; Tchoumakov, S.; Crassee, I.; Kuba, J.; Goerbig, M.O.; Homes, C.C.; Caha, O.; Novák, J.; Teppe, F.; et al. Magneto-Optical Signature of Massless Kane Electrons in Cd_3As_2. *Phys. Rev. Lett.* **2016**, *117*, 136401. [CrossRef] [PubMed]
46. Rodriguez, D.; Tsirlin, A.A.; Biesner, T.; Ueno, T.; Takahashi, T.; Kobayashi, K.; Dressel, M.; Uykur, E. Two Linear Regimes in Optical Conductivity of a Type-I Weyl Semimetal: The Case of Elemental Tellurium. *Phys. Rev. Lett.* **2020**, *124*, 136402. [CrossRef] [PubMed]
47. Uykur, E.; Li, W.; Kuntscher, C.A.; Dressel, M. Optical signatures of energy gap in correlated Dirac fermions. *NPJ Quantum Mater.* **2019**, *4*, 1–8. [CrossRef]
48. Xu, B.; Fang, Z.; Sánchez-Martínez, M.Á.; Venderbos, J.W.F.; Ni, Z.; Qiu, T.; Manna, K.; Wang, K.; Paglione, J.; Bernhard, C.; et al. Optical signatures of multifold fermions in the chiral topological semimetal CoSi. *Proc. Natl. Acad. Sci. USA* **2020**, *117*, 27104–27110. [CrossRef]
49. Blaha, P.; Schwarz, K.; Madsen, G.; Kvasnicka, D.; Luitz, J.; Laskowski, R.; Tran, F.; Marks, L.D. *Wien2k, An Augmented Plane Wave + Local Orbitals Program for Calculating Crystal Properties*; Schwarz, K., Ed.; Vienna University of Technology: Vienna, Austria, 2019; ISBN 3-9501031-1-2.
50. Blaha, P.; Schwarz, K.; Tran, F.; Laskowski, R.; Madsen, G.K.H.; Marks, L.D. WIEN2k: An APW+lo program for calculating the properties of solids. *J. Chem. Phys.* **2020**, *152*, 074101. [CrossRef]
51. Rarita, W.; Schwinger, J. On a Theory of Particles with Half-Integral Spin. *Phys. Rev.* **1941**, *60*, 61. [CrossRef]
52. Ambrosch-Draxl, C.; Sofo, J. Linear optical properties of solids within the full-potential linearized augmented planewave method. *Comput. Phys. Commun.* **2006**, *175*, 1–14. [CrossRef]

Article
Effect of Deformation on Topological Properties of Cobalt Monosilicide

Sergey Nikolaev [†], Dmitry Pshenay-Severin [*,†], Yuri Ivanov [†] and Alexander Burkov [†]

Ioffe Institute, 26 Politekhnicheskaya, 194021 St Petersburg, Russia; sergey.nikolaev.w@mail.ru (S.N.); yu.ivanov@mail.ioffe.ru (Y.I.); a.burkov@mail.ioffe.ru (A.B.)
* Correspondence: d.pshenay@mail.ru
† These authors contributed equally to this work.

Abstract: Recently, it was shown that materials with certain crystal structures can exhibit multifold band crossings with large topological charges. CoSi is one such material that belongs to non-centrosymmetric space group P2$_1$3 (#198) and possesses multifold band crossing points with a topological charge of 4. The change of crystal symmetry, e.g., by means of external stress, can lift the degeneracy and change its topological properties. In the present work, the influence of uniaxial deformation on the band structure and topological properties of CoSi is investigated on the base of ab initio calculations. The $\mathbf{k} \cdot \mathbf{p}$ Hamiltonian taking into account deformation is constructed on the base of symmetry consideration near the Γ and R points both with and without spin-orbit coupling. The transformation of multifold band crossings into nodes of other types with different topological charges, their shift both in energy and in reciprocal space and the tilt of dispersion around nodes are studied in detail depending on the direction of uniaxial deformation.

Keywords: topological semimetal; cobalt monosilicide; mechanical deformation

1. Introduction

Cobalt monosilicide crystallizes in the cubic noncentrosymmetric space group #198 (P2$_1$3). The unit cell and the Brillouin zone of CoSi are shown in Figure 1a,b. The band structure, magnetic, optical, transport and, in particular, thermoelectric properties of CoSi have been extensively studied [1–15]. Initially, the interpretation of experimental results was based on a simple semimetallic band structure model with small energy overlap of parabolic valence and conduction bands [1,2]. With the development of first-principle density functional theory (DFT) methods, a more realistic CoSi band structure has emerged [3–8]. Band structures calculated with and without the account of spin-orbit coupling (SOC) are plotted in Figure 1c,d, respectively. Earlier calculations [3,4] without the account of SOC revealed the presence of multiple band crossings at the Γ and R points of the Brillouin zone, but they did not consider the topology of the band structure. The symmetry analysis allowed to predict the existence of chiral fermions and multifold band crossings with high topological charges in crystals belonging to several space groups (including space group #198) in the presence of time-reversal symmetry [16,17]. In CoSi, multifold linear band crossing and spin texture was initially investigated around the Γ point, based on first-principle fully-relativistic calculations [5]. Later, detailed studies of band structure topology were made for CoSi [6,8] and for isostructural RhSi [7]. Effective $\mathbf{k} \cdot \mathbf{p}$ Hamiltonians around the time-reversal invariant momentum (TRIM) points were written down in Ref. [17] for R point and in Ref. [8] for Γ point. It was shown [6,8] that the topological charges at the Γ and R points are equal to ± 4 and there are four surface Fermi arcs, connecting projections of these points on the surface Brillouin zone. Because spin-orbit coupling in CoSi is not strong, the Chern numbers were also calculated without SOC [6,18]. It was shown that multifold nodes have large topological charges of ± 2 even without SOC (see Figure 1d for illustration). The existence of multifold fermions and surface Fermi arcs in CoSi was recently confirmed by angle resolved photoemission spectroscopy (ARPES) [18–20].

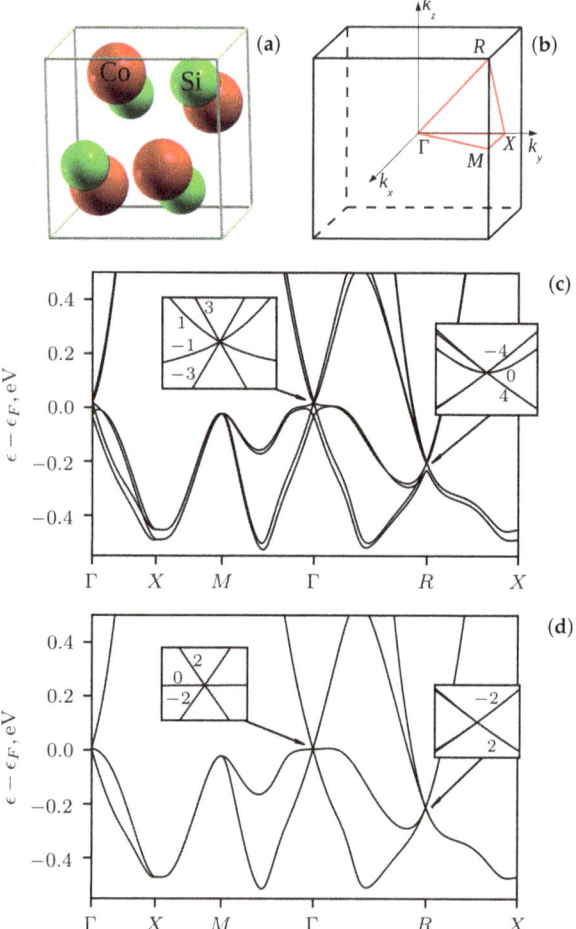

Figure 1. The unit cell (**a**), the Brillouin zone (**b**) and the band structure of CoSi, calculated with (**c**) and without (**d**) the account of spin-orbit coupling. Insets in (**c**,**d**) show band structure around multi-fold band crossings at the Γ and R points (numbers are topological charges).

The theoretical study of the band structure beyond DFT, taking into account dynamic on-site correlations of d-electrons, revealed that, in contrast to FeSi, the electronic states in CoSi are only moderately influenced by electronic correlations [21]. Band broadening in CoSi is small in the range of ± 0.3 eV near the Fermi level and decreases with the temperature. Thus, DFT description of CoSi band structure should give quite accurate results, that is confirmed by ARPES experiments [18–20] and by the better agreement of calculated lattice constants and elastic modules with experimental results for CoSi, compared to other monosilicides of the elements of the 4th period [22].

New information on the band structure of CoSi prompted to study the manifestation of its non-trivial topology and provided a base for correct interpretation of experimental results on conventional transport properties of the compound. For example, the account of real band structure and energy dependent relaxation time allowed to adequately explain the concentration dependencies of thermoelectric and galvanomagnetic properties of $Co_{1-x}Fe_xSi$ and $Co_{1-x}Ni_xSi$ alloys [10–12]. Recently, the effects of nonstoichiometry of CoSi-based materials on thermoelectric [9] and magnetic [14] properties were studied. In particular, in samples with the excess of Co, magnetically ordered states with helical and skyrmionic spin structures were observed near room temperature [14]. Quantum oscillations of thermopower with a beating pattern were observed in high-quality CoSi crystals [13]. They were successfully interpreted by the coexistence of two close Fermi surfaces in agreement with DFT results for the band structure. The influence of chiral fermions and charge density waves on magnetic field dependent electrical transport was studied in [23]. The experimental and theoretical investigation of optical conductivity of CoSi revealed various exotic multifold quasiparticles [15]. Moreover, low-frequency part of optical conductivity spectrum confirmed the existence of previously experimentally unobserved four-fold spin-3/2 node at the Γ point [15].

As the features of the band structure topology are due to particular crystal symmetry of CoSi, it is interesting to investigate the evolution of these properties when the symmetry changes. Such changes can appear due to mechanical stress, for example, in thin film devices or experimental setups, and can be important for device operation or interpretation of experimental data. In addition to the change of symmetry, mechanical deformation, in principle, can lead to the opening of a gap in the energy spectrum and the disappearance of the topological nodes. The possibility of using CMOS-compatible CoSi thin films for thermoelectric and sensor applications were considered recently in Ref. [24]. The stability of CoSi under hydrostatic pressure was theoretically investigated in Ref. [25], where it was predicted that the transition to CsCl structure ($Pm\bar{3}m$) take place at hight pressure of 270 GPa. In the present work, we theoreticaly investigate another possibility—the change of band structure under uniaxial strain. In contrast to isotropic strain, uniaxial deformation changes the crystal symmetry even at low pressure. We considered deformation in [100], [110] and [111] directions. Based on symmetry analysis, the $\mathbf{k} \cdot \mathbf{p}$ Hamiltonian, taking into account deformation, was constructed for both the Γ and R points. Combining ab initio calculations, analytical model and symmetry considerations, the band splitting at the Γ and R points, the types of nodes arising from multifold band crossings and their energy and k-space positions were carefully studied both with and without SOC.

2. Method of Calculation

DFT calculations were performed in an integrated suite of Open-Source computer codes for electronic-structure calculations—Quantum ESPRESSO (QE) [26], using fully relativistic optimized normconserving Vanderbilt pseudopotentials (ONCV) [27]. The plane wave cut-off energy was 80 eV. The calculations were performed on $8 \times 8 \times 8$ Monkhorst–Pack(MP) grid with the optimized lattice parameter $a_0 = 4.438$ Å. Four atomic positions of each of atomic species in the unit cell of undeformed CoSi are (x_A, x_A, x_A), $(-x_A + 1/2, -x_A, x_A + 1/2)$, $(-x_A, x_A + 1/2, -x_A + 1/2)$, and $(x_A + 1/2, -x_A + 1/2, -x_A)$. Their optimization gives $x_{Co} = 0.144$, $x_{Si} = 0.843$.

Under uniaxial deformation, we set the unit cell parameters based on corresponding strain tensor and performed the relaxation of atomic positions, that allowed to determine the space group of deformed crystal.

For detailed study of the band structure, we performed Wannier interpolation using Wannier90 [28]. The position of nodes, topological charges and Fermi arcs were calculated using WannierTools [29] software package.

In order to analyze low-energy excitations around the nodes at Γ and R points, we constructed $\mathbf{k} \cdot \mathbf{p}$ Hamiltonian $\hat{H}$ in the presence of deformation from symmetry considerations. This allowed to independently verify the position of nodes and topological charges. As the effects of strain was assumed to be small, we considered only zeroth order in k terms in Hamiltonian proportional to strain tensor [30,31]: $D_{ij}\epsilon_{ij}$, where ϵ_{ij} are strain tensor components and D_{ij} are deformation potential parameters. The independent terms can be identified, applying symmetry operations of the considered space group ($P2_13$, #198), as it was made for the construction of Hamiltonian without stain [8,16,17]. We took into account that ϵ_{ij} is transformed under symmetry operations as a product of wave vector components $k_i k_j$, and used irreducible representations of space (double space) groups from Bilbao Crystallographic Server [32] for the case without (with) spin-orbit coupling. Since the spin-orbit coupling is also small in CoSi, we did not consider terms in $\hat{H}$ that depend on both strain and spin-orbit interaction. As will be seen from what follows, this approximation is sufficient.

The form of obtained Hamiltonians and their parameters are given in Appendix A. In the equations we used eV as units of energy. The wave vector components $k_i, i = 1, 2, 3$ (in crystal coordinates) are measured in fractions of the reciprocal lattice vectors. The wave vector components $k_i, i = x, y, z$ (in Cartesian coordinates) are measured in the units of $2\pi/a_0 = 1.416\,\text{Å}^{-1}$. If not stated otherwise, the latter units were used in band structure plots.

The deformation potential parameters were obtained using shifts of energy levels from ab initio calculations of undeformed and deformed crystal. The deformation potential parameters at the diagonal elements of strain tensor ϵ_{ii} in $\mathbf{k} \cdot \mathbf{p}$ Hamiltonian determine the absolute shift of energy levels upon deformation. For CoSi, as metallic material, the absolute shift of energy level ϵ_n due to deformation can be calculated as $\Delta \epsilon_n = (\epsilon_n^{(d)} - \epsilon_F^{(d)}) - (\epsilon_n^{(u)} - \epsilon_F^{(u)})$, where $\epsilon_n^{(d(u))}$ are energy levels in deformed (undeformed) crystal, and $\epsilon_F^{(u(d))}$ are corresponding Fermi levels (see Appendix B for details).

3. Results without SOC

The band structure of CoSi without SOC features a triply-degenerate energy level at the Γ point close to the Fermi level. It is plotted in the inset of the Figure 1d and in the Figure 2 with dotted lines. The wave functions are transformed according to the three-dimensional single-valued representation Γ_4 of the little group of the Γ point of P2$_1$3 (#198). The low-energy excitations around this point can be considered as effective spin-1 quasiparticles [33]. The topological charges of lower and upper linear branches are -2 and 2 respectively, while nearly flat band has zero charge.

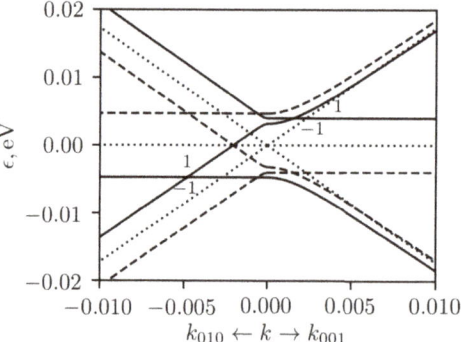

Figure 2. The splitting of energy levels around the Γ point under uniaxial strain along [100] direction. Dotted lines represent the spectrum of undeformed crystal, solid (dashed) lines represent the spectrum in the case of compressive (tensile) strain. The absolute value of strain is $|e| = 0.01$. The wave vectors are measured in $2\pi/a_0$ units.

Let us consider the simplest deformation of a crystal along the crystallographic direction [100]. When stretched along this direction, the spatial symmetry of group P2$_1$3 (#198) is lowered to P2$_1$2$_1$2$_1$ (#19), and essential remaining symmetry elements are: $\{C_{2x}|\frac{1}{2}0\frac{1}{2}\}$, $\{C_{2y}|\frac{1}{2}\frac{1}{2}0\}$, $\{C_{2z}|0\frac{1}{2}\frac{1}{2}\}$. At the Γ point, this group has only one-dimensional irreducible representations and, using character theory, we can expect that the three-dimensional representation Γ_4 of the space group P2$_1$3 (#198) splits into three one-dimensional representations of $P2_12_12_1$ (#19) as: $\Gamma_4 \to \Gamma_2 + \Gamma_3 + \Gamma_4$. As $\Gamma_{2(3,4)}$ are real single-valued representations, they are not combined due to time-reversal symmetry (TRS) [32].

Thus, without taking into account the spin-orbit interaction, the triply-degenerate level at the Γ point is split into three with different energies. The low-energy band structure around the Γ point in CoSi under 1% uniaxial deformation in [100] direction is shown in the Figure 2 with solid lines for compressive strain and with dashed lines for tensile strain.

As the time-reversal symmetry is preserved in the considered cases, the whole energy spectrum around the TRIM point is symmetric with respect to the change of the sign of the wave vector $\mathbf{k} \to -\mathbf{k}$. In addition, our $\mathbf{k} \cdot \mathbf{p}$ Hamiltonian is linear both in $\mathbf{k}$ and in components of deformation tensor $\hat{\epsilon}$. Hence, the low-energy band structure for stretched crystal can be obtained from the band structure of compressed crystal by changing the sign of energy $\epsilon(\mathbf{k}, -\hat{\epsilon}) = -\epsilon(\mathbf{k}, \hat{\epsilon})$, that can be seen by comparing solid and dashed curves in the Figure 2. It should be noted that this conclusion applies to all considered cased with the exception of eight-band Hamiltonian around the R point including SOC, as the latter contains terms independent of both wave vector and deformation tensor.

In compressed crystal there are nodes shifted in k_z and k_y directions upwards and downwards in energy relative to unstrained case, as shown in Figure 2. The topological charges of both nodes are equal to ± 1. In stretched crystal, the sign of the energy changes, and the nodes swap. In both cases, we have two doubly degenerate (spinless) nodes at the same energy at the positions $\pm k_{nz}$ with the total topological charge of ± 2 and similar nodes at positions $\pm k_{ny}$. In the case, when only $\epsilon_{11} = e$ is not zero, the node positions for small deformation can be obtained from eigenvalues of $\mathbf{k} \cdot \mathbf{p}$ Hamiltonian, and are equal to $k_{nz} = \sqrt{(D_1 - D_2)(D_3 - D_2)e}/v$ and $k_{ny} = \sqrt{(D_3 - D_1)(D_3 - D_2)e}/v$. In these expressions v is the Fermi velocity at the Γ point in unstrained crystal and D_i are the deformation potential parameters, defined in Appendix A after Equations (A1) and (A2).

It can be seen also, that the dispersion around doubly degenerate nodal points is tilted. As was shown in the Ref. [34], the general form of the Hamiltonian for Weyl point is the following: $H(\mathbf{k}) = \sum_{i,j} k_i A_{ij} \sigma_j$, where A_{ij} is a 3×4 matrix of coefficients and σ_j are the 2×2 unit matrix and the three Pauli matrices for $j = 0$ and $j = 1, 2, 3$ respectively. The spectrum can be written as $\epsilon_{\pm}(\mathbf{k}) = T(\mathbf{k}) \pm U(\mathbf{k})$, where $T(\mathbf{k}) = \sum_{i=1}^{3} k_i A_{i0}$ and $U(\mathbf{k}) = \sqrt{\sum_{j=1}^{3} \left(\sum_{i=1}^{3} k_i A_{ij}\right)^2}$. The nodal point is of the type II if there is a direction, in which $T(\mathbf{k}) > U(\mathbf{k})$. In the present case, it can be shown that in linear approximation $T(\mathbf{k}) = U(\mathbf{k})$ in k_{010} or k_{001} directions independently of the magnitude of strain e. Thus, under strain the nodal points are at the border of transition from type I to type II nodal points. However, it should be emphasized that, in contrast to ordinary type-II Weyl fermions, fermion states discussed here are spin degenerate.

The shift of nodes in reciprocal space implies the modification of the shape of surface Fermi arcs, that should emanate from the projections of the nodal points on the (100) surface Brillouin zone. In CoSi, it appeared that due to large extension of the Fermi arcs between the projections of the Γ and R point, their general shape changes quite moderately (at the scale of the full Brillouin zone) compared to undeformed case, presented in Refs. [6,8]. Therefore here we illustrate their variation around the Γ point only for several selected cases. The Figure 3 shows the Fermi arcs in the (100) surface Brillouin zone for the case of compressive deformation in the [100] direction for $e = -0.01$. For better visualisation, Fermi level was shifted to the energy of nodal points. The position of nodes, obtained by $\mathbf{k} \cdot \mathbf{p}$ calculations, are plotted in the figure by black asterisks. It can be seen, that two nodes are shifted along k_z direction, and their positions correlate with the sources of two surface Fermi arcs.

When deforming in [110] direction, off-diagonal elements of the strain tensor begin to play a role. The spatial symmetry of deformed cobalt monosilicide is described by the space group $P2_1$ (#4) with the only symmetry element $\{C_{2z}|00\frac{1}{2}\}$ (except lattice translations). Therefore, without taking into account the spin-orbit interaction, the three-dimensional representation Γ_4 of the group $P2_13$(#198) splits into three one-dimensional representations of $P2_1$(#4) as: $\Gamma_4 \to \Gamma_1 + 2\Gamma_2$. In this way, the degeneracy at the Γ point is completely lifted, as in the case of the deformation along the main unit cell directions. In the most simple case, compatible with considered symmetry, where the only non-zero components of stain tensor are $\epsilon_{12} = \epsilon_{21} = e/2$, two effective spin-1/2 nodes symmetrically diverge from Γ point along [110] ([1$\bar{1}$0]) crystallographic direction and shift to lower energies in the case of compressive (tensile) strain $e < 0$ ($e > 0$). Similar nodes appear at higher energies but they are shifted along [1$\bar{1}$0] ([110]) directions for $e < 0$ ($e > 0$). In more general case, when $\epsilon_{11} = \epsilon_{22} = \epsilon_{12} = e/2$, that corresponds to the absence of deformation in directions normal to [110], the nodes split along the line, that is rotated by a small angle (about $\phi = 5°$ at $e = 0.01$) from [110] ([1$\bar{1}$0]) axis. Let's denote these directions by k^ϕ_{110} ($k^\phi_{1\bar{1}0}$). The low-energy band structure for these directions and topological charges are given in the Figure 4. The situation is somewhat similar to [100] case (see, Figure 2), but the shift of nodes in both energy and k-space are larger. In this case we obtain again effective spin-1/2 nodes with the tilt intermediate between tilts of the type-I and type-II nodes. The total topological charge of each pair of the nodes is ± 2.

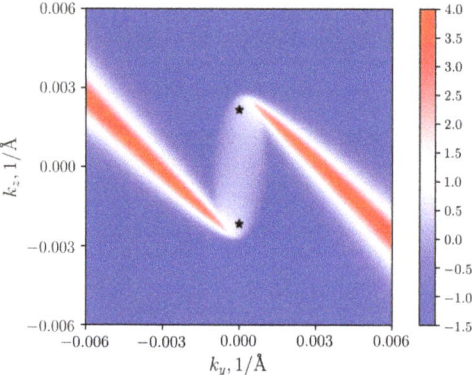

Figure 3. The details of surface Fermi arcs around the Γ point under uniaxial strain along [100] direction ($e = -0.01$) without the account of spin-orbit coupling (SOC). Asterisks depict the positions of nodal points.

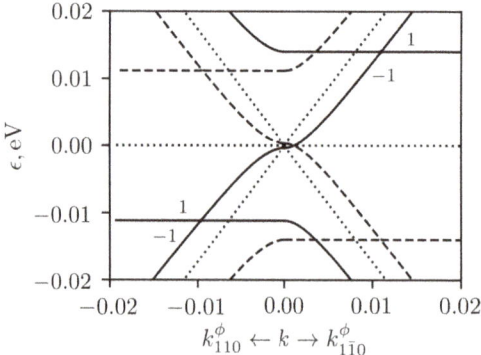

Figure 4. The splitting of energy levels around the Γ point under uniaxial stain along [110] direction. Dotted lines represent the spectrum of undeformed crystal, solid (dashed) lines represent the spectrum in the case of compressive (tensile) strain. The absolute value of strain is $|e| = 0.01$.

The deformation along the [111] crystallographic direction needs special consideration for CoSi. When deformed in [111] direction, the symmetry of cobalt monosilicide is reduced to $R3$(#146) space group with the single 3-fold rotation axis. Character theory suggests that without SOC, the three-dimensional representation Γ_4 of $P2_13$(#198) space group splits into three one-dimensional representations of $R3$(#146) as: $\Gamma_4 \to \Gamma_1 + (\Gamma_2 + \Gamma_3)$. Since the representations Γ_2 and Γ_3 are mutually conjugate, they should be combined due to time reversal symmetry. The triply degenerate level is split into two (nondegenerate and doubly degenerate) levels, in contrast to other types of deformation in which the degeneracy is completely lifted at the Γ point. In this case, strain tensor was taken in the form $\epsilon_{ij} = e/3$ for all i, j. In deformed crystal, one unusual node is located at the Γ point and two other nodes are displaced along the [111] direction at the positions $\pm k_{n,111}$ with $k_{n,111} = D_4 e / v(1+e)$ (see the Figure 5). In this case we obtained one node with topological charge ± 2 at the Γ point and two nodes with charges ± 1 at $\pm k_{n,111}$ points. The spectrum for compressive and tensile strains are again can be obtained by the energy sign change. Thus the number of nodes between the two upper bands depends on the sign of deformation e. Another way to see this result is to plot Fermi arcs in the (001) surface Brillouin zone for compressive and tensile strain (see Figure 6). Consider a compressed crystal. Below the Fermi level, there are two nodes shifted in [111] direction. Their projections on (001) plane are sources of two Fermi arcs (left panel). The starting points of the arcs are shifted towards the projections of the nodes (black asterisks) but do not coincide with them exactly, since the Fermi level is located above these nodes. In the case of expansion, the node with topological charge of 2 is below the Fermi level, and both Fermi arcs start from the Γ point (right panel).

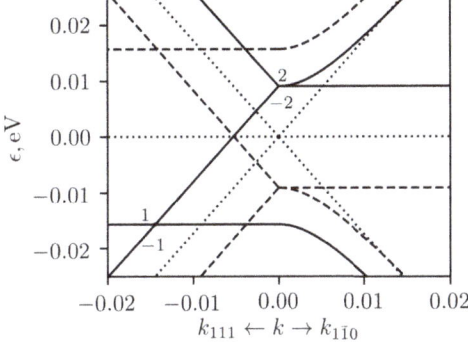

Figure 5. The splitting of energy levels around the Γ point under uniaxial stain along [111] direction. Dotted lines represent the spectrum of undeformed crystal, solid (dashed) lines represent the spectrum in the case of compressive (tensile) strain. The absolute value of strain is $|e| = 0.01$.

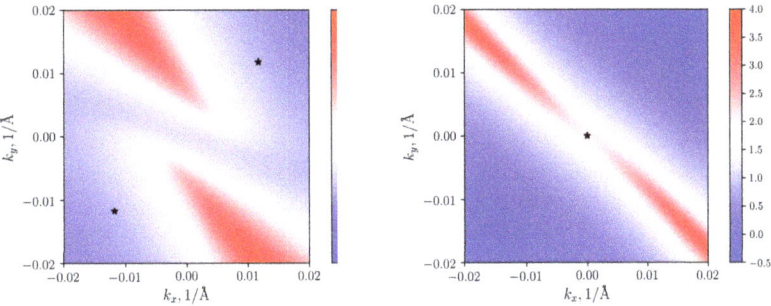

Figure 6. The details of surface Fermi arcs around the Γ point under uniaxial compression (**left** panel) and extension (**right** panel) along [111] direction ($|e| = 0.01$) without the account of SOC. Asterisks depict the position of nodal points.

The fermions around the node with topological charge of 2 at the Γ point are similar to that of quadratic double-Weyl fermions in SrSi$_2$, described in Ref. [35], but they arise for another reason. In SrSi$_2$ without SOC, on the four-fold rotation axes of the crystal, there are two-fold band crossings with linear dispersion. The bands are spin degenerate. The account of spin-orbit coupling adds terms independent of wave vector to the Hamiltonian that leads to a partial lifting of the degeneracy and to a change of linear dispersion to quadratic in certain directions. In CoSi, the k-independent terms in $\hat{H}$ appear due to strain even without SOC. Counting energy relative to the charge-2 node in the Figure 5, the dispersion in [111] direction remains linear: $\Delta\epsilon = \pm k_{111} v(1+e)$. While, in perpendicular direction, it becomes quadratic, $\Delta\epsilon = D_4 e/2 - \text{sign}(e)\sqrt{(D_4 e/2)^2 + (k_{\perp,111} v)^2}$ or flat. Thus, in CoSi under [111] deformation, there is a strain induced transition from spin-1 quasiparticles to quadratic effective-spin-1/2 fermions.

Let us now consider low-energy band structure around the R point without spin-orbit coupling. In this case in unstrained CoSi, the energy level at the R point is four-fold degenerate not considering spin (see Figure 1d). Low energy excitations around the R point are double spin-1/2 fermions [33] with the Chern number −2 [6]. The wave functions are transformed according to the direct sum of single-valued mutually conjugated complex two-dimensional representations R_1 and R_3, combined due to TRS. The switching to $P2_12_12_1$ (#19) space group under [100] uniaxial deformation does not lead to the energy level splitting, because the representation $R_1 + R_3$ is transformed into the direct sum of the pseudoreal representations $R_1 + R_1$ of $P2_12_12_1$. Thus the node at the R point remains intact.

Under uniaxial [110] stress, the space group $P2_13$ is reduced to $P2_1$ group and the R point goes into the E point, which is also located at the vertex of the deformed Brillouin zone. The representation $R_1 + R_3$ is transformed into $2(E_1 + E_2)$. The E_1 and E_2 representations of $P2_1$ are one-dimensional and mutually conjugated, therefore they are combined due to TRS. Thus, four-fold degenerate energy level splits into two doubly degenerated levels (see Figure 7). The nodes are split along k_z direction and are situated at $k_{nz} = \pm\sqrt{D_2^2 + D_3^2}e/2v$, where deformation potential constants are given in Appendix A after Equation (A3). The topological charges of these two nodes are ∓ 1. Two crossing points at the R point (E point of $P2_12_12_1$ space group) in the Figure 7 are not nodes as the states are degenerate on the (001) surface of the deformed Brillouin zone.

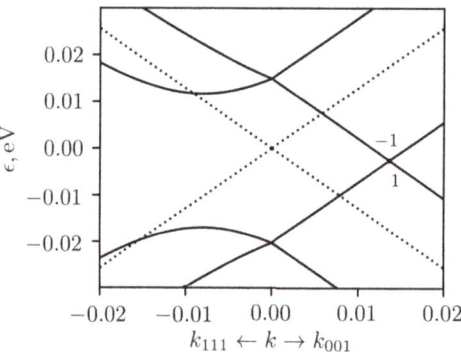

Figure 7. The splitting of energy levels around the R point under uniaxial stain along [110] direction (E point, $P2_1$ space group). Dotted lines represent the spectrum of undeformed crystal, solid lines represent the spectrum in the case of compressive strain. The value of strain is $e = -0.01$.

In the case of [111] deformation, the four-fold degenerate level at the R point splits into three levels (two nondegenerate, and one doubly degenerate) at the corner (T point) of deformed Brillouin zone (see Figure 8). Representations transform according to the expression $R_1 + R_3 \rightarrow 2T_1 + (T_2 + T_3)$. All representations at the T point are one-dimensional, but T_2 and T_3 are mutually conjugated and should be combined due to TRS. Similarly to the case of Γ point, doubly degenerate node at the T point has topological charge of ∓ 2 and has quadratic dispersion in the direction perpendicular to [111]. There are also nodes with tilted dispersion, shifted in the [111] direction by $k_{n,111} = \pm(2D_2^2 - D_3^2)e/2\sqrt{3}D_2v$. Their topological charge is ∓ 1.

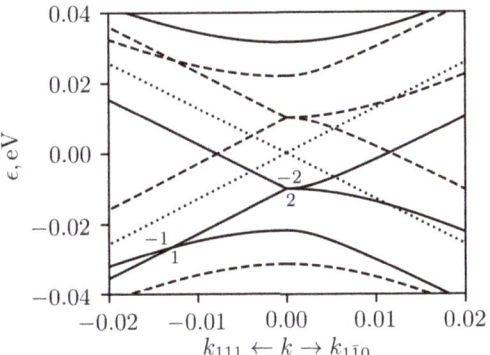

Figure 8. The splitting of energy levels around the R point under uniaxial stain along [111] direction (T point of $R3$ space group). Dotted lines represent the spectrum of undeformed crystal, solid (dashed) lines represent the spectrum in the case of compressive (tensile) strain. The absolute value of strain is $|e| = 0.01$.

4. Results with SOC

Taking into account the spin-orbital coupling in the crystal without deformation, the 6-fold degenerate level at the Γ point splits into a doublet and 4-fold degenerate levels. Their wave functions are transformed according to the $\bar{\Gamma}_5$ irreducible representation and mutually conjugated $\bar{\Gamma}_6$ and $\bar{\Gamma}_7$ irreducible representations, combined due to time-reversal symmetry [8]. The low-energy excitations around the 4-fold degenerate node at the Γ point are spin-3/2 fermions [6,33] with topological charge of 4. Its dispersion is shown in the Figure 1c, and is also plotted with dotted lines in the Figure 9. The doublet does not move from the Γ point due to deformation, so we consider in more details the evolution of fourfold node at the Γ point under the influence of deformation along the main crystallographic directions.

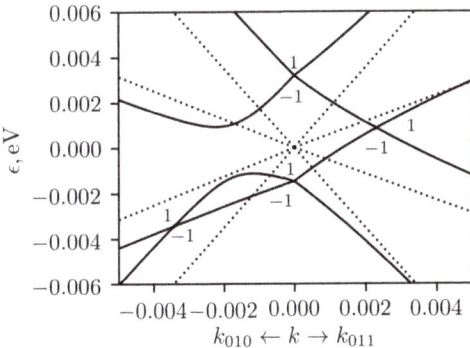

Figure 9. The splitting of energy levels around the Γ point under uniaxial stain along [100] direction. Dotted lines represent the spectrum of undeformed crystal, solid lines represent the spectrum in the case of compressive strain with $e = -0.01$.

Under the deformation along [100] the fourfold degenerate level splits into two twofold degenerate levels, both corresponding to $\bar{\Gamma}_5$ representation of the $P2_12_12_1$ (#19) group, as this two-dimensional representation is time-reversal invariant. The low-energy Hamiltonian for these levels is given by Equations (A4) and (A5) of Appendix A. When the only non-zero component of deformation is $\epsilon_{11} = e$, the gap between two levels at the Γ point is equal to $2|D_3|e$. In general case, it is equal to $2|D_3|e(1+\nu_P)$, where ν_P is the Poisson ratio. The low-energy spectrum is shown in the Figure 9. The doublets at the Γ point form Weyl nodes with unit topological charge. Four nodes are shifted from the Γ point along the diagonals of the $k_y - k_z$ plane and each of them has a unit topological charge. In addition, two Weyl nodes shifted from the Γ point in the $\pm k_y$ directions appear between two lower branches of the spectrum, and two similar Weyl nodes shifted in the $\pm k_z$ directions (not shown in Figure 9) appear between two upper branches of the spectrum. The tensile and compressive strain spectra differ from each other by a change in the sign of the energy.

Without deformation, there are four surface Fermi arcs, emanating from the projection of the nodal point at Γ, as the topological charge is 4. The shift of the node positions for [100] deformation ($e = -0.01$) is accompanied by a change in the surface Fermi arcs, shown in the Figure 10, for the case when the Fermi level coincides with the nodes located along the diagonals of the $k_y - k_z$ plane. The projections of the nodes are marked with asterisks. Their positions, calculated by the $\mathbf{k} \cdot \mathbf{p}$ method, quite well coincide with the sources of four Fermi arcs.

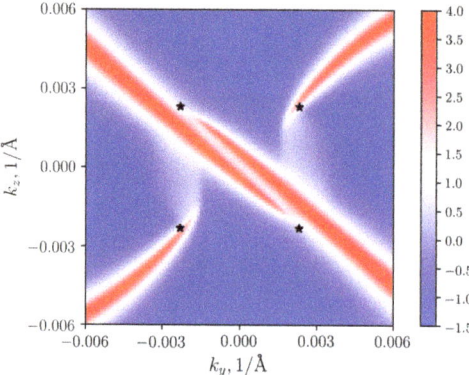

Figure 10. The details of surface Fermi arcs around the Γ point under uniaxial strain along [100] direction ($e = -0.01$) with the account of SOC. Asterisks depict the positions of nodal points.

Considering the deformation along [110] axis, we found similar splitting of four-fold degenerate level at the Γ point into 2 doublets: $\overline{\Gamma}_6 + \overline{\Gamma}_7 \to 2(\overline{\Gamma}_3 + \overline{\Gamma}_4)$, where irreducible representations $\overline{\Gamma}_{3(4)}$ of the space group $P2_1$ (#4) are one-dimensional and combined together due to TRS. The energy gap at the Γ point is equal to $e\sqrt{D_2^2 + D_3^2}$. When the only non-zero components of stain tensor are $\epsilon_{12} = \epsilon_{21} = e/2$, the four-fold degenerate node splits into 4 nodes, moving along crystallographic directions [100], [$\overline{1}$00], [010], [0$\overline{1}$0] by the distance $D_2 e/2\sqrt{b^2 - a^2}$. Due to distortion, small deviation from corresponding Cartesian axis appears by an angle of $\phi = \arctan(e/2)$, which is equal, for example, to $0.3°$ at $e = 0.01$. In the case of the absence of deformations in the directions, normal to [110], when $\epsilon_{11} = \epsilon_{22} = \epsilon_{12} = e/2$, the shift of energy levels due to volume change leads to additional deviation of nodes from Cartesian axes, which is about $\phi = 6°$ at $e = 0.01$. Similar to the case of [100] deformations, there are also two Weyl nodes below and two Weyl nodes above the node in unstrained crystal, but here they are shifted close to the diagonals of $k_x - k_y$ plane. To within a change of the directions of node shifts, the low-energy spectrum around the Γ point for this case is qualitatively very similar to the case of [100] deformations (see the Figure 9).

When the stress is applied along [111] axis, we obtain similar 4-fold level slitting into two doublets at the Γ point with $\overline{\Gamma}_6 + \overline{\Gamma}_7 \to (\overline{\Gamma}_4 + \overline{\Gamma}_4) + (\overline{\Gamma}_5 + \overline{\Gamma}_6)$, where all irreducible representations $\overline{\Gamma}_{4(5,6)}$ of the space group $R3$ (#146) are one-dimensional. $\overline{\Gamma}_4$ is real and it is doubled due to TRS, while $\overline{\Gamma}_{5(6)}$ are complex conjugated and they are combined together due to TRS. These two band crossings at the Γ point are shown in the Figure 11. The lower one is a Weyl node. The node at higher energy has linear dispersion in the [111] direction and nonlinear dispersion in the perpendicular plane (this branch is not shown in the figure). It looks like the triple-Weyl node [36–38] with topological charge ±3, but it is located at the TRIM point. In addition, near the Γ point, there are two groups of nodes connected by time-reversal symmetry. Each of these groups consist of 4 nodes. One of them k_{n1} is shifted from the Γ point along the [111] axis by a distance $k = D_2 e(a + \sqrt{a^2 + 2b^2})/\sqrt{3}b^2$, which is about 0.007 at $|e| = 0.01$ (see Figure 11). In the case of compressive (tensile) strain the energy of the node shifts downwards (upwards) relative to the node at the Γ point in unstrained crystal. More detailed calculations showed that there are another 3 nodes in each group: one of them k_{n2} is shifted from k_{n1} into $[11\bar{2}]$ direction and positions of two other nodes $k_{n3(4)}$ can be obtained using $2\pi/3$ rotation around [111] axis. The distance between nodes is rather small, about 0.0003 at $e = -0.01$. The calculation of topological charge showed that three equivalent nodes $k_{n2(3,4)}$ have topological charge of 1 each, and the node k_{n1} has a charge of -1. Thus total topological charge of each group is 2, giving 4 for both groups together. The dispersion around the nodes is rather complex and is given in the Figure 12. It can be seen that the electronic velocities are very different in different directions, and the nodes are tilted. In addition to these groups of nodes, there are also two tilted Weyl nodes in the directions [111] and $[\bar{1}\bar{1}\bar{1}]$. The lowest band crossing in Figure 11 is one of these node.

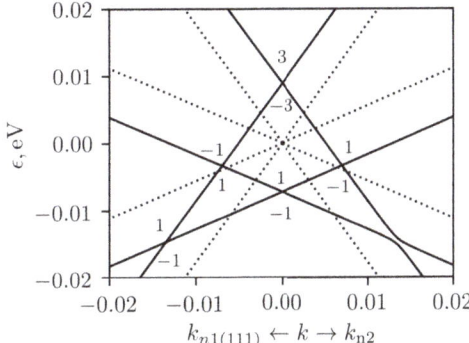

Figure 11. The splitting of energy levels around the Γ point under uniaxial stain along [111] direction. Dotted lines represent the spectrum of undeformed crystal, solid lines represent the spectrum in the case of compressive strain for $e = -0.01$.

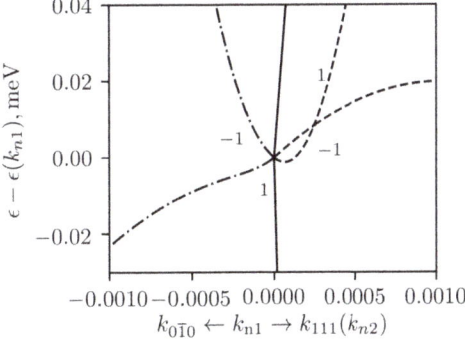

Figure 12. The dispersion around the nodes shifted from the Γ point under uniaxial compressive strain along [111] direction. The dispersions along [111] (solid lines), $[1\bar{1}0]$ (dot-dashed lines) and $[11\bar{2}]$ (towards the node k_{n2}, dashed lines) directions are plotted for $e = -0.01$.

Let us now consider the effect of deformation on the low-energy spectrum around the R point in the presence of spin-orbit coupling. In unstrained crystal, the 8-fold degenerate level at the R point splits into 6-fold degenerate level $\bar{R}_7 + \bar{R}_7$ (double spin-1 quasiparticles) and doublet $\bar{R}_5 + \bar{R}_6$ due to SOC. The doublet is not split by the strain, so we will consider only 6-fold degenerate level (see the Figure 1c). In the case of [100] deformation, it is split into 3 doublets with the wave functions, transforming according to the representations $\bar{R}_2 + \bar{R}_2$, $\bar{R}_3 + \bar{R}_3$ and $\bar{R}_4 + \bar{R}_4$ of the P2$_1$2$_1$2$_1$ (#19) group. The change of the dispersion around the R point is shown in the Figure 13. Two nodes at lower energy are shifted along positive and negative k_x (k_z) directions under compressive (tensile) strain. There is a crossing of four energy branches at each of these nodal points. They are a tilted double spin-1/2 nodes [33] with Chern numbers of ∓ 2. In the case of eight-band Hamiltonian, the equality $\epsilon(\mathbf{k}, -\hat{e}) = -\epsilon(\mathbf{k}, \hat{e})$ does not hold exactly. But in the case of [100] deformation the spectrum for six considered bands approximately follows this rule. This implies that there are the two additional double spin-1/2 nodes in k_z (k_x) directions for compressive (tensile) strain (see Figure 13).

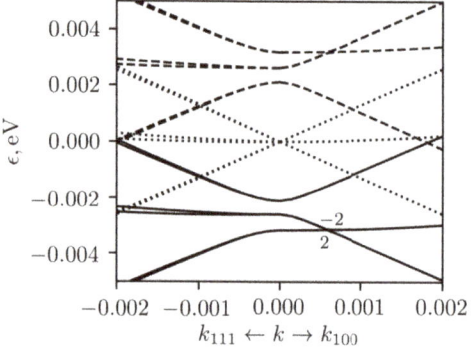

Figure 13. The splitting of energy levels around the R point under uniaxial stain along [100] direction. Dotted lines represent the spectrum of undeformed crystal, solid (dashed) lines represent the spectrum in the case of compressive (tensile) strain of $|e| = 0.01$.

The deformation in [110] direction again leads to the splitting of 6-fold degenerate level into 3 doublets at the vertex of deformed Brillouin zone (E point). Wave functions of two doublets are transformed according to the $\bar{E}_3 + \bar{E}_3$ representation and one doublet according to the $\bar{E}_4 + \bar{E}_4$ representation, where both $\bar{E}_{3(4)}$ are real one-dimensional. These doublets do not form Weyl nodes, as the energy branches, starting from them are degenerate at the edges of the Brillouin zone parallel to (001) plane. Four simple Weyl nodes are formed near the E point. They shifted mainly into k_z direction to the points with coordinates $\pm k_n$, where $k_n = (\pm 0.001, \mp 0.001, 0.014)$ at $e = -0.01$ (see Figure 14). In the case of tensile strain the shift appeared to be almost the same. As the degeneracy of the bands is completely lifted under this deformation, the topological charge of each of the 4 nodes is ∓ 1.

The case of [111] deformation is similar to the two previously considered cases in the sense that one obtains 3 doublets instead of 6-fold degenerate level at the vertex of the Brillouin zone ($2\bar{R}_7 \rightarrow (\bar{T}_4 + \bar{T}_4) + 2(\bar{T}_5 + \bar{T}_6)$, where $\bar{T}_4$ is real one-dimensional representations, $\bar{T}_5$ and $\bar{T}_6$, are complex conjugated one dimensional representations of the little group of the T point of the $R3$(#146) space group). Each of these doublets corresponds to a Weyl node. The two band crossings at the T point are the conventional Weyl nodes with Chern number of ∓ 1. The third band crossing looks like the triple-Weyl node with the topological charge of ∓ 3. It is similar to triple-Weyl node at the Γ point. In addition, near the T point, there are two groups of nodes connected by time-reversal symmetry, as in the case of the Γ point. Two of them are simple Weyl nodes shifted into [111] and $[\bar{1}\bar{1}\bar{1}]$ directions, but they have topological charge 1. Around each of them, there are three conventional Weyl nodes with topological charges -1. The total charge of these eight nodes is -4. For example, in the case of compressive strain with $e = -0.01$, one of the nodes at the [111] direction have coordinates $k_{n1} = (0.00197, 0.00197, 0.00197)$ relative to the T point. One of its satellites have coordinates $k_{n2} = (0.00169, 0.00196, 0.00227)$, and the coordinates of another two satellites $k_{n3(4)}$ can be obtained by cyclic permutations. The dispersion around the T point towards nodes k_{n1} and k_{n2} is plotted in the Figure 15. It is almost linear. At the same time, the dispersion along the line connecting the central node with one of its satellites (Figure 16) looks like a result of the crossing of two nonlinear bands.

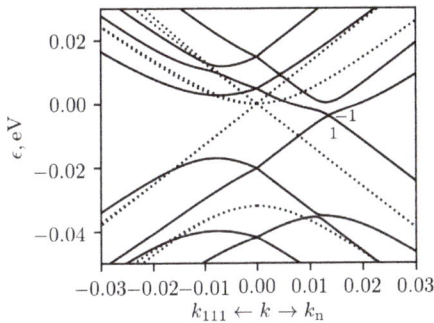

Figure 14. The splitting of energy levels around the R point (E point, P2$_1$ space group) under uniaxial stain along [110] direction. Dotted lines represent the spectrum of undeformed crystal, solid lines represent the spectrum in the case of compressive strain of $e = -0.01$.

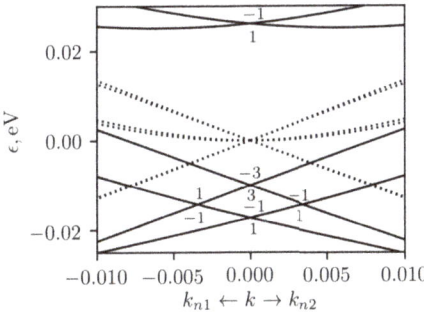

Figure 15. The splitting of energy levels around the R point under uniaxial stain along [111] direction (T point, R3 space group). Dotted lines represent the spectrum of undeformed crystal, solid lines represent the spectrum in the case of compressive strain of $e = -0.01$.

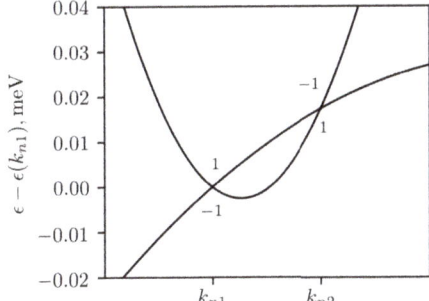

Figure 16. The electronic dispersion along the direction from central node k_{n1} towards to one of its satellites under uniaxial stain along [111] direction at $e = -0.01$.

5. Conclusions

In the present work the influence of deformation on the band structure and topological properties of CoSi was studied using both ab initio calculations, and symmetry considerations. The symmetry prescribed $\mathbf{k} \cdot \mathbf{p}$ Hamiltonians at the Γ and R TRIM points taking into account deformation were written down for the cases with and without SOC. It was shown that in almost all considered cases, the degeneracy is partially lifted at the TRIM points. The only exception is the fourfold degenerate level at the R point (without SOC) under [100] strain. A lowering in symmetry leads to the appearance of a significant number of different band crossings with topological charges from ± 1 to ± 3 around the TRIM points. The nodes often have a tilted dispersion.

The unusual results were obtained upon deformation of CoSi along the [111] direction. Without spin-orbit coupling, the doubly degenerate nodes with quadratic dispersion in the plane orthogonal to the [111] direction appear at the Γ and T points of the deformed Brillouin zone. These band crossings have Chern numbers of ± 2 and resemble the well-known double-Weyl nodes, but they are spin degenerate. Calculation with account of SOC revealed doubly degenerate nodes with the topological charges of ± 3 at the TRIM points. These band crossings are located on the threefold rotation axis and are analogous to triple-Weyl nodes.

The band structure with SOC around the R point under [100] strain exhibits another example of the change of node type. The double spin-1 node with topological charge of 4 splits into pairs of double spin-1/2 nodes with topological charges of 2 per node. Thus, using mechanical deformation, the transition between different types of topological nodes can be realized in the same material.

A lowering of the crystal symmetry under strain also leads to a modification of the surface Fermi arcs shape. A change in the sign of the deformation and the Fermi level position switches the ends of the Fermi arcs from one group of nodes to another. However, the number of Fermi arcs always remains equal to two without taking into account SOC and four with SOC.

As a byproduct of low-energy Hamiltonian fitting, the absolute deformation potential parameters were obtained for considered energy states, and the work function of CoSi was calculated (4.55 eV), which correlates with available experimental data.

Author Contributions: Conceptualization, Y.I. and A.B.; methodology, Y.I.; investigation, S.N. and D.P.-S.; writing—original draft preparation, S.N. and D.P.-S.; writing—review and editing, Y.I. and A.B.; supervision, A.B. All authors have read and agreed to the published version of the manuscript.

Funding: The study was supported by the Russian Foundation for basic Reseach, project 18-52-80005 (BRICS).

Conflicts of Interest: The authors declare no conflict of interest.

Appendix A. $\mathbf{k} \cdot \mathbf{p}$ Hamiltonians and Their Parameters

In this section, the form of $\mathbf{k} \cdot \mathbf{p}$ Hamiltonians and their parameters will be given. We used eV units for energy, and the dimensionless wave vector components $k_i, i = 1, 2, 3$ are measured in fractions of the reciprocal lattice vectors.

Without spin-orbital coupling linear in wave vector part of Hamiltonian at the Γ point is given by the following equation:

$$H_{\Gamma 1} = \begin{pmatrix} 0 & ivk_3 & -ivk_2 \\ -ivk_3 & 0 & ivk_1 \\ ivk_2 & -ivk_1 & 0 \end{pmatrix}, \quad (A1)$$

where $v = 1.73$ eV. The node at the Γ point lies 3.6 meV above the Fermi level.

The perturbation Hamiltonian in the linear approximation in the deformation tensor ϵ_{ik} and in the zero approximation in the wave vector has the following form:

$$H_{\Gamma 2} = \begin{pmatrix} S_1(\hat{e}) & D_4\epsilon_{12} & D_4\epsilon_{13} \\ D_4\epsilon_{12} & S_2(\hat{e}) & D_4\epsilon_{23} \\ D_4\epsilon_{13} & D_4\epsilon_{23} & S_3(\hat{e}) \end{pmatrix}, \quad (A2)$$

where $S_1(\hat{e}) = D_1\epsilon_{11} + D_2\epsilon_{22} + D_3\epsilon_{33}$, $S_2(\hat{e}) = D_3\epsilon_{11} + D_1\epsilon_{22} + D_2\epsilon_{33}$, $S_3(\hat{e}) = D_2\epsilon_{11} + D_3\epsilon_{22} + D_1\epsilon_{33}$, $D_1 = -0.319$ eV, $D_2 = -0.400$ eV, $D_3 = 0.470$ eV and $D_4 = 2.479$ eV.

At the R point the Hamiltonian, linear in k-vector, was given in Ref. [16]. It can be represented as $H_{R1} = v\hat{1} \otimes (\sigma \cdot \mathbf{k})$ with $v = 1.28$ eV. The node at the R point lies 0.211 eV below the Fermi level. The perturbation due to elastic strain reads:

$$H_{R2} = \begin{pmatrix} D_1\mathrm{Tr}\hat{e} - D_2\epsilon_{12} & -D_2(\epsilon_{23} - i\epsilon_{13}) & iD_3\epsilon_{12} & D_3(v_6^*\epsilon_{23} + iv_6\epsilon_{13}) \\ -D_2(\epsilon_{23} + i\epsilon_{13}) & D_1\mathrm{Tr}\hat{e} + D_2\epsilon_{12} & D_3(v_6^*\epsilon_{23} - iv_6\epsilon_{13}) & -iD_3\epsilon_{12} \\ -iD_3^*\epsilon_{12} & D_3^*(v_6\epsilon_{23} + iv_6^*\epsilon_{13}) & D_1\mathrm{Tr}\hat{e} + D_2\epsilon_{12} & D_2(\epsilon_{23} - i\epsilon_{13}) \\ D_3^*(v_6\epsilon_{23} - iv_6^*\epsilon_{13}) & iD_3^*\epsilon_{12} & D_2(\epsilon_{23} + i\epsilon_{13}) & D_1\mathrm{Tr}\hat{e} - D_2\epsilon_{12} \end{pmatrix}, \quad (A3)$$

where $\mathrm{Tr}\hat{e}$ is a trace of strain tensor, $v_6 = e^{i\pi/6}$, $D_1 = 0.264$ eV, $D_2 = -1.29$ eV and $D_3 = 3.27$ eV.

Taking into account spin-orbit coupling, linear Hamiltonian at the Γ point was written down in Ref. [8] and has the following form:

$$H_{\Gamma 1}^{(SOC)} = \begin{pmatrix} ak_3 & a(k_1 - ik_2) & b(v_3k_1 - v_6k_2) & bk_3 \\ a(k_1 + ik_2) & -ak_3 & bk_3 & -b(v_3k_1 + v_6k_2) \\ b^*(v_3^*k_1 - v_6^*k_2) & b^*k_3 & -ak_3 & -a(k_1 + ik_2) \\ b^*k_3 & -b^*(v_3^*k_1 + v_6^*k_2) & -a(k_1 - ik_2) & ak_3 \end{pmatrix}, \quad (A4)$$

where $v_3 = e^{i\pi/3}$, $a = 0.56$ eV and $b = 1.19$ eV [8]. The 4-fold degenerate node position is 21 meV above the Fermi level, and the Weyl cone at the Γ point is shifted down due to SOC by 54 meV relative to this node.

The perturbation due to deformation reads:

$$H_{\Gamma 2}^{(SOC)} = \begin{pmatrix} D_1\mathrm{Tr}\hat{e} + D_2\epsilon_{12} & D_2(\epsilon_{23} - i\epsilon_{13}) & 0 & D_3\Sigma(\hat{e}) \\ D_2(\epsilon_{23} + i\epsilon_{13}) & D_1\mathrm{Tr}\hat{e} - D_2\epsilon_{12} & -D_3\Sigma(\hat{e}) & 0 \\ 0 & -D_3^*\Sigma^*(\hat{e}) & D_1\mathrm{Tr}\hat{e} + D_2\epsilon_{12} & D_2(\epsilon_{23} + i\epsilon_{13}) \\ D_3^*\Sigma^*(\hat{e}) & 0 & D_2(\epsilon_{23} - i\epsilon_{13}) & D_1\mathrm{Tr}\hat{e} - D_2\epsilon_{12} \end{pmatrix}, \quad (A5)$$

where $\Sigma(\hat{e}) = \epsilon_{11} - v_3\epsilon_{22} + v_3^2\epsilon_{33}$, $D_1 = -0.085$ eV, $D_2 = 1.40$ eV. Parameter D_3 is complex. Eigenvalues at $k = 0$ does not depend on its phase, but it affects the spectrum for nonzero k values. The fitting gives $D_3 \approx 0.233 e^{-i\pi/6}$ eV.

At the R point the Hamiltonian for 6-fold degenerate node including SOC was given in Ref. [17]. After uniaxial deformation this node splits into three doubly-degenerate nodes. Under deformation in [100] direction, the shift of energy levels at the R point is linear in deformation. If the deformation is applied in [111] direction, only for small $e < 0.004$, the shift of energy levels can be considered as linear, and the deformation along [110] axis leads to nonlinear shift of the two pairs of energy levels (see Figure A1). It was shown in Ref. [16] in the framework of a simple model that a linear Hamiltonian that includes SOC in the zeroth order with respect to the wave vector and takes into account all eight bands leads to the correct nonlinear band dispersion near the R point (see, e.g., Figure 3b–c in Ref. [8]). So, we consider both nodes together and obtain 8×8 Hamiltonian at the R point. The zero-order Hamiltonian has only nonzero matrix elements $(H_{R0}^{(SOC)})_{ii} = -\Delta, i = 7, 8$, which describe energy shift of doublet downwards in energy due to SOC. Including SOC, the position of the 6-fold degenerate node is 0.202 eV below ϵ_F, while the band splitting $\Delta = 32$ meV. The zero- and linear-order in k parts together reads:

$$H_{R01}^{(SOC)} = \begin{pmatrix} 0 & a_1k_3 & -a_1^*k_2 & 0 & a_2k_3 & -a_2k_2 & a_3k_1 & a_4k_1 \\ a_1^*k_3 & 0 & a_1k_1 & a_2^*k_3 & 0 & a_2k_1 & v_3^*a_3k_2 & v_3^*a_4k_2 \\ -a_1k_2 & a_1^*k_1 & 0 & -a_2k_2 & a_2k_1 & 0 & -v_3^*a_3k_3 & -v_3a_4k_3 \\ 0 & a_2^*k_3 & -a_2^*k_2 & 0 & -a_1^*k_3 & a_1k_2 & a_4^*k_1 & -a_3^*k_1 \\ a_2^*k_3 & 0 & a_2^*k_1 & -a_1k_3 & 0 & -a_1^*k_1 & v_3a_4^*k_2 & -v_3^*a_3^*k_2 \\ -a_2^*k_2 & a_2^*k_1 & 0 & a_1^*k_2 & -a_1k_1 & 0 & -v_3^*a_4^*k_3 & v_3a_3^*k_3 \\ a_3^*k_1 & v_3^*a_3^*k_2 & -v_3a_3^*k_3 & a_4k_1 & v_3^*a_4k_2 & -v_3a_4k_3 & -\Delta & 0 \\ a_4^*k_1 & v_3a_4^*k_2 & -v_3^*a_4^*k_3 & -a_3k_1 & -v_3a_3k_2 & v_3^*a_3k_3 & 0 & -\Delta \end{pmatrix}, \quad (A6)$$

where parameters a_i are complex. Their values were obtained by fitting to electron spectrum around R point. They are not unique, but they were checked to give correct values of topological charges. These values are $a_1 = (0.342 - 0.686i)$ eV, $a_2 = (1.043 + 0.060i)$ eV, $a_3 = (-0.459 - 0.657i)$ eV and $a_4 = (0.181 - 0.100i)$ eV.

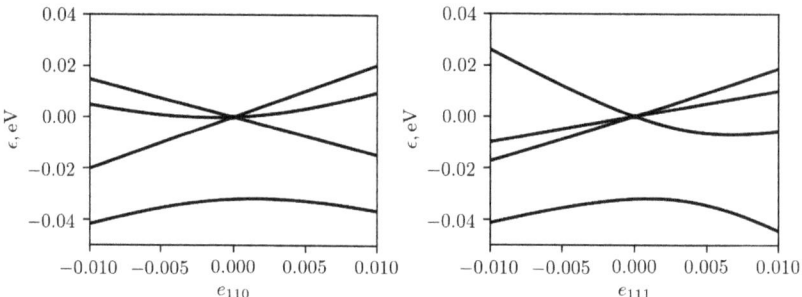

Figure A1. The splitting of energy levels at the R point with uniaxial stress of magnitude e in [110] (**left** panel) and in [111] (**right** panel) directions.

The perturbation due to deformation is:

$$H_{R2}^{(SOC)} = \begin{pmatrix} S_1(\hat{e}) & D_5\epsilon_{12} & -D_5^*\epsilon_{13} & 0 & D_6\epsilon_{12} & D_6\epsilon_{13} & D_7\epsilon_{23} & D_8\epsilon_{23} \\ D_5^*\epsilon_{12} & S_2(\hat{e}) & D_5\epsilon_{23} & -D_6\epsilon_{12} & 0 & D_6\epsilon_{23} & D_7\epsilon_{13}v_3 & D_8\epsilon_{13}v_3^* \\ -D_5\epsilon_{13} & D_5^*\epsilon_{23} & S_3(\hat{e}) & -D_6\epsilon_{13} & -D_6\epsilon_{23} & 0 & -D_7\epsilon_{12}v_3^* & -D_8\epsilon_{12}v_3 \\ 0 & -D_6^*\epsilon_{12} & -D_6^*\epsilon_{13} & S_1(\hat{e}) & D_5^*\epsilon_{12} & -D_5\epsilon_{13} & -D_8^*\epsilon_{23} & D_7^*\epsilon_{23} \\ D_6^*\epsilon_{12} & 0 & -D_6^*\epsilon_{23} & D_5\epsilon_{12} & S_2(\hat{e}) & D_5^*\epsilon_{23} & -D_8^*\epsilon_{13}v_3 & D_7^*\epsilon_{13}v_3^* \\ D_6^*\epsilon_{13} & D_6^*\epsilon_{23} & 0 & -D_5^*\epsilon_{13} & D_5\epsilon_{23} & S_3(\hat{e}) & D_8^*\epsilon_{12}v_3^* & -D_7^*\epsilon_{12}v_3 \\ D_7^*\epsilon_{23} & D_7^*\epsilon_{13}v_3^* & -D_7^*\epsilon_{12}v_3 & -D_8\epsilon_{23} & -D_8\epsilon_{13}v_3^* & D_8\epsilon_{12}v_3 & D_4\text{Tr}\hat{e} & 0 \\ D_8^*\epsilon_{23} & D_8^*\epsilon_{13}v_3 & -D_8^*\epsilon_{12}v_3^* & D_7\epsilon_{23} & D_7\epsilon_{13}v_3 & -D_7\epsilon_{12}v_3^* & 0 & D_4\text{Tr}\hat{e} \end{pmatrix}, \quad (A7)$$

where $D_1 = 0.318$ eV, $D_2 = 0.211$ eV, $D_3 = 0.261$ eV, $D_4 = 0.270$ eV are real and determine the shift of each pair of energy levels under [100] deformation. The splitting of levels under the compressive or tensile strain e in [110] direction also can be obtained analytically. Two doublets linearly shift with deformation e

$$\epsilon_R = \left(2D_1 + D_2 + D_3 \pm \sqrt{(D_2 - D_3)^2 + 4(|D_5|^2 + |D_6|^2)}\right)e/4, \quad (A8)$$

from which $\sqrt{|D_5|^2 + |D_6|^2} = 3.5$ eV can be obtained. But another four levels shift nonlinearly

$$\epsilon_R = \left((D_2 + D_3 + 2D_4)e - 2\Delta \pm \sqrt{((D_2 + D_3 - 2D_4)e + 2\Delta)^2 + 4e^2(|D_7|^2 + |D_8|^2)}\right)/4. \quad (A9)$$

$\sqrt{|D_7|^2 + |D_8|^2} = 3.36$ eV. Other parameters were obtained from fitting to band structures of deformed crystal. They are non-unique, one of possible parameter sets is $D_5 = (-1.107 - 2.916i)$ eV, $D_6 = (0.713 + 1.420i)$ eV, $D_7 = (1.147 + 1.048i)$ eV, $D_8 = (-1.667 + 2.469i)$ eV.

Appendix B. Absolute Deformation Potentials and Work Function of CoSi

In order to obtain absolute shift of energy level ϵ_n after deformation, it is necessary to have common reference energy in deformed and undeformed crystals or to determine the shift of the reference due to deformation. For example, energy can be measured from macroscopic average of effective self-consistent potential V_e. Then absolute shift of energy level ϵ_n due to deformation is equal to $\Delta \epsilon_n = (\epsilon_n^{(d)} - V_e^{(d)}) - (\epsilon_n^{(u)} - V_e^{(u)}) + \Delta V_e$, where ΔV_e is the reference energy offset due to strain and superscript $d(u)$ corresponds to bulk calculation for deformed (undeformed) crystal.

The vacuum level can be used as a common reference energy, but it is not accessible in bulk DFT calculation. Hence we apply approach similar to that used for work function calculations. The superlattice configuration was considered with alternating layers of material and vacuum gaps. Average effective potential inside material layer V_e was calculated relative to its value inside vacuum gap (vacuum energy level). Then, the change of average effective potential ΔV_e due to deformation can be calculated as a deference between the values obtained from separate calculations for strained and unstrained layers.

Alternative approach was used in Ref. [39], where another superlattice method was proposed in order to obtain reference energy offset. The superlattice was formed from layers, extended or compressed along the direction of superlattice axis, and the layers were undeformed in the plane. In all-electron calculations, performed in Ref. [39], localized core levels, used as an energy reference, can be associated with each of the layers. The difference in their energy positions in the limit of thick layers allowed to obtain the reference energy offset due to deformation. Similar approach was used in Ref. [40], where pseudopotential calculations were used and, instead of core levels, macroscopic average effective potential in deformed $V_e^{(DL)}$ and undeformed $V_e^{(UL)}$ layers was used to determine the change of the energy reference due to deformation $\Delta V_e = V_e^{(DL)} - V_e^{(UL)}$. We also used the latter approach and made similar calculations for superlattice of strained/unstrained layers of CoSi for [100], [110] and [111] directions. We checked the convergence of ΔV_e with respect to the layer thickness. The accuracy of 1–2 meV was reached for the layer thickness of $10a_0$.

Inside thick metallic layers, thicker then screening length, the difference $(V_e - \epsilon_F)$ is determined only by its bulk properties, and the superlattice made of strained/unstrained layers should have common Fermi level ϵ_F. Hence, the same ΔV_e can be obtained from bulk calculations for deformed and undeformed crystal $\Delta V_e = (V_e^{(d)} - \epsilon_F^{(d)}) - (V_e^{(u)} - \epsilon_F^{(u)})$. Then, the absolute shift of energy level ϵ_n due to deformation can be calculated as $\Delta \epsilon_n = (\epsilon_n^{(d)} - \epsilon_F^{(d)}) - (\epsilon_n^{(u)} - \epsilon_F^{(u)})$.

All three considered approaches should give the same results for metallic material. Although CoSi is considered as semimetallic, the comparison gave the same results for ΔV_e to within 1–2 meV. In addition, we obtained work function for CoSi, equal to 4.55 eV which compares favourably with experimental values of 4.47–4.54 eV [41].

References

1. Asanabe, S.; Shinoda, D.; Sasaki, Y. Semimetallic Properties of $Co_{1-x}Fe_xSi$ Solid Solutions. *Phys. Rev.* **1964**, *134*, A774. [CrossRef]
2. Fedorov, M.I.; Zaitsev, V.K. Semimetals as materials for thermoelectric generators. In *CRC Handbook of Thermoelectrics*; Rowe, D.M., Ed.; CRC Press: Boca Raton, FL, USA, 1995; Chapter 27.
3. Pan, Z.; Zhang, L.; Wu, J. Electronic structure and transport properties of doped CoSi single crystal. *J. Appl. Phys.* **2007**, *101*, 033715. [CrossRef]
4. Sakai, A.; Ishii, F.; Onose, Y.; Tomioka, Y.; Yotsuhashi, S.; Adachi, H.; Nagaosa, N.; Tokura, Y. Thermoelectric power in transition-metal monosilicides. *J. Phys. Soc. Jpn.* **2007**, *76*, 093601. [CrossRef]
5. Ishii, F.; Kotaka, H.; Onishi, T. Spin–Orbit Interaction Effects in the Electronic Structure of B20-Type CoSi: First-Principles Density Functional Study. *JPS Conf. Proc.* **2014**, *3*, 016019. [CrossRef]
6. Tang, P.; Zhou, Q.; Zhang, S.C. Multiple Types of Topological Fermions in Transition Metal Silicides. *Phys. Rev. Lett.* **2017**, *119*, 206402. [CrossRef]
7. Chang, G.; Xu, S.Y.; Wieder, B.J.; Sanchez, D.S.; Huang, S.M.; Belopolski, I.; Chang, T.R.; Zhang, S.; Bansil, A.; Lin, H.; et al. Unconventional Chiral Fermions and Large Topological Fermi Arcs in RhSi. *Phys. Rev. Lett.* **2017**, *119*, 206401. [CrossRef]
8. Pshenay-Severin, D.A.; Ivanov, Y.V.; Burkov, A.A.; Burkov, A.T. Band structure and unconventional electronic topology of CoSi. *J. Phys. Condens. Matter* **2018**, *30*, 135501. [CrossRef]
9. Yu, J.; Kuang, J.; Long, J.; Ke, X.; Duan, X.; Liu, Z. Effects of nonstoichiometry on thermoelectric properties of CoSi-based materials. *J. Mater. Sci. Mater. Electron.* **2020**, *31*, 2139–2144. [CrossRef]
10. Pshenay-Severin, D.A.; Ivanov, Y.V.; Burkov, A.T.; Novikov, S.V.; Zaitsev, V.K.; Reith, H. Electronic Structure and Thermoelectric Properties of Transition Metal Monosilicides. *J. Electron. Mater.* **2018**, *47*, 3277–3281. [CrossRef]

11. Pshenay-Severin, D.A.; Ivanov, Y.V.; Burkov, A.T. The effect of energy-dependent electron scattering on thermoelectric transport in novel topological semimetal CoSi. *J. Phys. Condens. Matter* **2018**, *30*, 475501. [CrossRef]
12. Antonov, A.; Ivanov, Y.; Konstantinov, P.; Kuznetsova, V.; Novikov, S.; Ovchinnikov, A.; Pshenay-Severin, D.; Burkov, A. Thermoelectric and galvanomagnetic properties of topologically non-trivial (Co-M)Si semimetals (M = Fe, Ni) at high temperatures. *J. Appl. Phys.* **2019**, *126*, 245103. [CrossRef]
13. Xu, X.; Wang, X.; Cochran, T.A.; Sanchez, D.S.; Chang, G.; Belopolski, I.; Wang, G.; Liu, Y.; Tien, H.J.; Gui, X.; et al. Crystal growth and quantum oscillations in the topological chiral semimetal CoSi. *Phys. Rev. B* **2019**, *100*, 045104. [CrossRef]
14. Balasubramanian, B.; Manchanda, P.; Pahari, R.; Chen, Z.; Zhang, W.; Valloppilly, S.R.; Li, X.; Sarella, A.; Yue, L.; Ullah, A.; et al. Chiral Magnetism and High-Temperature Skyrmions in B20-Ordered Co-Si. *Phys. Rev. Lett.* **2020**, *124*, 057201. [CrossRef] [PubMed]
15. Xu, B.; Fang, Z.; Sanchez-Martinez, M.A.; Venderbos, J.W.F.; Ni, Z.; Qiu, T.; Manna, K.; Wang, K.; Paglione, J.; Bernhard, C.; et al. Optical signatures of multifold fermions in the chiral topological semimetal CoSi. *Proc. Natl. Acad. Sci. USA* **2020**, *117*, 27104–27110. [CrossRef]
16. Manes, J.L. Existence of bulk chiral fermions and crystal symmetry. *Phys. Rev. B* **2012**, *85*, 155118. [CrossRef]
17. Bradlyn, B.; Cano, J.; Wang, Z.; Vergniory, M.G.; Felser, C.; Cava, R.J.; Bernevig, B.A. Beyond Dirac and Weyl fermions: Unconventional quasiparticles in conventional crystals. *Science* **2016**, *353*, aaf5037. [CrossRef]
18. Sanchez, D.S.; Belopolski, I.; Cochran, T.A.; Xu, X.; Yin, J.X.; Chang, G.; Xie, W.; Manna, K.; Süß, V.; Huang, C.Y.; et al. Topological chiral crystals with helicoid-arc quantum states. *Nature* **2019**, *567*, 500–505. [CrossRef]
19. Takane, D.; Wang, Z.; Souma, S.; Nakayama, K.; Nakamura, T.; Oinuma, H.; Nakata, Y.; Iwasawa, H.; Cacho, C.; Kim, T.; et al. Observation of Chiral Fermions with a Large Topological Charge and Associated Fermi-Arc Surface States in CoSi. *Phys. Rev. Lett.* **2019**, *122*, 076402. [CrossRef]
20. Rao, Z.; Li, H.; Zhang, T.; Tian, S.; Li, C.; Fu, B.; Tang, C.; Wang, L.; Li, Z.; Fan, W.; et al. Observation of unconventional chiral fermions with long Fermi arcs in CoSi. *Nature* **2019**, *567*, 496–499. [CrossRef]
21. Dutta, P.; Pandey, S.K. Effects of correlations and temperature on the electronic structures and related physical properties of FeSi and CoSi: A comprehensive study. *J. Phys. Condens. Matter* **2019**, *31*, 145602. [CrossRef]
22. Pshenay-Severin, D.A.; Burkov, A.T. Electronic Structure of B20 (FeSi-Type) Transition-Metal Monosilicides. *Materials* **2019**, *12*, 2710. [CrossRef] [PubMed]
23. Schnatmann, L.; Geishendorf, K.; Lammel, M.; Damm, C.; Novikov, S.; Thomas, A.; Burkov, A.; Reith, H.; Nielsch, K.; Schierning, G. Signatures of a Charge Density Wave Phase and the Chiral Anomaly in the Fermionic Material Cobalt Monosilicide CoSi. *Adv. Electron. Mater.* **2020**, *6*, 1900857. [CrossRef]
24. Krishna Nichenametla, C.; Calvo, J.; Riedel, S.; Gerlich, L.; Hindenberg, M.; Novikov, S.; Burkov, A.; Kozelj, P.; Cardoso-Gil, R.; Wagner-Reetz, M. Doping Effects in CMOS-compatible CoSi Thin Films for Thermoelectric and Sensor Applications. *Z. Anorg. Allg. Chem.* **2020**, *646*, 1231–1237. [CrossRef]
25. Hernandez, J.; Vočadlo, L.; Wood, I. High pressure stability of the monosilicides of cobalt and the platinum group elements. *J. Alloys Compd.* **2015**, *626*, 375–380. [CrossRef]
26. Giannozzi, P.; Baroni, S.; Bonini, N.; Calandra, M.; Car, R.; Cavazzoni, C.; Ceresoli, D.; Chiarotti, G.L.; Cococcioni, M.; Dabo, I.; et al. QUANTUM ESPRESSO: A modular and open-source software project for quantum simulations of materials. *J. Phys. Condens. Matter* **2009**, *21*, 395502. [CrossRef]
27. Hamann, D.R. Optimized norm-conserving Vanderbilt pseudopotentials. *Phys. Rev. B* **2013**, *88*, 085117. [CrossRef]
28. Mostofi, A.A.; Yates, J.R.; Pizzi, G.; Lee, Y.S.; Souza, I.; Vanderbilt, D.; Marzari, N. An updated version of wannier90: A tool for obtaining maximally-localised Wannier functions. *Comput. Phys. Commun.* **2014**, *185*, 2309. [CrossRef]
29. Wu, Q.; Zhang, S.; Song, H.F.; Troyer, M.; Soluyanov, A.A. WannierTools: An open-source software package for novel topological materials. *Comput. Phys. Commun.* **2018**, *224*, 405. [CrossRef]
30. Bir, G.L.; Pikus, G.E. *Symmetry and Strain-Induced Effects in Semiconductors*; Wiley: New York, NY, USA, 1974.
31. Voon, L.C.L.Y. *Electronic and Optical Properties of Semiconductors: A Study Based on the Empirical Tight Binding Model*; Universal-Publishers: Parkland, FL, USA, 1997.
32. Elcoro, L.; Bradlyn, B.; Wang, Z.; Vergniory, M.G.; Cano, J.; Felser, C.; Bernevig, B.A.; Orobengoa, D.; Flor, G.; Aroyo, M.I. Double crystallographic groups and their representations on the Bilbao Crystallographic Server. *J. Appl. Crystallogr.* **2017**, *50*, 1457–1477. [CrossRef]
33. Flicker, F.; de Juan, F.; Bradlyn, B.; Morimoto, T.; Vergniory, M.G.; Grushin, A.G. Chiral optical response of multifold fermions. *Phys. Rev. B* **2018**, *98*, 155145. [CrossRef]
34. Soluyanov, A.A.; Gresch, D.; Wang, Z.; Wu, Q.; Troyer, M.; Dai, X.; Bernevig, B.A. Type-II Weyl semimetals. *Nature* **2015**, *527*, 495–498. [CrossRef] [PubMed]
35. Huang, S.M.; Xu, S.Y.; Belopolski, I.; Lee, C.C.; Chang, G.; Chang, T.R.; Wang, B.; Alidoust, N.; Bian, G.; Neupane, M.; et al. New type of Weyl semimetal with quadratic double Weyl fermions. *Proc. Natl. Acad. Sci. USA* **2016**, *113*, 1180. [CrossRef] [PubMed]
36. Fang, C.; Gilbert, M.J.; Dai, X.; Bernevig, B.A. Multi-Weyl Topological Semimetals Stabilized by Point Group Symmetry. *Phys. Rev. Lett.* **2012**, *108*, 266802. [CrossRef]
37. Tsirkin, S.S.; Souza, I.; Vanderbilt, D. Composite Weyl nodes stabilized by screw symmetry with and without time-reversal invariance. *Phys. Rev. B* **2017**, *96*, 045102. [CrossRef]

38. Chang, G.; Wieder, B.J.; Schindler, F.; Sanchez, D.S.; Belopolski, I.; Huang, S.M.; Singh, B.; Wu, D.; Chang, T.R.; Neupert, T.; et al. Topological quantum properties of chiral crystals. *Nat. Mater.* **2018**, *17*, 978–985. [CrossRef] [PubMed]
39. Franceschetti, A.; Wei, S.H.; Zunger, A. Absolute deformation potentials of Al, Si, and NaCl. *Phys. Rev. B* **1994**, *50*, 17797–17801. [CrossRef]
40. Murphy, A.R.; Murphy-Armando, F.; Fahy, S.; Savić, I. Acoustic deformation potentials of *n*-type PbTe from first principles. *Phys. Rev. B* **2018**, *98*, 085201. [CrossRef]
41. Kedzierski, J.; Nowak, E.; Kanarsky, T.; Zhang, Y.; Boyd, D.; Carruthers, R.; Cabral, C.; Amos, R.; Lavoie, C.; Roy, R.; et al. Metal-gate FinFET and fully-depleted SOI devices using total gate silicidation. In Proceedings of the Digest, International Electron Devices Meeting, San Francisco, CA, USA, 8–11 December 2002; pp. 247–250. [CrossRef]

Article

Faraday Rotation Due to Quantum Anomalous Hall Effect in Cr-Doped (Bi,Sb)$_2$Te$_3$

Alexey Shuvaev [1,*], Lei Pan [2], Peng Zhang [2], Kang L. Wang [2] and Andrei Pimenov [1]

[1] Institute of Solid State Physics, Vienna University of Technology, 1040 Vienna, Austria; andrei.pimenov@tuwien.ac.at

[2] Department of Electrical and Computer Engineering, University of California, Los Angeles, CA 90095, USA; leipan@ucla.edu (L.P.); echozp@ucla.edu (P.Z.); wang@seas.ucla.edu (K.L.W.)

* Correspondence: alexey.shuvaev@tuwien.ac.at

Abstract: Quantum anomalous Hall effect (QAHE) represents a quantized version of the classical anomalous Hall effect. In the latter case the magnetization takes over the role of magnetic field and induces nonzero off-diagonal elements in the conductivity matrix. In magnetic topological insulators with the band inversion the QAHE can be reached due to quantized conduction channel at the sample edge if the Fermi energy is tuned into the surface magnetic gap. In the static regime the QAHE is seen as a zero-field step in the Hall resistivity. At optical frequencies this step is transformed into a quantized value of the polarization rotation approaching the fine structure constant $\alpha = e^2/2\varepsilon_0 hc \approx 1/137$. However, due to material issues the steps reach the predicted values at millikelvin temperatures only. In this work we investigate the Faraday polarization rotation in thin films of Cr-doped topological insulator and in the sub-terahertz frequency range. Well defined polarization rotation steps can be observed in transmittance in Faraday geometry. At temperatures down to $T = 1.85$ K the value of the rotation reached about 20% of the fine structure constant and disappeared completely for $T > 20$ K.

Keywords: quantum anomalous Hall effect; Faraday rotation; topological insulators; terahertz spectroscopy

Citation: Shuvaev, A.; Pan, L.; Zhang, P.; Wang, K.L.; Pimenov, A. Faraday Rotation Due to Quantum Anomalous Hall Effect in Cr-Doped (Bi,Sb)$_2$Te$_3$. Crystals 2021, 11, 154. https://doi.org/10.3390/cryst11020154

Academic Editor: Artem Pronin
Received: 24 December 2020
Accepted: 30 January 2021
Published: 3 February 2021

Publisher's Note: MDPI stays neutral with regard to jurisdictional claims in published maps and institutio-nal affiliations.

Copyright: © 2021 by the authors. Licensee MDPI, Basel, Switzerland. This article is an open access article distributed under the terms and conditions of the Creative Commons Attribution (CC BY) license (https://creativecommons.org/licenses/by/4.0/).

1. Introduction

Topological insulators [1,2] are materials with insulating bulk but revealing conducting surface states. These states possess different helicity thus making them symmetry protected against non-magnetic scattering processes. In two-dimensional (2D) systems and in external magnetic fields the quantized off-diagonal conductivity is observed proportional to an integer times the conductivity quantum e^2/h. However, the application of external magnetic fields can be avoided in magnetically-doped topological insulators [3], see Refs. [4,5] for reviews. In that case the coupling between magnetic moments of the dopants must be strong enough to obtain a magnetically ordered state with finite static magnetization [6]. In addition, the Fermi level must be shifted into the surface magnetic gap thus leading to a single quantized conducting channel at the edge. QAHE in magnetically-doped topological insulators can be seen as a last station starting from the classical Hall resistivity via time reversal breaking and quantization effects [7].

The predicted QAHE has been first observed [8] in Cr-doped (Bi,Sb)$_2$Te$_3$ and at millikelvin temperatures. In these, as well as in several similar experiments [9,10], the temperature range at that well-quantized conduction states are observed is substantially lower than the transition temperature to a magnetically ordered state of typically 20 K. This discrepancy is normally attributed to the sample issues like presence of additional dissipative channels [4,5]. More recently, QAHE in several magnetic topological insulators [11–13] could be achieved at temperatures close to 1 K.

In conducting materials a step in the Hall resistivity should normally lead to a step in optical properties. We note here an existing discrepancy in interpretation of the quantum Hall effect in statics and dynamics of the 2D systems [14]. In the former case the quantization is explained by counting the quantum conducting channels at the edge [2,15]. In the optical case, the edges are normally excluded due to contact-free technique. Therefore, to explain the quantization of the optical data, one have to return to the quantization of the bulk conduction [16,17]. In the dynamic regime, one of the typical observation in two-dimensional systems is the polarization rotation of linearly-polarized light in transmission geometry, see Figure 1.

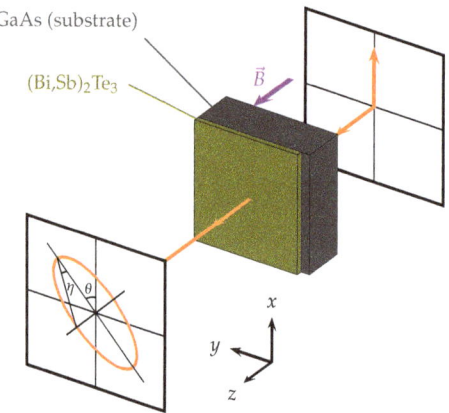

Figure 1. Scheme of the optical experiment. Linearly polarized incident light is transformed into the elliptical polarization after the sample, and is characterized by Faraday rotation angle θ and ellipticity η. The analyzer in front of the detector projects the ellipse either into the same direction as the incident beam leading to parallel transmittance t_{xx} or to perpendicular direction leading to the crossed transmittance t_{xy}. An external magnetic field is applied parallel to the propagation direction (Faraday geometry).

Full expressions for the polarization rotation include the influence of the substrate and are given elsewhere [18–20]. However, two important approximations substantially simplify the interpretation of the data. First, the influence of the substrate can be removed if the field-dependent experiment is done in the maximum of the Fabry-Pérot resonances of the substrate (see Figure 6). At such frequencies the expressions for the Faraday rotation reduce to the substrate-free result [18,21]. Second, in most cases the thin film approximation can be used assuming that the influence of the conducting film is small: $(\sigma_{xx} Z_0, \sigma_{xy} Z_0) \ll 1$. Here σ_{xx} is the 2D diagonal conductivity, σ_{xy} is the 2D Hall conductivity and $Z_0 \approx 377\,\Omega$ is the impedance of free space.

In the following we assume that the incident radiation is linearly polarized with the ac electric field along the x-axis and is propagating along the z-axis. In the thin film approximation the transmittance amplitudes in the parallel t_{xx} and perpendicular t_{xy} channels are given by [18]

$$t_{xx} \approx 1 - \sigma_{xx} Z_0 / 2 \approx 1 \quad \text{and} \quad t_{xy} \approx \sigma_{xy} Z_0 / 2, \tag{1}$$

respectively. In present experiments, t_{xx} and t_{xy} are measured putting the analyzer parallel and perpendicular to the polarization of the incident beam. The phase shift (or optical thickness) of both signals are obtained using the Mach-Zehnder interferometer arrangement, see Methods Section.

Further on, especially for the samples of the present work, the scattering time of the charge carriers is rather small, thus the frequency dependent terms $\omega\tau$ in conductivities σ_{xx} and σ_{xy} can be neglected. This can be derived from the fact that we do not observe any signs of the cyclotron resonance in the present range of frequencies and magnetic fields. This indicates that the resonance terms in the Drude conductivity with typical width $\omega\tau$ are negligible. In the same approximation the (Faraday) rotation angle θ can be written as [18–20]:

$$\theta \approx \tan(2\theta)/2 \approx \Re(t_{xy}/t_{xx}) \approx t_{xy} \approx \sigma_{xy}Z_0/2. \quad (2)$$

In the quantum regime we expect only a single conduction channel with $\sigma_{xy} = e^2/h$ leading to

$$\theta \approx \sigma_{xy}Z_0/2 = \alpha, \quad (3)$$

where $\alpha = e^2 Z_0/2h = e^2/2\varepsilon_0 hc \approx 7.3 \times 10^{-3}$ rad is the fine structure constant.

2. Results and Discussion

Figure 2 shows typical magnetic field dependence of the transmittance in crossed polarizers geometry that is most sensitive to weak polarization rotations. In these experiments the amplitude of the signal corresponds to the transmittance amplitude $|t_{xy}|$ and the optical thickness is related to the phase shift of the transmittance. The absolute values of the optical thickness are mainly determined by the thickness and refractive index of the substrate $\varphi \approx n_s d_s$ (see Section 4). The magnetic field-induced changes can be attributed to the film properties that are basically determined by σ_{xy} in this geometry in agreement with Equation (1). The data reveal a clear step at zero magnetic fields with a hysteresis of about 0.09 T. Compared to the *dc* data shown in Figure 5 below, the transmittance is not affected by the contact resistivity and, therefore, provides more direct information on the sample conductivity.

After a calibration to absolute values, the complex polarization rotation angle $\theta + i\eta$ can be calculated either using the simplified Equations (1) and (2) or via the exact procedure [18–20].

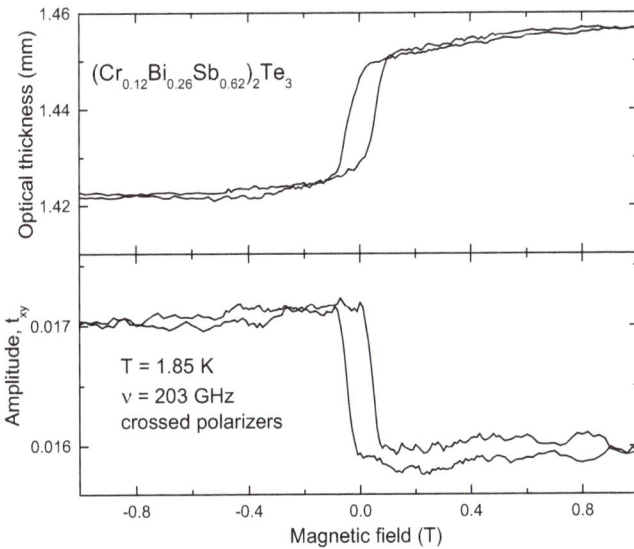

Figure 2. Magnetic field scans of the transmittance in $(Cr_{0.12}Bi_{0.26}Sb_{0.62})_2Te_3$ film and in crossed polarizers geometry $t_{xy} = |t_{xy}|e^{i\varphi}$. The external field is applied parallel to the propagation direction (Faraday geometry, see Figure 1). The parameters of the experiment are given in the plot. Bottom panel: amplitude of the crossed signal. Top panel: relative optical thickness (phase shift) of the sample.

Complex polarization rotation angles at the lowest temperature of our experiments ($T = 1.85$ K) and at various frequencies are shown in Figure 3. We observe that in the frequency range of the present experiment the rotation angle is approximately a real number, as the ellipticity corresponds roughly to the noise level of the spectrometer. Similarly to the raw transmittance data in Figure 2, the Faraday rotation angle shows a clear step-like function across zero magnetic field. The inset in Figure 3 shows the absolute values of the rotation angle step at zero magnetic field and as a function of frequency.

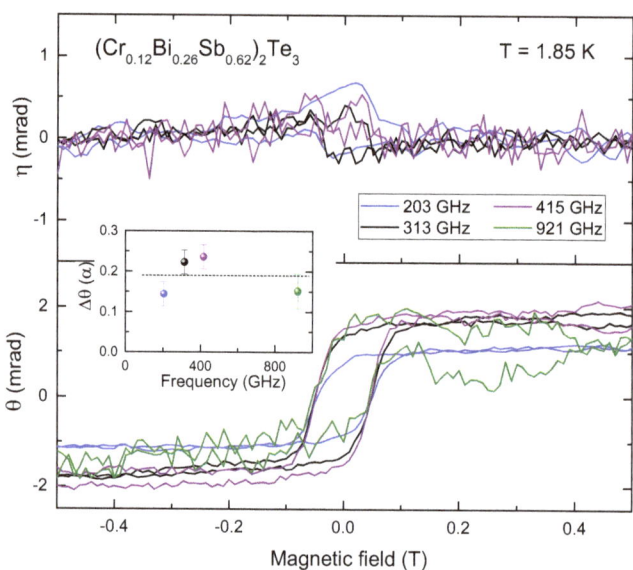

Figure 3. Complex polarization rotation angle $\theta + i\eta$ in $(Cr_{0.12}Bi_{0.26}Sb_{0.62})_2Te_3$ at $T = 1.85$ K and at different frequencies. The frequencies were selected at the maxima of the Fabry-Pérot interferences to suppress the effect of the substrate in the spectra. Bottom panel: Faraday rotation angle θ, top panel: ellipticity η. The inset shows the absolute values of the rotation angle due to quantum anomalous Hall effect (QAHE) in the units of the fine structure constant at zero magnetic field and as a function of frequency. Straight dashed line is to guide the eye.

We conclude that in the frequency range of the present experiment the Faraday angle is roughly frequency independent at the value $\theta \approx 0.2\alpha$ and the variation of the data corresponds to the uncertainties of the experiment. In order to get more arguments on the absolute values of the step across the zero field, we investigated the temperature dependence of the Faraday rotation. These results are shown in Figure 4. As also seen in the frequency-dependent rotation angles, Figure 3, the ellipticity in our data is close to zero within the experimental uncertainties. The Faraday rotation, as shown in the bottom panel and in the inset to Figure 4, decreases with increasing temperature. In our experiments the step disappears around 20 K that agrees reasonably well with Curie temperature estimated [9] as $T_C \approx 30$ K. The Faraday step at our lowest temperatures is $\Delta\theta(0) \approx 1.3$ mrad $\approx 0.18\alpha$. This value is substantially smaller than 1.0α expected within simple arguments. However, it is still possible that scattering processes suppressing $\Delta\theta$ will freeze out at millikelvin temperatures. We conclude that at temperatures down to 1.85 K additional dissipative channels like residual carriers from bulk bands or scattering by impurities [4,5,22] are still present, which impedes the dissipationless character of the chiral states and suppresses the universally quantized values of the Hall resistance and of the Faraday rotation.

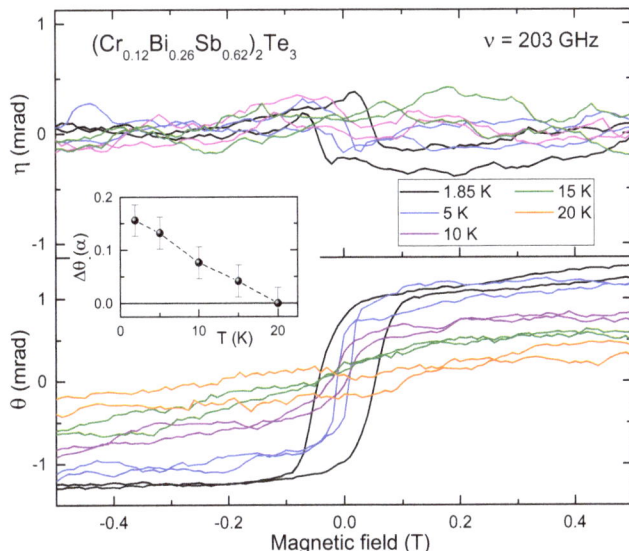

Figure 4. Complex polarization rotation angle $\theta + i\eta$ in $(Cr_{0.12}Bi_{0.26}Sb_{0.62})_2Te_3$ at $\nu = 203$ GHz and at different temperatures. Bottom panel: Faraday rotation angle θ, top panel: ellipticity η. The inset shows the absolute values of the step of the rotation angle in the units of the fine structure constant at zero magnetic field and as a function of temperature.

As the transmission experiments are done in the Faraday geometry and the sample is magnetic, the magneto-optical Faraday effect [23] cannot be a priori neglected. In fact, in the small angle approximation, the rotation angles due to the off-diagonal conductivity σ_{xy} and due to the static magnetization M_0 are simply added. To estimate the value of the last effect, we use Equation (8) of the Methods Section. The value of the static magnetization in our samples $\mu_0 M_0 \approx 0.9 \times 10^{-2}$ T has been measured in Ref. [9]. It agrees well with an estimate assuming fully ordered moments of Cr^{3+} ions. Putting the numbers into Equation (8) we finally get:

$$\theta_m \sim 10^{-8} \text{ rad} \ll \alpha. \tag{4}$$

We see that in most cases dealing with QAHE the classical Faraday effect can be neglected.

Finally, we compare the static and dynamic results in our sample. In agreement with Equations (1) and (2) direct correspondence between both properties may be expected. As discussed in the Methods Section, the resistivity of indium contacts was too high thus distorting the magnetic field dependencies of the diagonal and Hall resistivity. Reasonable step-like Hall resistivity data could be obtained for $T \geq 5$ K only, see Figure 5. Although the Hall data were distorted, we still could estimate the steps across zero field (inset to Figure 5) and compare them with the dynamic data in Figures 3 and 4. We see that both steps disappear at temperatures close to 20 K. The absolute values of the Hall resistivity in Figure 5 correspond to $\Delta R_{xy} \sim 0.5 h/e^2$ in our lowest temperature of 1.85 K that deviates from the values of Faraday rotation $\sim 0.2\alpha$ observed in the transmittance data. We recall, however, that the resistivity was strongly affected by highly resistive contacts, although the rotation is measured by a contact-free technique.

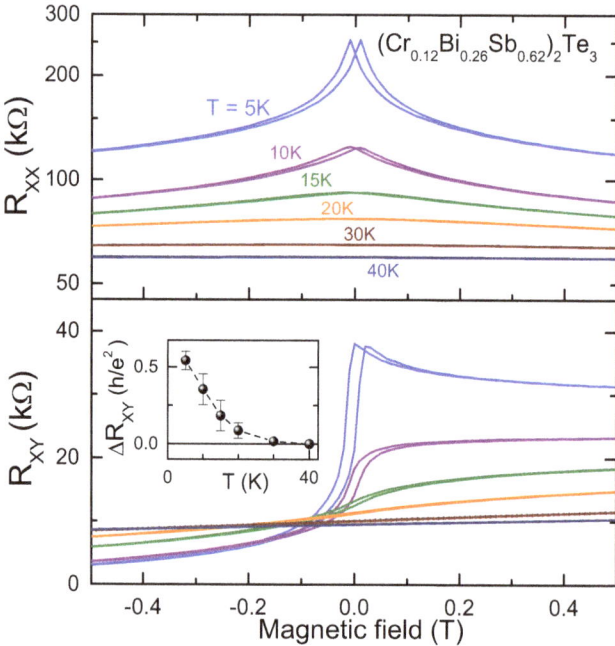

Figure 5. Magnetoresistance data in $(Cr_{0.12}Bi_{0.26}Sb_{0.62})_2Te_3$ film at various temperatures. Top: diagonal resistivity; bottom: Hall resistivity. The inset shows the absolute values of the step in the Hall resistance at zero magnetic field and as a function of temperature.

3. Conclusions

In this work we investigated the polarization rotation of the sub-terahertz light in thin films of Cr-doped topological insulator $(Cr_{0.12}Bi_{0.26}Sb_{0.62})_2Te_3$. The optical data are compared to the step in the quantum Hall conductivity measured by static technique. Well defined polarization rotation steps can be observed in transmittance at different frequencies and temperatures. At the lowest temperature of $T = 1.85$ K the value of the rotation angle reached about 20% of the fine structure constant and disappeared completely for $T > 20$ K. We estimate that pure magnetic contribution to the Faraday rotation can be neglected in the present case.

4. Materials and Methods

Single-crystalline $(Cr_{0.12}Bi_{0.26}Sb_{0.62})_2Te_3$ films on insulating (111) GaAs substrates were grown by molecular beam epitaxy [9,10,24]. Both the Cr doping level (12%) and the (Bi/Sb) ratio (0.3/0.7) were optimized so that the Fermi level positions of the as-grown samples were close to the charge neutrality point. The growth was monitored by reflection high-energy electron diffraction and the films with a thickness of 6 quintuple layers (~6 nm) were obtained. After the film growth, a 2 nm Al was evaporated to passivate the films. During the growth procedure the back side of the sample was fully covered with indium film that was nontransparent for the terahertz radiation. Therefore, prior to the optical experiments this film was removed by polishing. To measure the static resistivity, indium contacts were made at the corners of the hexagon-like sample at soldering temperature of 560 K. Unfortunately, this procedure did not provide good contacts, thus reasonable static Hall resistivity could be measured at $T \geq 5$ K only (see Figure 5).

Terahertz transmittance experiments at frequencies 0.1 THz $< \nu < 1.0$ THz were carried out in a quasioptical arrangement [18,25] which allows measurements of the amplitude and phase shift of the electromagnetic radiation in a geometry with controlled polarization.

The spectrometer utilizes linearly polarized monochromatic radiation which is provided by backward-wave oscillators, and a He-cooled bolometer as a detector. The amplitude $|t|$ and the phase shift φ of the radiation transmitted through the sample are measured by using the Mach-Zehnder interferometer setup. Static magnetic field up to 7 Tesla is applied to the sample using a split-coil superconducting magnet with mylar windows. The polarization state of the transmitted beam is determined by measuring the amplitude and phase shift of the radiation both with parallel and crossed polarizer and analyzer. This procedure provides the complex values of t_{xx} and t_{xy}, respectively (see Figure 1).

Figure 6 shows the transmittance spectra of the $(Cr_{0.12}Bi_{0.26}Sb_{0.62})_2Te_3$ thin film in the frequency range of the present experiment. Due to Fabry-Pérot resonances within the substrate a clear periodic modulation is seen in the spectra. The frequency positions of the maxima correspond to a resonance relation $2n_s d_s \nu = m$, where m is an integer, $d_s = 0.478$ mm is the sample thickness and $n_s = 3.02$ is the refractive index of the substrate. As mentioned in the Introduction section, doing magnetic field-dependent experiments at the maxima of the resonances lead to the Faraday rotation angle that is close to that of the free-standing film, thus strongly simplifying the interpretation of the data. We stress, however, that exact expressions given in detail elsewhere [18,21] have been used to calculate the angle of the polarization rotation. The transmittance maxima in the frequency range 120–500 GHz are close to unity supporting the approximation of a weakly conducting sample. In the frequency range close to 1 THz the absolute values of the transmittance are by about 20 % less than unity. We attribute this effect to a slight non-parallel surfaces of the substrate that appeared after polishing of the backside of the sample. This effect is expected to produce an amplitude correction proportional to the ratio $\delta \cdot n_s/(\lambda/D)$. Here $\delta \cdot n_s$ is the deviation angle δ enhanced by the substrate refractive index n_s, and λ/D is the diffraction angle as a ratio of the radiation wavelength and the sample aperture. At high frequencies the wavelength becomes smaller, thus enhancing the effect.

Finally, we estimate the value of the magnetooptical Faraday effect on the polarization rotation in terahertz experiments. In calculations below, we neglect the influence of the substrate as the measurements are done in the maxima of the Fabry-Pérot interferences. In addition, we assume isotropic electromagnetic susceptibilities and the normal incidence. Then, in a thin sample approximation, i.e. for $\varepsilon d/\lambda \ll 1$; $\mu_\pm d/\lambda \ll 1$, the boundary conditions can be written in an extended manner that includes the sample as part of the surface [26,27]. The transmittance of eigenmodes for a magnetic thin film can then be written as

$$t_\pm \approx 1 - \frac{i\pi d}{\lambda}(\varepsilon + \mu_\pm) \,. \tag{5}$$

Here d is the sample thickness, ε is the permittivity, $\mu_\pm$ is the permeability for two circular polarizations, and λ is the radiation wavelength. We recall that in the present geometry circularly polarized waves are the eigenmodes of the system and that Equation (5) is closely similar to Equation (1) and to the purely magnetic case in Ref. [28].

We apply now the definitions given in Equation (2) to obtain the magnetic part of the polarization rotation via $2t_{xx} = t_+ + t_-$ and $2it_{xy} = t_+ - t_-$:

$$\theta_m \approx \frac{i\pi d}{\lambda}(\chi_+ - \chi_-) \,. \tag{6}$$

Here $\chi_\pm = (\mu_\pm - 1)$ are magnetic susceptibilities. Similar expression for the polarization rotation including magnetoelectric susceptibilities has been obtained in Ref. [27]. For a ferromagnetic material $\chi_\pm$ can be written as [28,29]:

$$\chi_\pm = \frac{\gamma M_0}{\omega_0 \mp \omega + ig\omega}, \tag{7}$$

where $\omega_0 = \gamma|H - M_0|$ is the ferromagnetic resonance frequency in the Faraday geometry, M_0 is the static magnetization, γ is the gyromagnetic ratio, g is the Gilbert damping parameter and H is the external magnetic field (here we avoid using usual notation α for the Gilbert damping).

The ferromagnetic resonance frequency can be estimated as $\omega_0 = \gamma |H - M_0| \sim \gamma H \sim 3 - 10\,\text{GHz}$ for fields below $\mu_0 H \sim 0.3\,\text{T}$. Therefore, the useful approximation in the present case is $\omega_0, g\omega \ll \omega$ leading to a simple expression for the magnetic Faraday angle:

$$\theta_m = \gamma M_0 \frac{d}{2c} \,. \tag{8}$$

Finally, it should be noted that Equation (6) differs substantially from the expression $\theta'_m = \frac{\pi d}{\lambda}(n_+ - n_-)$ used in the classical books by a factor of $\sqrt{\varepsilon} \sim 10$ for Bi_2Te_3 [30]. The latter case is derived for a thick sample and it neglects the influence of the surfaces that are dominating in the thin-film geometry.

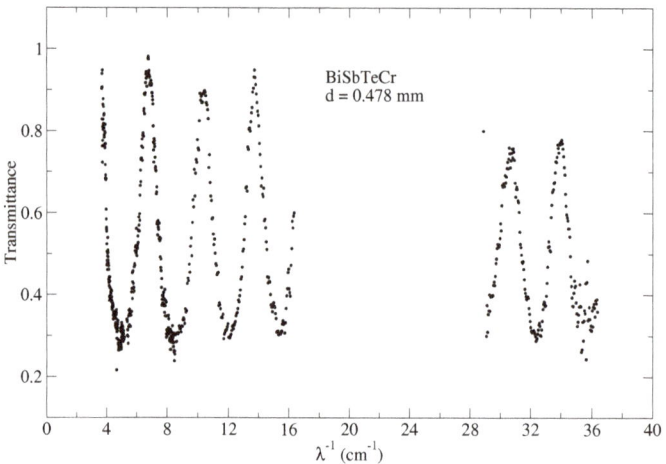

Figure 6. Transmittance spectrum of the sample used in this work in zero magnetic field and at temperature $T = 1.85\,\text{K}$. This spectrum was measured in the parallel polarizers geometry, t_{xx}, and shows a series of Fabry-Pérot resonances due to reflections on the substrate surfaces.

Author Contributions: Terahertz experiments, A.S.; Sample preparation, L.P., P.Z. and K.L.W.; writing of the manuscript A.P.; Project administration, A.P. and A.S. All authors have read and agreed to the published version of the manuscript.

Funding: This work was supported by Austrian Science Funds (Grants No. W-1243, No. P27098-N27, and No. I3456-N27). Open Access was funded by Austrian Science Funds (FWF).

Institutional Review Board Statement: Not applicable.

Informed Consent Statement: Not applicable.

Data Availability Statement: The data presented in this study are available on request from the corresponding author.

Conflicts of Interest: The authors declare no conflict of interest.

References

1. Qi, X.L.; Hughes, T.L.; Zhang, S.C. Topological field theory of time-reversal invariant insulators. *Phys. Rev. B* **2008**, *78*, 195424. [CrossRef]
2. Hasan, M.Z.; Kane, C.L. *Colloquium*: Topological insulators. *Rev. Mod. Phys.* **2010**, *82*, 3045–3067. [CrossRef]
3. Yu, R.; Zhang, W.; Zhang, H.J.; Zhang, S.C.; Dai, X.; Fang, Z. Quantized Anomalous Hall Effect in Magnetic Topological Insulators. *Science* **2010**, *329*, 61–64. [CrossRef]

4. He, K.; Wang, Y.; Xue, Q.K. Topological Materials: Quantum Anomalous Hall System. *Annu. Rev. Condens.* **2018**, *9*, 329–344. [CrossRef]
5. Tokura, Y.; Yasuda, K.; Tsukazaki, A. Magnetic topological insulators. *Nat. Rev. Phys.* **2019**, *1*. [CrossRef]
6. Zhang, J.; Chang, C.Z.; Tang, P.; Zhang, Z.; Feng, X.; Li, K.; Wang, L.l.; Chen, X.; Liu, C.; Duan, W.; et al. Topology-Driven Magnetic Quantum Phase Transition in Topological Insulators. *Science* **2013**, *339*, 1582–1586. [CrossRef]
7. Liu, C.X.; Zhang, S.C.; Qi, X.L. The Quantum Anomalous Hall Effect: Theory and Experiment. *Annu. Rev. Condens.* **2016**, *7*, 301–321. [CrossRef]
8. Chang, C.Z.; Zhang, J.; Feng, X.; Shen, J.; Zhang, Z.; Guo, M.; Li, K.; Ou, Y.; Wei, P.; Wang, L.L.; et al. Experimental Observation of the Quantum Anomalous Hall Effect in a Magnetic Topological Insulator. *Science* **2013**, *340*, 167–170. [CrossRef]
9. Kou, X.; Guo, S.T.; Fan, Y.; Pan, L.; Lang, M.; Jiang, Y.; Shao, Q.; Nie, T.; Murata, K.; Tang, J.; et al. Scale-Invariant Quantum Anomalous Hall Effect in Magnetic Topological Insulators beyond the Two-Dimensional Limit. *Phys. Rev. Lett.* **2014**, *113*, 137201. [CrossRef]
10. Kou, X.; Pan, L.; Wang, J.; Fan, Y.; Choi, E.; Lee, W.L.; Nie, T.; Murata, K.; Shao, Q.; Zhang, S.C.; et al. Metal-to-insulator switching in quantum anomalous Hall states. *Nat. Commun.* **2015**, *6*, 8474. [CrossRef]
11. Mogi, M.; Yoshimi, R.; Tsukazaki, A.; Yasuda, K.; Kozuka, Y.; Takahashi, K.S.; Kawasaki, M.; Tokura, Y. Magnetic modulation doping in topological insulators toward higher-temperature quantum anomalous Hall effect. *Appl. Phys. Lett.* **2015**, *107*, 182401. [CrossRef]
12. Okada, K.N.; Takahashi, Y.; Mogi, M.; Yoshimi, R.; Tsukazaki, A.; Takahashi, K.S.; Ogawa, N.; Kawasaki, M.; Tokura, Y. Observation of topological Faraday and Kerr rotations in quantum anomalous Hall state by terahertz magneto-optics. *Nat. Commun.* **2016**, *7*, 12245. [CrossRef] [PubMed]
13. Ou, Y.; Liu, C.; Jiang, G.; Feng, Y.; Zhao, D.; Wu, W.; Wang, X.X.; Li, W.; Song, C.; Wang, L.L.; et al. Enhancing the Quantum Anomalous Hall Effect by Magnetic Codoping in a Topological Insulator. *Adv. Mater.* **2018**, *30*, 1703062. [CrossRef] [PubMed]
14. Avron, J.E.; Osadchy, D.; Seiler, R. A Topological Look at the Quantum Hall Effect. *Phys. Today* **2003**, *56*, 38–42. [CrossRef]
15. Qi, X.L.; Zhang, S.C. Topological insulators and superconductors. *Rev. Mod. Phys.* **2011**, *83*, 1057–1110. [CrossRef]
16. Wu, L.; Salehi, M.; Koirala, N.; Moon, J.; Oh, S.; Armitage, N.P. Quantized Faraday and Kerr rotation and axion electrodynamics of the surface states of three-dimensional topological insulators. *Science* **2016**, *354*, 1124. [CrossRef]
17. Lubatsch, A.; Frank, R. Behavior of Floquet Topological Quantum States in Optically Driven Semiconductors. *Symmetry* **2019**, *11*. [CrossRef]
18. Shuvaev, A.M.; Astakhov, G.V.; Brüne, C.; Buhmann, H.; Molenkamp, L.W.; Pimenov, A. Terahertz magneto-optical spectroscopy in HgTe thin films. *Semicond. Sci. Technol.* **2012**, *27*, 124004. [CrossRef]
19. Shuvaev, A.; Dziom, V.; Kvon, Z.D.; Mikhailov, N.N.; Pimenov, A. Universal Faraday Rotation in HgTe Wells with Critical Thickness. *Phys. Rev. Lett.* **2016**, *117*, 117401. [CrossRef]
20. Dziom, V.; Shuvaev, A.; Mikhailov, N.N.; Pimenov, A. Terahertz properties of Dirac fermions in HgTe films with optical doping. *2D Mater.* **2017**, *4*, 024005. [CrossRef]
21. Dziom, V.; Shuvaev, A.; Pimenov, A.; Astakhov, G.V.; Ames, C.; Bendias, K.; Böttcher, J.; Tkachov, G.; Hankiewicz, E.M.; Brüne, C.; et al. Observation of the universal magnetoelectric effect in a 3D topological insulator. *Nat. Commun.* **2017**, *8*, 15197. [CrossRef] [PubMed]
22. Onoda, M.; Nagaosa, N. Quantized Anomalous Hall Effect in Two-Dimensional Ferromagnets: Quantum Hall Effect in Metals. *Phys. Rev. Lett.* **2003**, *90*, 206601. [CrossRef] [PubMed]
23. Zvezdin, A.K.; Kotov, V.A. *Modern Magnetooptics and Magnetooptical Materials*; Condensed Matter Physics; Taylor & Francis: New York, NY, USA, 2010.
24. Bestwick, A.J.; Fox, E.J.; Kou, X.; Pan, L.; Wang, K.L.; Goldhaber-Gordon, D. Precise Quantization of the Anomalous Hall Effect near Zero Magnetic Field. *Phys. Rev. Lett.* **2015**, *114*, 187201. [CrossRef] [PubMed]
25. Volkov, A.A.; Goncharov, Y.G.; Kozlov, G.V.; Lebedev, S.P.; Prokhorov, A.M. Dielectric measurements in the submillimeter wavelength region. *Infrared Phys.* **1985**, *25*, 369. [CrossRef]
26. Oksanen, M.I.; Tretiakov, S.A.; Lindell, I.V. Vector circuit-theory for isotropic and chiral slabs. *J. Electromagn. Waves Appl.* **1990**, *4*, 613. [CrossRef]
27. Szaller, D.; Shuvaev, A.; Mukhin, A.A.; Kuzmenko, A.M.; Pimenov, A. Controlling of light with electromagnons. *Phys. Sci. Rev.* **2020**, *5*, 20190055. [CrossRef]
28. Weymann, L.; Shuvaev, A.; Pimenov, A.; Mukhin, A.A.; Szaller, D. Magnetic equivalent of electric superradiance: Radiative damping in yttrium-iron-garnet films. *arXiv* **2020**, arXiv:2012.09440.
29. Gurevich, A.; Melkov, G. *Magnetization Oscillations and Waves*; CRC Press: Boca Raton, FL, USA, 1996.
30. Greenaway, D.L.; Harbeke, G. Band structure of bismuth telluride, bismuth selenide and their respective alloys. *J. Phys. Chem. Sol.* **1965**, *26*, 1585. [CrossRef]

Article

Isotropic Nature of the Metallic Kagome Ferromagnet Fe₃Sn₂ at High Temperatures

Rebecca L. Dally [1,*], Daniel Phelan [2], Nicholas Bishop [3], Nirmal J. Ghimire [3,4] and Jeffrey W. Lynn [1]

1. NIST Center for Neutron Research, National Institute of Standards and Technology, Gaithersburg, MD 20899-6102, USA; jeffrey.lynn@nist.gov
2. Materials Science Division, Argonne National Laboratory, Lemont, IL 60439, USA; dphelan@anl.gov
3. Department of Physics and Astronomy, George Mason University, Fairfax, VA 22030, USA; nbishop3@masonlive.gmu.edu (N.B.); nghimire@gmu.edu (N.J.G.)
4. Quantum Science and Engineering Center, George Mason University, Fairfax, VA 22030, USA
* Correspondence: rebecca.dally@nist.gov

Abstract: Anisotropy and competing exchange interactions have emerged as two central ingredients needed for centrosymmetric materials to exhibit topological spin textures. Fe_3Sn_2 is thought to have these ingredients as well, as it has recently been discovered to host room temperature skyrmionic bubbles with an accompanying topological Hall effect. We present small-angle inelastic neutron scattering measurements that unambiguously show that Fe_3Sn_2 is an isotropic ferromagnet below $T_C \approx 660$ K to at least 480 K—the lower temperature threshold of our experimental configuration. Fe_3Sn_2 is known to have competing magnetic exchange interactions, correlated electron behavior, weak magnetocrystalline anisotropy, and lattice (spatial) anisotropy; all of these features are thought to play a role in stabilizing skyrmions in centrosymmetric systems. Our results reveal that at the elevated temperatures measured, there is an absence of significant magnetocrystalline anisotropy and that the system behaves as a nearly ideal isotropic exchange interaction ferromagnet, with a spin stiffness $D(T = 480\text{ K}) = 168$ meV Å², which extrapolates to a ground state spin stiffness $D(T = 0\text{ K}) = 231$ meV Å².

Keywords: inelastic neutron scattering; topological materials; anomalous Hall effect; isotropic ferromagnet; kagome; frustrated magnetism; skyrmion; magnetization

1. Introduction

The two-dimensional kagome lattice lends itself to hosting a variety of phenomena depending on the chemical species occupying the network of corner-sharing triangles. For example, the tight-binding model for itinerant electrons leads to an electronic spectrum with a flat band and two Dirac crossings at the symmetry protected K and K' corner points of the hexagonal Brillouin zone. Chemical tuning can drive the Fermi level to meet the Dirac points (a Dirac semimetal) to realize chiral massless charge carriers such as that in graphene [1,2]. The prediction of the flat band—on the extreme opposite from a Dirac band—is the result of destructive interference of Bloch waves from the lattice geometry. Consequently, this nontrivial flat band can exhibit interesting physics such as flat-band ferromagnetism and a finite Chern number. Experimentally, FeSn was shown to host both flat bands and Dirac fermions [3] due to the isolated Fe kagome layers rendering it a nearly perfect realization of 2D kagome physics. Fe_3Sn_2 is similar in structure, but features isolated breathing kagome bilayers, as shown in Figure 1a–c. Interestingly, the bilayers and breathing structure were still theorized to have a band structure with similar features. Instead of one Dirac crossing at each K and K' point, there are two which are symmetric about each point [4], and the fermions are both spin-polarized due to the breaking of time-reversal symmetry and massive due to the opening of a gap from spin-orbit coupling. The combination of these effects gives rise to a non-zero Berry curvature which is consistent with the quadratic relationship of the anomalous Hall resistivity with the longitudinal resistivity [5], implying the intrinsic Karplus and Luttinger mechanism [6] is responsible for the large anomalous Hall effect. It was also recently shown that nearly flat bands near the Fermi surface exist, which may contribute to the observed high-temperature ferromagnetism [7].

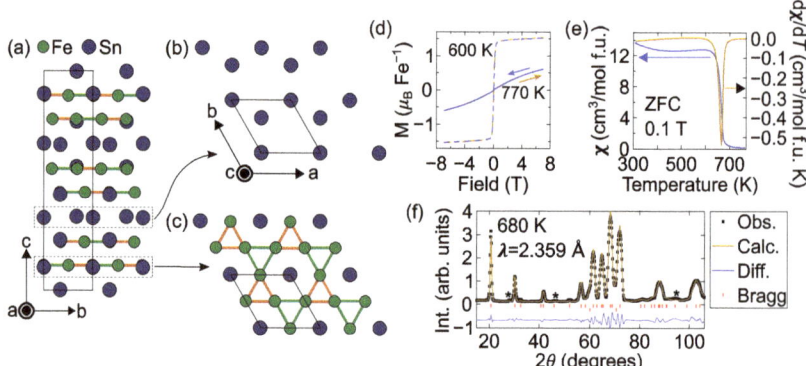

Figure 1. Crystal structure and characterization of Fe$_3$Sn$_2$. The crystallographic space group is $R\bar{3}m$ with reported lattice parameters $a = b = 5.344$ Å and $c = 19.845$ Å [8]. (**a**) View along the **a**-axis. The solid black line represents the unit cell and Fe atoms are shown as the smaller green circles and Sn atoms are shown as the larger blue circles. A single Fe site is offset from any high symmetry position ($x/a = 0.4949$, $y/b = 0.5051$, and $z/c = 0.1134$) leading to two different Fe-Fe bond lengths in the ab-plane (the so-called "breathing" kagome). Two Fe-Fe bond lengths are shown, where the shorter bond is in orange, and the longer bond is in green. (**b**) A Sn-only layer viewed along the c-axis, where the Sn atoms are arranged on a honeycomb lattice. (**c**) An Fe-Sn layer viewed along the c-axis, showing the breathing kagome lattice made up of Fe atoms. The axes labels for (**c**) are the same as in (**b**), and the parallelogram outlined by a solid black line for both panels represents the unit cell. (**d**) Magnetization measurements taken at 770 K (solid lines) and 600 K (dashed lines). The samples show no signs of coercivity as the sweep down in field (blue lines) coincides with the sweep up (orange lines) in field. (**e**) Zero-field cooled (ZFC) magnetic susceptibility measurement taken in a 0.1 T applied magnetic field. The derivative (right axis) clearly shows the ferromagnetic transition at $T_C \approx 665$ K. (**f**) Neutron powder diffraction data taken above the magnetic transition at 680 K. The data demonstrate the structure is consistent with that reported. The upper set of red tic marks denote Fe$_3$Sn$_2$ Bragg peak positions and the lower set denote Al Bragg peak positions coming from the sample canister. A few small impurity peaks were observed but not identified, and these are marked by the * symbol.

Metallic kagome ferromagnets clearly exhibit elegant physics; however, they are elusive with only two reported: Co$_3$Sn$_2$S$_2$, a semimetal [9], and the aforementioned Fe$_3$Sn$_2$. As alluded to thus far, the electronic structure has signatures of non-trivial topology, but recently, Fe$_3$Sn$_2$ has garnered growing attention for the discovery of topologically nontrivial spin textures. The observation of room temperature skyrmion bubbles [10] quickly led to reports of nanostructured skyrmionic devices [11–14] and studies of the associated properties such as the topological Hall effect [15–17] and skyrmion thermopower [18]. The space group of Fe$_3$Sn$_2$ is the centrosymmetric $R\bar{3}m$, meaning the mechanism for skyrmion bubble formation is not due to the conventional breaking of crystalline inversion symmetry with Dzyaloshinshkii-Moriya interactions found in conventional B20 skyrmion systems. Instead, topological magnetic structures in centrosymmetric systems are due to the presence of anisotropy and/or frustration. The underlying source of each which is needed to stabilize skyrmions has become widely studied in recent years. One common model is the triangular lattice with frustrated Heisenberg antiferromagnetic exchange interactions. [19] Although the magnetic frustration alone was shown to lead to a skyrmion phase, either lattice and/or spin anisotropy [20], particularly easy-axis anisotropy [21,22], was shown to be helpful in stabilizing the skyrmions.

From a frustrated magnetism perspective, Fe_3Sn_2 has been of interest for quite some time. Original neutron powder diffraction measurements indicated collinear ferromagnetic order below the onset of magnetism at $T_C \approx 660$ K with moments oriented along the c-axis [23]. A spin-reorientation transition to the *ab*-plane starting below 250 K was identified and later measurements implied a slightly non-collinear structure was more likely starting below 300 K [24] and that the spin-reorientation transition was actually first-order in nature and occurs at $\approx$150 K [25,26]. The non-collinearity is thought to be due to frustrated magnetic exchange, and would also explain the large anomalous Hall effect [5,27] and possibly some of the temperature regimes where the topological Hall effect is observed if the scaler spin chirality is finite. Bulk magnetic measurements have also shown Fe_3Sn_2 to be an extremely soft ferromagnet at all temperatures with no coercivity, implying any easy-axis magnetic anisotropy must be very weak.

Here, we present our small-angle inelastic neutron scattering study of the magnetic excitations in Fe_3Sn_2 between 480 K and 660 K and unambiguously show that no significant spin wave gap is observed within experimental uncertainties between these temperatures. Below 480 K, the spin stiffness parameter, $D(T)$, becomes too large and the spin wave full-width-at-half-maximum in energy, $\Gamma(q)$, has narrowed to the point that the excitations move outside our measurement window. However, our results show that down to at least 480 K, Fe_3Sn_2 behaves as an ideal isotropic ferromagnet, and any onset of significant magnetic anisotropy that may contribute to the topological spin textures must develop below this point.

2. Materials and Methods

Polycrystalline samples of Fe_3Sn_2 were synthesized by solid state reaction. Stoichiometric amounts of Fe powder (Alfa Aesar 99+%) and Sn powder (Alfa Aesar 99.995%) were mixed and pelletized. The pellet was sealed in a fused silica ampoule under vacuum. The sealed ampoule was heated to 800 °C at the rate of 1 °C/hour and was kept at 800 °C for 1 week. After 1 week, the ampule at 800 °C was quenched into ice water. The pellet was reground, re-pelletized, and sealed into the fused silica ampoule under vacuum and was annealed at 800 °C for 1 week.

Magnetic measurements were performed on a piece of pressed pellet of Fe_3Sn_2 powder employing a Quantum Design MPMS3 magnetometer with an oven heater stick between 300 K and 756 K.

Neutron powder diffraction (NPD) measurements were taken using the triple-axis spectrometer, BT-7, at the NIST Center for Neutron Research [28]. A 17 g sample of polycrystalline Fe_3Sn_2 was sealed in a cylindrical aluminum canister, which was mounted inside a closed cycle refrigerator. Data were collected in two-axis mode using a position sensitive detector and wavelength of 2.359 Å. Söller collimators of $50' - 40'R$ were used before and after the sample, respectively (where R indicates radial), and pyrolytic graphite (PG) filters were employed both in the reactor beam and after the sample to suppress higher order wavelength contributions. Data were refined using the Rietveld method and the program, FullProf [29].

Inelastic neutron scattering data were also taken using BT-7 and the same 17 g sample as in NPD. Two different small-angle inelastic neutron scattering configurations were used in order to obtain data over a wider temperature range. For higher temperatures (630 K to 660 K), PG(002) monochromator crystals with vertical focusing and PG(002) analzyer crystals were used, and constant-Q scans were taken with a fixed incident energy of 13.7 meV. Söller collimators of $10' - 10' - 10' - 25'$ were used before and after the monochromator and before and after the analyzer, and the reactor beam PG filter was once again employed. The vertical resolution was measured using a graphite crystal and found to be 0.16 Å^{-1}. For lower temperatures (480 K to 610 K), PG(004) monochromator crystals with vertical focusing and PG(004) analzyer crystals were used, and constant-Q scans were taken with a fixed incident energy of 35 meV. A velocity selector in the reactor beam was employed to suppress higher and lower order wavelengths. The same collimations as the $E_i = 13.7$ meV experiment were used and the vertical resolution at this higher energy was found to be 0.24 Å^{-1}. The same scans taken at high temperatures were also taken at much lower temperatures (300 K for the $E_i = 13.7$ meV experiment and 250 K for the $E_i = 35$ meV experiment), and these data were used for background subtraction.

In the small-angle inelastic neutron scattering configuration, spin waves are probed in the long-wavelength (i.e., small-q) limit, and the dispersion for a ferromagnet is

$$\hbar\omega(q) = \Delta + D(T)q^2, \tag{1}$$

where Δ is any anisotropy gap and $D(T)$ is the spin wave stiffness which in mean field theory is proportional to the magnetization. The kinematic constraints for the scattering severely restrict the range of energy transfers accessible, so that the spin waves can only be observed if there is little to no anisotropy gap. The point in reciprocal space where the spin waves are being probed can be viewed by the schematic in Figure 2a. Here, a parabolic dispersion about $Q = 0$ and energy transfer, $E = 0$, is shown. About this point, the dispersion of an isotropic ferromagnet powder sample is identical to that of a single crystal. Similar experiments on amorphous alloys [30] and powder samples of manganites [31] have been widely used to establish their isotropic nature.

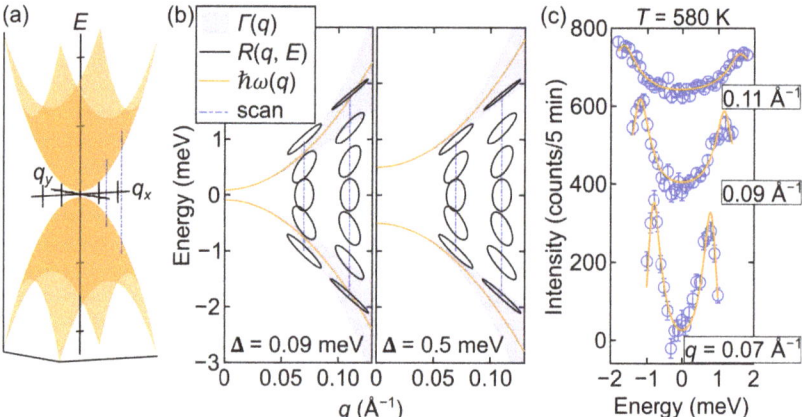

Figure 2. (a) A three-dimensional schematic of an isotropic parabolic spin wave dispersion near $Q = 0$ and energy transfer, $E = 0$. The dispersion is shown as the orange surface, and dashed blue lines show the direction of constant-Q scans cutting through the dispersion surface along E. (b) A two-dimensional schematic demonstrating how the experiment captures the intensity from the spin wave excitations. The orange solid line represents the dispersion, $\hbar\omega(q) = \Delta + D(T)q^2$, and the surrounding blue surface represents the full-width-at-half-maximum of the spread in energy of the dispersion, $\Gamma(q)$, due to thermally induced magnon-magnon interactions. Dashed blue lines are examples of constant-Q scans made in the experiment. Overlayed on these lines are the instrumental resolution ellipses, $R(Q,E)$, along $Q = 0.07$ Å^{-1} and 0.11 Å^{-1}. The left panel uses the refined values for the dispersion from the actual data at $T = 580$ K in the $E_i = 35$ meV experiment. The right panel uses the same parameters, but increased the gap to be 0.5 meV in order to demonstrate the sensitivity of the technique to the size of the gap. Here, the scans performed during the experiment wouldn't be able to reach the signal of the spin waves. (c) The actual data at $T = 580$ K in the $E_i = 35$ meV experiment. The solid orange lines are the refined fits to the data, shown as blue circles. The three constant-Q scans are vertically offset from one another for clarity.

One advantage of studying the spin waves in the long-wavelength limit (i.e., about $Q = 0$) is that the instrumental resolution is focused on both the energy gain and energy loss side, unlike with a Bragg point where there is a focused and de-focused side. More details on the resolution function in the small-angle limit can be found in Ref. [32] The intensity detected in a neutron scattering experiment represents a convolution of the instrumental resolution, $R(Q, E)$, and the scattering function, $S(q, \hbar\omega)$, making it necessary to include the convolution when analyzing the data. Using the Cooper-Nathans approximation for the resolution, we used the program ResLib [33] to fit each set of data (where a set of data consists of all the constant-Q scans at a single temperature) to the scattering function,

$$S(q, \hbar\omega) \propto F(q, \hbar\omega) \frac{\hbar\omega}{1 - e^{-\hbar\omega/k_B T}}, \quad (2)$$

where $F(q, \hbar\omega)$ is the spectral weight function, k_B is the Boltzmann constant, and T is the temperature. At finite temperatures, magnon-magnon interactions lead to damping effects in energy for the spin waves. For Heisenberg ferromagnets below T_C, and in the energy regime $\hbar\omega \ll k_B T$, the excitation width in energy has been calculated [34] as

$$\Gamma(q) \propto q^4 T^2 \left\{ \frac{1}{6} \ln^2\left(\frac{k_B T}{\hbar\omega}\right) + \frac{5}{9} \ln\left(\frac{k_B T}{\hbar\omega}\right) - 0.05 \right\}. \quad (3)$$

The shape of the broadening in energy is approximated using a Lorentzian function as the spectral weight function, $F(q, \hbar\omega)$, centered about $\hbar\omega(q)$, with $\Gamma(q)$ as the full-width-at-half maximum.

3. Results

3.1. Characterization

Figure 1d shows the magnetization both above (770 K) and below (600 K) the ferromagnetic transition temperature. No coercivity was observed for either temperature, meaning Fe_3Sn_2 is a soft ferromagnet. Figure 1e shows the magnetic susceptibility as a function of temperature at an applied magnetic field of 0.1 T. The derivative of the susceptibility with respect to temperature shows the ferromagnetic transition to be ≈665 K, which is consistent with previous reports that show the Curie temperature to vary anywhere between 640 K and 660 K [5,16,24].

The observed NPD profile and Rietveld refined fit are shown in Figure 1f. The data were taken at 680 K and confirm the structure to be Fe_3Sn_2 with refined lattice parameters of $a = b = 5.3787 \pm 0.0004$ Å and $c = 19.863 \pm 0.002$ Å. The refined atomic positions for Fe are $x/a = 0.4940 \pm 0.0004$, $y/b = 0.5060 \pm 0.0004$, and $z/c = 0.1132 \pm 0002$. The Sn positions are $z/c = 0.1039 \pm 0.0007$ and $z/c = 0.3318 \pm 0.0007$ for the Sn1 and Sn2 sites, respectively. The isotropic thermal parameters (B) were refined to 0.8 ± 0.1 Å^2, 4.1 ± 0.5 Å^2, and 2.6 ± 0.4 Å^2 for the Fe, Sn1, and Sn2 sites, respectively. There were three small impurity peaks in the pattern that were unable to be identified. They are marked with an * in Figure 1f.

3.2. Inelastic Neutron Scattering

We first demonstrate the sensitivity of the small-angle inelastic scattering configuration to the size of the gap in order to discern between isotropic and anisotropic ferromagnets. A schematic of a dispersion following Equation (1) near $\mathbf{Q} = 0$ is shown in Figure 2a. The neutron scattering plane is defined by two arbitrary orthogonal vectors, $\mathbf{q}_x$ and $\mathbf{q}_y$, and constant-Q cuts are shown as blue dashed lines to show how the experimental scans can cut through the dispersion along energy, E.

Each temperature set of constant-Q scans was fit globally to obtain the spin wave parameters, and the parameters for $T = 580$ K were used to create Figure 2b. The spin stiffness parameter was found to be $D(T = 580 \text{ K}) = 135 \pm 3$ meV Å^2 and the gap, $\Delta = 0.09 \pm 0.02$ meV, where the uncertainties throughout represent one standard deviation due to statistical counting. These parameters were used to create the solid orange line representing $\hbar\omega(q)$. We note that even for an ideal isotropic spin system a small dipolar gap is expected due to ferromagnetic magnetization. The full-width-at-half-maximum of the spin waves in energy, $\Gamma(q)$, is shown as the shaded blue region following Equation (3), and the instrumental resolution, $R(q, E)$, is shown as black ellipses. The maxima and minima of the ellipses along energy represent the allowed scan region which satisfies the required conservation of momentum and energy represented by the scattering triangle (i.e., scanning farther in energy is not possible). Two representative constant-Q scans are shown as dashed blue lines at 0.07 Å^{-1} and 0.11 Å^{-1}, and with the small gap of 0.09 meV, the center of the instrumental resolution ellipses for both scans is able to pass over the peak of the dispersion on the energy gain and loss sides. This is not possible if the gap is increased to 0.5 meV, as shown in the right panel of Figure 2b (all other parameters from the $T = 580$ K fit were fixed). The actual data from $T = 580$ K are shown in Figure 2c as blue circles and the fits are shown as solid orange lines.

The spin stiffness parameter, $D(T)$, was extracted from the fits for each temperature and is shown in Figure 3. The dashed line is a power law fit to the data: $D(T) = D_0 \left(\frac{T_C - T}{T_C}\right)^{\nu - \beta}$, where $D_0 = 271 \pm 9$ meV Å^2, $T_C = 662.4 \pm 0.8$ K, and $\nu - \beta = 0.34 \pm 0.02$. The solid line is a fit to the Dyson formalism of two spin-wave interactions in a Heisenberg ferromagnet, where $D(T) = D_0 \left[1 - A \left(\frac{k_B T}{4 \pi D_0}\right)^{5/2} \zeta\left(\frac{5}{2}\right)\right]$, $\zeta\left(\frac{5}{2}\right)$ is the Riemann integral and A is a constant proportional to the interaction range [35]. The $T^{5/2}$ temperature dependence is not valid near the critical regime, and only the lowest four temperatures were used in the fit, resulting in $D_0 = 231 \pm 7$ meV Å^2.

The gap was not found to have any meaningful temperature dependence, ranging between 0.06 meV and 0.09 meV, and was the same within plus or minus one standard deviation. It should also be noted that the instrumental resolution in energy for the scans taken is on the order of these values (see Figure 2b), meaning the exact fitted value for the gap is not well-defined. For example, in the $E_i = 13.7$ meV experiment, the resolution in energy at $Q = 0.07$ Å^{-1} and $E = 0$ meV is 0.29 meV, and at $E = 0.6$ meV the resolution is 0.07 meV.

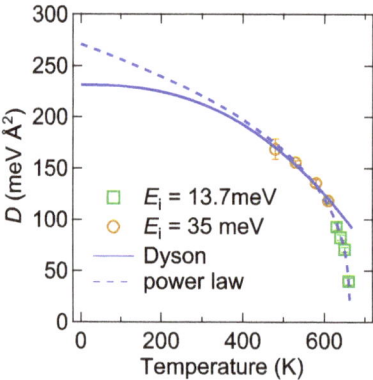

Figure 3. The temperature dependence of the spin wave stiffness parameter, $D(T)$. Data from both the $E_i = 13.7$ meV and $E_i = 35$ meV experiments were included in the power law fit, $D(T) = D_0 \left(\frac{T_C - T}{T_C}\right)^{\nu - \beta}$, shown as the dashed line. Only the lowest four temperatures were used in the Dyson fit, $D(T) = D_0 \left[1 - A \left(\frac{k_B T}{4 \pi D_0}\right)^{5/2} \zeta\left(\frac{5}{2}\right)\right]$, shown as the solid line.

4. Discussion

The temperature renormalization of the spin stiffness for Heisenberg ferromagnets is expected to follow a power law on approach to T_C with the critical exponents $\nu - \beta = 0.34$ [36], which is the exponent found in this study, further showing that magnetically, Fe$_3$Sn$_2$ is a typical exchange ferromagnet at elevated temperatures. In fact, the $\nu - \beta$ exponent from the power law fit is strikingly similar to those for elemental Fe [37] ($\nu - \beta = 0.37$) and Ni [38] ($\nu - \beta = 0.39$), in addition to the amorphous iron magnets already mentioned in Ref. [30], using the same technique. We remark that the T_C of 631 K for Ni is comparable to Fe$_3$Sn$_2$, but the spin stiffness of $D = 550$ meV Å^2 in the ground state of this itinerant magnet is much larger [39]. However, the extrapolation of $D(T)$ to $T = 0$ K for Fe$_3$Sn$_2$ using the power law fit is likely over estimated due to its validity only near T_C. The value of $D(T = 0 \text{ K}) = 231 \pm 7$ meV Å^2 using the Dyson formalism is a better estimate of the ground state spin stiffness, although the limited temperature range accessible in this study still results in a large extrapolation window.

All ferromagnets have a gap due to the magnetic dipole-dipole interaction between different atoms [40]. This gap is typically small and often out of the range of resolution for inelastic neutron scattering experiments. The dipole-dipole interaction or resolution/instrumental alignment effects are both probable reasons for the observation of a small gap in this study (on the order of 0.06 meV to 0.09 meV), which is quite small compared to the exchange energy rendering Fe$_3$Sn$_2$ an isotropic ferromagnet to an excellent approximation. However, the magnetic anisotropy energy due to magnetocrystalline anisotropy was recently calculated to be close to our gap value, at 0.037 meV per Fe atom for the ground state when the easy-axis and spins are oriented within the kagome plane [41]. The ground state for which this value was calculated, though, is in a different temperature regime and spin configuration than that of the present experiment, so it is unclear whether the gap observed is solely due to magnetic anisotropy energy coming from dipolar interactions and/or magnetocrystalline effects.

We now discuss the meaning surrounding the term "anisotropy" in our discussion. Previous studies have cited the uniaxial anisotropy in Fe$_3$Sn$_2$ as one of the necessary ingredients for the formation of the topologically protected skyrmionic bubbles [10], and many of the centrosymmetric skyrmion systems discovered thus far are well-known to be a result of competition between frustrated magnetic exchange and spin anisotropy [21,22]. Unsurprisingly, measurements of the anisotropy energy density, K_u, have therefore been published [11,14,15] and show that the onset of a magnetic anisotropy precedes the temperatures at which the skyrmion bubbles are found. However, anisotropy can range from preferred orientation of a spin—which all ordered crystalline magnets have—to an appreciable energy required to pull spins away from a preferred direction. As a soft ferromagnet, Fe$_3$Sn$_2$ falls into the former category and can be considered an isotropic ferromagnet in accordance with our results. This is in contrast to the large anisotropies required for permanent magnet devices for magnetostatic energy storage [42]. In fact, one of the appealing properties of skyrmion-based devices may be that the weak anisotropy requirements open up the field for potential skyrmion candidate materials, especially when considering inducing small anisotropies into materials via doping is quite common.

An example of a system that internally tunes its anisotropy is Nd$_2$Fe$_{14}$B, a hard uniaxial ferromagnet used in permanent magnet applications but also exhibits a spin-reorientation transition such as that in Fe$_3$Sn$_2$. It was found that the rotating spins act to tune the overall anisotropy in the system [43], although in contrast with Fe$_3$Sn$_2$, the anisotropy is due to the lanthanide crystal field effect. It is also instructive to recall that spin anisotropy is not required for skyrmion formation in inversion symmetric systems [19,20], although these theories have not been specifically applied yet to Fe$_3$Sn$_2$. Another metallic breathing kagome lattice to host a skyrmion spin texture is Gd$_3$Ru$_4$Al$_{12}$ [44]. In contrast to Fe$_3$Sn$_2$, the ordered magnetic state is antiferromagnetic and a weak anisotropy is of the easy-plane type. Future work on either of these kagome materials to directly probe the anisotropy gap in proximity to the skyrmion phases would be of interest to explore the role of the anisotropy versus magnetic exchange frustration. Inelastic neutron scattering can be used to achieve this below the temperatures accessible in the work presented here but would require a comparable mass of co-aligned single crystals and sub-meV instrumental resolution in a wide-angle scattering experiment.

Author Contributions: Material synthesis, N.J.G. and N.B.; Magnetization measurements, D.P.; neutron experiment design, J.W.L. and R.L.D.; neutron experiment analysis, J.W.L. and R.L.D.; writing—original draft preparation, R.L.D.; writing—review and editing, J.W.L., R.L.D., D.P., and N.J.G. All authors have read and agreed to the published version of the manuscript.

Funding: Synthesis and characterization work (N.J.G.) were supported by the U.S. Department of Energy, Office of Science, Basic Energy Sciences, Materials Science and Engineering Division. Work in the Materials Science Division at Argonne National Laboratory was supported by the U.S. Department of Energy, Office of Science, Basic Energy Sciences, Materials Science and Engineering Division.

Institutional Review Board Statement: Not applicable.

Informed Consent Statement: Not applicable.

Data Availability Statement: Data is available upon request to the corresponding author.

Conflicts of Interest: The identification of any commercial product or trade name does not imply endorsement or recommendation by the National Institute of Standards and Technology. The authors declare no conflict of interest. The funders had no role in the design of the study; in the collection, analyses, or interpretation of data; in the writing of the manuscript, or in the decision to publish the results.

References

1. Guo, H.M.; Franz, M. Topological insulator on the kagome lattice. *Phys. Rev. B* **2009**, *80*, 113102. [CrossRef]
2. Mazin, I.; Jeschke, H.O.; Lechermann, F.; Lee, H.; Fink, M.; Thomale, R.; Valentí, R. Theoretical prediction of a strongly correlated Dirac metal. *Nat. Commun.* **2014**, *5*, 1–7. [CrossRef] [PubMed]
3. Kang, M.; Ye, L.; Fang, S.; You, J.S.; Levitan, A.; Han, M.; Facio, J.I.; Jozwiak, C.; Bostwick, A.; Rotenberg, E.; et al. Dirac fermions and flat bands in the ideal kagome metal FeSn. *Nat. Mater.* **2020**, *19*, 163–169. [CrossRef]
4. Ye, L.; Kang, M.; Liu, J.; Von Cube, F.; Wicker, C.R.; Suzuki, T.; Jozwiak, C.; Bostwick, A.; Rotenberg, E.; Bell, D.C.; et al. Massive Dirac fermions in a ferromagnetic kagome metal. *Nature* **2018**, *555*, 638–642. [CrossRef] [PubMed]
5. Wang, Q.; Sun, S.; Zhang, X.; Pang, F.; Lei, H. Anomalous Hall effect in a ferromagnetic Fe_3Sn_2 single crystal with a geometrically frustrated Fe bilayer kagome lattice. *Phys. Rev. B* **2016**, *94*, 075135. [CrossRef]
6. Karplus, R.; Luttinger, J.M. Hall Effect in Ferromagnetics. *Phys. Rev.* **1954**, *95*, 1154–1160. [CrossRef]
7. Lin, Z.; Choi, J.H.; Zhang, Q.; Qin, W.; Yi, S.; Wang, P.; Li, L.; Wang, Y.; Zhang, H.; Sun, Z.; et al. Flatbands and Emergent Ferromagnetic Ordering in Fe_3Sn_2 Kagome Lattices. *Phys. Rev. Lett.* **2018**, *121*, 096401. [CrossRef] [PubMed]
8. Malaman, B.; Roques, B.; Courtois, A.; Protas, J. Structure cristalline du stannure de fer Fe_3Sn_2. *Acta Crystallogr. Sect. B* **1976**, *32*, 1348–1351. [CrossRef]
9. Vaqueiro, P.; Sobany, G.G. A powder neutron diffraction study of the metallic ferromagnet $Co_3Sn_2S_2$. *Solid State Sci.* **2009**, *11*, 513–518. doi:10.1016/j.solidstatesciences.2008.06.017. [CrossRef]
10. Hou, Z.; Ren, W.; Ding, B.; Xu, G.; Wang, Y.; Yang, B.; Zhang, Q.; Zhang, Y.; Liu, E.; Xu, F.; et al. Observation of Various and Spontaneous Magnetic Skyrmionic Bubbles at Room Temperature in a Frustrated Kagome Magnet with Uniaxial Magnetic Anisotropy. *Adv. Mater.* **2017**, *29*, 1–8. [CrossRef]
11. Tang, J.; Kong, L.; Wu, Y.; Wang, W.; Chen, Y.; Wang, Y.; Li, J.; Soh, Y.; Xiong, Y.; Tian, M.; et al. Target Bubbles in Fe_3Sn_2 Nanodisks at Zero Magnetic Field. *ACS Nano* **2020**, *14*, 10986–10992. [CrossRef]
12. Hou, Z.; Zhang, Q.; Xu, G.; Zhang, S.; Gong, C.; Ding, B.; Li, H.; Xu, F.; Yao, Y.; Liu, E.; et al. Manipulating the Topology of Nanoscale Skyrmion Bubbles by Spatially Geometric Confinement. *ACS Nano* **2019**, *13*, 922–929. [CrossRef]
13. Hou, Z.; Zhang, Q.; Zhang, X.; Xu, G.; Xia, J.; Ding, B.; Li, H.; Zhang, S.; Batra, N.M.; Costa, P.M.F.J.; et al. Current-Induced Helicity Reversal of a Single Skyrmionic Bubble Chain in a Nanostructured Frustrated Magnet. *Adv. Mater.* **2020**, *32*, 1904815. doi:10.1002/adma.201904815. [CrossRef]
14. Hou, Z.; Zhang, Q.; Xu, G.; Gong, C.; Ding, B.; Wang, Y.; Li, H.; Liu, E.; Xu, F.; Zhang, H.; et al. Creation of Single Chain of Nanoscale Skyrmion Bubbles with Record-High Temperature Stability in a Geometrically Confined Nanostripe. *Nano Lett.* **2018**, *18*, 1274–1279. [CrossRef]
15. Li, H.; Ding, B.; Chen, J.; Li, Z.; Hou, Z.; Liu, E.; Zhang, H.; Xi, X.; Wu, G.; Wang, W. Large topological Hall effect in a geometrically frustrated kagome magnet Fe_3Sn_2. *Appl. Phys. Lett.* **2019**, *114*, 192408. [CrossRef]
16. O'Neill, C.D.; Wills, A.S.; Huxley, A.D. Possible topological contribution to the anomalous Hall effect of the noncollinear ferromagnet Fe_3Sn_2. *Phys. Rev. B* **2019**, *100*, 174420. [CrossRef]
17. Wang, Q.; Yin, Q.; Lei, H. Giant topological Hall effect of ferromagnetic kagome metal Fe_3Sn_2. *Chin. Phys. B* **2020**, *29*, 017101. [CrossRef]
18. Du, Q.; Han, M.G.; Liu, Y.; Ren, W.; Zhu, Y.; Petrovic, C. Room-Temperature Skyrmion Thermopower in Fe_3Sn_2. *Adv. Quantum Technol.* **2020**, *3*, 2000058. doi:10.1002/qute.202000058. [CrossRef]

19. Okubo, T.; Chung, S.; Kawamura, H. Multiple-q States and the Skyrmion Lattice of the Triangular-Lattice Heisenberg Antiferromagnet under Magnetic Fields. *Phys. Rev. Lett.* **2012**, *108*, 017206. [CrossRef] [PubMed]
20. Hayami, S.; Lin, S.Z.; Batista, C.D. Bubble and skyrmion crystals in frustrated magnets with easy-axis anisotropy. *Phys. Rev. B* **2016**, *93*, 184413. [CrossRef]
21. Leonov, A.; Mostovoy, M. Multiply periodic states and isolated skyrmions in an anisotropic frustrated magnet. *Nat. Commun.* **2015**, *6*, 1–8. [CrossRef] [PubMed]
22. Lin, S.Z.; Hayami, S. Ginzburg-Landau theory for skyrmions in inversion-symmetric magnets with competing interactions. *Phys. Rev. B* **2016**, *93*, 064430. [CrossRef]
23. Malaman, B.; Fruchart, D.; Caer, G.L. Magnetic properties of Fe_3Sn_2. II. Neutron diffraction study (and Mossbauer effect). *J. Phys. Met. Phys.* **1978**, *8*, 2389–2399. [CrossRef]
24. Fenner, L.A.; Dee, A.A.; Wills, A.S. Non-collinearity and spin frustration in the itinerant kagome ferromagnet Fe_3Sn_2. *J. Phys. Condens. Matter* **2009**, *21*, 452202. [CrossRef]
25. Kumar, N.; Soh, Y.; Wang, Y.; Xiong, Y. Magnetotransport as a diagnostic of spin reorientation: Kagome ferromagnet as a case study. *Phys. Rev. B* **2019**, *100*, 214420. [CrossRef]
26. Heritage, K.; Bryant, B.; Fenner, L.A.; Wills, A.S.; Aeppli, G.; Soh, Y.A. Images of a First-Order Spin-Reorientation Phase Transition in a Metallic Kagome Ferromagnet. *Adv. Funct. Mater.* **2020**, *30*, 1909163. doi:10.1002/adfm.201909163. [CrossRef]
27. Kida, T.; Fenner, L.A.; Dee, A.A.; Terasaki, I.; Hagiwara, M.; Wills, A.S. The giant anomalous Hall effect in the ferromagnet Fe_3Sn_2—A frustrated kagome metal. *J. Phys. Condens. Matter* **2011**, *23*, 112205. [CrossRef]
28. Lynn, J.; Chen, Y.; Chang, S.; Zhao, Y.; Chi, S.; Ratcliff, W. Double-focusing thermal triple-axis spectrometer at the NCNR. *J. Res. NIST* **2012**, *117*, 61. [CrossRef]
29. Rodríguez-Carvajal, J. Recent advances in magnetic structure determination by neutron powder diffraction. *Phys. B* **1993**, *192*, 55–69. doi:10.1016/0921-4526(93)90108-I. [CrossRef]
30. Lynn, J.W.; Fernandez-Baca, J.A. Neutron Scattering Studies of the Spin Dynamics of Amorphous Alloys. In *The Magnetism of Amorphous Metals And Alloys*; Ching, W.Y., Fernandez-Baca, J.A., Eds.; World Scientific Publishing Company: Singapore, 1995; Chapter 5, pp. 221–260.
31. Lynn, J.W.; Erwin, R.W.; Borchers, J.A.; Huang, Q.; Santoro, A.; Peng, J.L.; Li, Z.Y. Unconventional Ferromagnetic Transition in $La_{1-x}Ca_xMnO_3$. *Phys. Rev. Lett.* **1996**, *76*, 4046–4049. [CrossRef]
32. Mitchell, P.W.; Cowley, R.A.; Higgins, S.A. The resolution function of triple-axis neutron spectrometers in the limit of small scattering angles. *Acta Crystallogr. Sect. A* **1984**, *40*, 152–160. [CrossRef]
33. Zheludev, A. ResLib v3.4c. 2009. Available online: https://neutron.ethz.ch/Methods/reslib.html (accessed on 15 January 2021).
34. Harris, A.B. Energy Width of Spin Waves in the Heisenberg Ferromagnet. *Phys. Rev.* **1968**, *175*, 674–679; Erratum in **1969**, *184*, 606–606. [CrossRef]
35. Mattis, D.C. *The Theory of Magnetism I: Statics and Dynamics*; Springer Science & Business Media: Berlin/Heidelberg, Germany, 2012; Volume 17.
36. Collins, M.F. *Magnetic Critical Scattering*; Oxford University Press: Oxford, UK, 1989.
37. Collins, M.F.; Minkiewicz, V.J.; Nathans, R.; Passell, L.; Shirane, G. Critical and Spin-Wave Scattering of Neutrons from Iron. *Phys. Rev.* **1969**, *179*, 417–430. [CrossRef]
38. Minkiewicz, V.J.; Collins, M.F.; Nathans, R.; Shirane, G. Critical and Spin-Wave Fluctuations in Nickel by Neutron Scattering. *Phys. Rev.* **1969**, *182*, 624–631. [CrossRef]
39. Lynn, J.; Mook, H. Temperature dependence of the dynamic susceptibility of nickel. *Phys. Rev. B* **1981**, *23*, 198. [CrossRef]
40. Holstein, T.; Primakoff, H. Field Dependence of the Intrinsic Domain Magnetization of a Ferromagnet. *Phys. Rev.* **1940**, *58*, 1098–1113. [CrossRef]
41. Lin, Z.Z.; Chen, X. Tunable Massive Dirac Fermions in Ferromagnetic Fe_3Sn_2 Kagome Lattice. *Phys. Status Solidi-(Rrl) Rapid Res. Lett.* **2020**, *14*, 1900705. doi:10.1002/pssr.201900705. [CrossRef]
42. Skomski, R.; Coey, J. Magnetic anisotropy—How much is enough for a permanent magnet? *Scr. Mater.* **2016**, *112*, 3–8. doi:10.1016/j.scriptamat.2015.09.021. [CrossRef]
43. Xiao, Y.; Morvan, F.J.; He, A.N.; Wang, M.K.; Luo, H.B.; Jiao, R.B.; Xia, W.X.; Zhao, G.P.; Liu, J.P. Spin-reorientation transition induced magnetic skyrmion in $Nd_2Fe_{14}B$ magnet. *Appl. Phys. Lett.* **2020**, *117*, 132402. [CrossRef]
44. Hirschberger, M.; Nakajima, T.; Gao, S.; Peng, L.; Kikkawa, A.; Kurumaji, T.; Kriener, M.; Yamasaki, Y.; Sagayama, H.; Nakao, H.; et al. Skyrmion phase and competing magnetic orders on a breathing kagomé lattice. *Nat. Commun.* **2019**, *10*, 1–9. [CrossRef] [PubMed]

Article

Fractional Power-Law Intraband Optical Conductivity in the Low-Dimensional Dirac Material CaMnBi$_2$

M. B. Schilling [1], C. X. Wang [2], Y. G. Shi [2], R. K. Kremer [3], M. Dressel [1] and A. V. Pronin [1,*]

[1] Physikalisches Institut, Universität Stuttgart, 70569 Stuttgart, Germany; micha.physiker@gmx.de (M.B.S.); martin.dressel@pi1.physik.uni-stuttgart.de (M.D.)
[2] Beijing National Laboratory for Condensed Matter Physics, Institute of Physics, Chinese Academy of Sciences, Beijing 100190, China; cxwang@iphy.ac.cn (C.X.W.); ygshi@iphy.ac.cn (Y.G.S.)
[3] Max-Planck-Institut für Festkörperforschung, 70569 Stuttgart, Germany; rekre@fkf.mpg.de
* Correspondence: artem.pronin@pi1.physik.uni-stuttgart.de

Abstract: We studied the broadband optical conductivity of CaMnBi$_2$, a material with two-dimensional Dirac electronic bands, and found that both components of the intraband conductivity follow a universal power law as a function of frequency at low temperatures. This conductivity scaling differs from the Drude(-like) behavior, generally expected for free carriers, but matches the predictions for the intraband response of an electronic system in a quantum critical region. Since no other indications of quantum criticality are reported for CaMnBi$_2$ so far, the cause of the observed unusual scaling remains an open question.

Keywords: Dirac materials; optical-conductivity scaling; topological semimetals

Citation: Schilling, M.B.; Wang, C.X.; Shi, Y.G.; Kremer, R.K.; Dressel, M.; Pronin, A.V. Fractional Power-Law Intraband Optical Conductivity in the Low-Dimensional Dirac Material CaMnBi$_2$. *Crystals* **2021**, *11*, 428. https://doi.org/10.3390/cryst11040428

Academic Editor: Andreas Hermann

Received: 30 March 2021
Accepted: 13 April 2021
Published: 16 April 2021

Publisher's Note: MDPI stays neutral with regard to jurisdictional claims in published maps and institutional affiliations.

Copyright: © 2021 by the authors. Licensee MDPI, Basel, Switzerland. This article is an open access article distributed under the terms and conditions of the Creative Commons Attribution (CC BY) license (https://creativecommons.org/licenses/by/4.0/).

1. Introduction

CaMnBi$_2$ and its sister compound SrMnBi$_2$ are some of the first materials in which bulk electronic bands with Dirac-like dispersion were experimentally confirmed [1,2]. Both materials are arranged in layers with square nets of Bi atoms (space group P4/*nmm*). The materials are believed to possess two-dimensional Dirac bands that are anisotropic and slightly gapped due to spin-orbit coupling [1–5]. The materials have antiferromagnetic in-plane ordering of Mn ions with Néel temperatures between 270 and 290 K [1,3,6,7]. In CaMnBi$_2$, another transition at $T_s \approx 50$ K was detected by various experimental techniques including transport [2,3,8,9], magnetoresistance [2], susceptibility [3], thermopower [8], and optical [10,11] measurements. The signatures of T_s are often tiny and not always resolved in DC transport [6]. No indications of a phase transition were detected in specific-heat [3] and neutron measurements [7]. The anomaly at T_s was first tentatively attributed to either weak ferromagnetic order [2] or spin canting [3]. Based on optical and magnetic torque measurements in combination with band-structure calculations, Yang et al. [11] recently concluded on a spin-canting-induced band reconstruction at T_s, therefore clarifying the nature of this transition. In this paper, we report on the optical conductivity measurements in CaMnBi$_2$. Below T_s, we found an unusual scaling of its intraband conductivity. This scaling was previously attributed to manifestations of quantum criticality. Hence, it might be an indication of quantum criticality in CaMnBi$_2$, although other explanations cannot be excluded.

2. Materials and Methods

Sample growth and characterization: single crystals of CaMnBi$_2$ were grown using a self-flux method similar to that described previously [6]. Elementary Ca (99.99%), Mn (99.9%), and Bi (99.99%) were mixed in the molar ratio Ca:Mn:Bi = 1:1:8 and put into an alumina tube before sealing it in a quartz tube. The mixture was heated up to 800 °C during 10 h, kept at this temperature for 5 h, then slowly cooled down to 450 °C at a rate of 3 °C/h. The excess Bi flux was decanted at this temperature in a centrifuge. As CaMnBi$_2$ is somewhat air-sensitive, its handling was carried out in an inert gas atmosphere. The obtained samples were carefully characterized by X-ray, transport, magnetic, and specific-heat measurements as described in the Appendix A.

Optical measurements: the near-normal-incidence optical reflectivity $R(\nu)$ was measured from a large (roughly 2 by 3 mm) (001) surface of a CaMnBi$_2$ crystal at a number of temperatures between 10 to 300 K over a broad frequency range from $\nu = 50$ to 22,000 cm^{-1} ($\approx$6 meV–2.75 eV) using two Fourier-transform spectrometers (Bruker IFS 113v and Bruker Vertex 80v equipped with a Hyperion IR microscope (all three devices are from Bruker Corporation, Billerica, MA, USA)). At low frequencies, an in situ gold evaporation technique was utilized for reference measurements. For frequencies above 1000 cm^{-1}, gold and protected silver mirrors served as references. The complex optical conductivity, $\sigma(\nu) = \sigma_1(\nu) + i\sigma_2(\nu)$, was obtained using Kramers–Kronig transformations. The high-frequency range was extended by involving the X-ray atomic scattering functions for high-frequency extrapolations [12]. The results of the four-point DC resistivity measurements were used for the low-frequency extrapolations. To avoid possible surface oxidation, all measurements were performed on freshly cleaved surfaces.

3. Results

The results of our optical experiments are shown in Figures 1 and 2. All measurements were obtained on (001) planes of CaMnBi$_2$ (in-plane response). Let us note here that, although the in-plane Dirac bands of CaMnBi$_2$ are known to be highly anisotropic [4,5], this band anisotropy is not expected to be seen in the linear optical response because of the four-fold in-plane symmetry. Indeed, our polarization-dependent reflectivity measurements do not reveal any optical anisotropy. Hence, we discuss the measurements performed with unpolarized light throughout the paper.

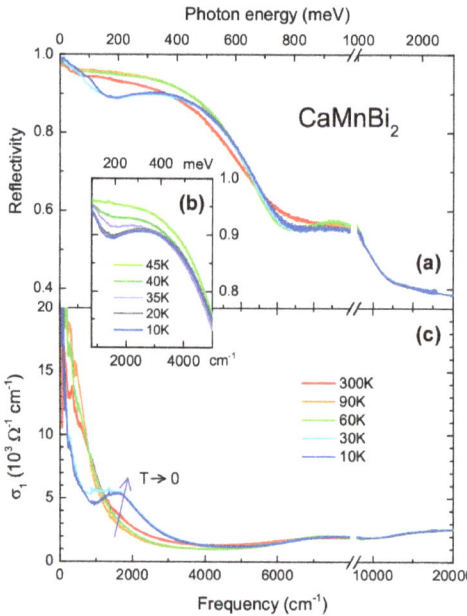

Figure 1. Frequency-dependent in-plane reflectivity $R(\nu)$ (panels (**a**,**b**)) and the real part of the optical conductivity $\sigma_1(\nu)$ (panel (**c**)) of CaMnBi$_2$ for select temperatures between 10 and 300 K. The development of a dip in $R(\nu)$ and a bump in $\sigma_1(\nu)$ at around 1500 cm^{-1} ($\approx$200 meV) is clearly seen at $T < 50$ K and marked with the arrow in panel (**c**). Note the change in frequency scale at 8000 cm^{-1}.

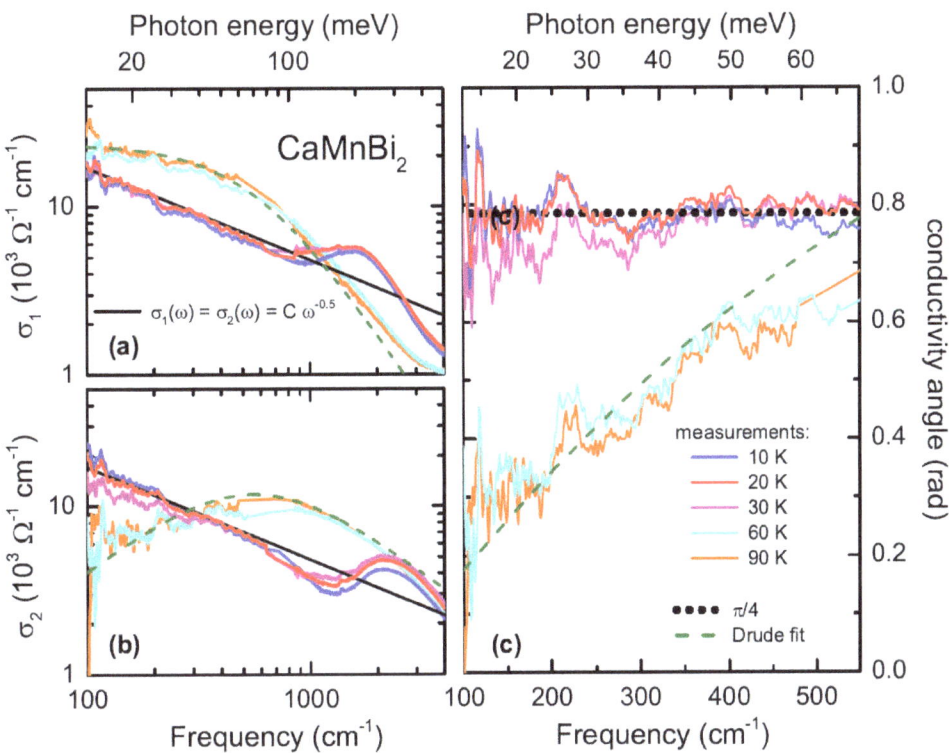

Figure 2. Scaling of the intraband complex optical conductivity in CaMnBi$_2$. The real (panel (**a**)) and imaginary (panel (**b**)) parts of the optical conductivity follow the Drude behavior for $T > T_s \sim 50$ K and scale as $1/\omega^{0.5}$ at low temperatures. The conductivity angle φ (panel (**c**)) is almost constant at these temperatures, while it increases quasi-linearly in the Drude case.

The obtained broadband optical spectra as functions of frequency are shown in Figure 1. The interband part of the optical conductivity has been analyzed in Reference [11]; our experimental findings are in full agreement with these results. The goal of our paper is to analyze the intraband low-energy response.

At low frequencies and for $T > 50$ K, the reflectivity $R(\nu)$ [$\nu = \omega/(2\pi)$] and both parts of the complex conductivity are dominated by intraband electronic transitions and are typically metallic: $R(\nu)$ approaches unity as ν diminishes, while $\sigma_1(\nu)$ and $\sigma_2(\nu)$ reveal typical Drude behavior, as can be seen best from Figure 2a,b. The conductivity angle, $\varphi = \arctan(\sigma_2/\sigma_1)$, is frequency dependent and follows the Drude model; see panel (c).

The low-energy interband transitions within the Dirac bands, which are known to provide a power-law contribution to low-frequency $\sigma_1(\nu)$ [13–17], are not seen in our measurements. The low-frequency response of CaMnBi$_2$ is completely dominated by free carriers. This situation is, in fact, rather typical for different Dirac systems, in which the Fermi level is situated far from the band crossings and/or the free-carrier contributions from non-Dirac bands are significant [18–23].

At the spin-canting temperature $T_s \approx 50$ K, dramatic changes occur in the optical spectra. Apart from the formation of a low-frequency mode at approximately 200 meV (Figure 2a,b) and a corresponding dip in reflectivity (Figure 1a) that were reported previously [10,11], the intraband absorption also drastically changes its shape. The single Drude term is unable to describe the low-energy spectra. (Let us note that the two-Drude approach used in Reference [11] is able to provide only a very rough description of the experimental $\sigma_1(\omega)$; see Figure 1b of Reference [11].) Instead, one can see that both components of the optical conductivity follow a power law. This power-law behavior is most apparent at low temperatures: below 30 K. As evidenced from our fit, $\sigma_1(\omega)$ and $\sigma_2(\omega)$ both depend on frequency as $1/\omega^{0.5}$; this power law is shown as black solid lines in Figure 2a,b. This behavior of conductivity strongly differs from the conventional Drude response. In particular, changes in the reactive part ($\sigma_2(\omega)$) are significant: instead of showing a broad maximum (which corresponds to the scattering rate in the Drude case), $\sigma_2(\omega)$ is now monotonic in frequency. Furthermore, the pre-factors in the frequency dependencies of $\sigma_1(\omega)$ and $\sigma_2(\omega)$ are identical, i.e., σ_1 and σ_2 are equal at a given frequency. This provides that $\varphi = \pi/4$.

4. Discussion

The strong non-Drude intraband response of $CaMnBi_2$ is rather surprising. Free electrons are generally expected to follow a Drude(-like) conductivity ansatz [24]. One can notice that the conductivity scaling observed here was widely discussed in the past in relation to quantum phase transitions (QPTs). The presence of a QPT leads to universal power-law scaling behaviors of the response functions [25]. In particular, the frequency-dependent complex conductivity should follow such a behavior. For the frequency region where $k_B T < \hbar\omega$, the conductivity can be a universal function of frequency [25]. In our case, this inequality is fulfilled. Van der Marel et al. [26] argued that scale invariance, causality, and time reversal symmetry require that, for a quantum critical system, the complex conductivity in this frequency region follows:

$$\sigma(\omega) = |\sigma(\omega)|e^{i\varphi(\omega)} = C\omega^{\gamma-2}e^{i\pi(1-\gamma/2)}, \qquad (1)$$

where γ is a critical exponent and C is a constant. This ansatz implies that both $\sigma_1(\omega)$ and $\sigma_2(\omega)$ depend on frequency as $\omega^{\gamma-2}$ and the phase φ is frequency independent and set by the same exponent γ. If we apply Equation (1) to the recorded spectra of σ_1 and σ_2, we find the critical exponent γ to be $3/2$. According to the scaling analysis, this value of the critical exponent should provide a frequency-independent value for the conductivity angle, $\varphi = \pi/4$. As noticed above, this result indeed follows from our data.

Interestingly, the same optical conductivity scaling (with $\gamma = 3/2$) was theoretically elaborated by Ioffe and Millis [27] in relation to a possible QPT in the superconducting cuprates. Van der Marel [28] suggested a generalized form of this relation (with the critical exponent not fixed at $3/2$) that merges with a proposition of Anderson [29] for a one-dimensional Luttinger liquid in the collision-less limit.

It should be noted that the Dirac bands in $CaMnBi_2$ are two-dimensional (due to the planar net of Bi atoms) and that they possess a very high anisotropy within this plane [4,5]. In fact, the electronic band structure can be viewed as a gapped dispersive nodal line in two dimensions, with the Fermi velocity in one direction being much smaller than the Fermi velocity in another one. It is known that the presence of a nodal line effectively reduces the dimensionality of electronic transport [16,17,30]. This reduction can possibly occur in $CaMnBi_2$, leading to a quasi-one-dimensional situation and, eventually, to the realization of a quantum critical state.

Certainly, the nature of the observed scaling has to be clarified in further theoretical and experimental studies; the observed scaling is not necessarily related to quantum criticality. The goal of this paper is to report this unusual conductivity behavior and to suggest a possible explanation. Still, one can note that the possible quantum criticality in $CaMnBi_2$ (if it is confirmed) should likely be related to the magnetism in this system and, particularly, to the spin-canting transition at T_s. This conclusion follows from the fact that the observed conductivity scaling appears only below this temperature.

5. Conclusions

In summary, we performed broadband optical conductivity measurements of $CaMnBi_2$ —a highly anisotropic material with two-dimensional nets of Bi atoms and anisotropic Dirac bands. We detected the formation of a finite-frequency absorption mode at $T < T_s = 50$ K, which is in agreement with previous studies. Most importantly, the optical response of itinerant electrons at these temperatures is not of the Drude type. Instead, it follows a fractional power-law behavior, $\sigma_1(\omega) \sim \sigma_2(\omega) \sim \omega^{-0.5}$, that is similar to the behavior proposed for quantum critical systems with the critical exponent $\gamma = 3/2$. These findings might indicate that CaMnBi$_2$ is in the vicinity of a quantum phase transition. More input from the theory side and further experiments are necessary to confirm this proposition.

Author Contributions: Conceptualization, A.V.P.; sample growth, C.X.W. and Y.G.S.; measurements, M.B.S. and R.K.K.; data analysis, M.B.S. and A.V.P.; writing—original draft preparation, M.B.S.; writing—review and editing, M.D. and A.V.P.; funding acquisition, Y.G.S., M.D. and A.V.P. All authors have read and agreed to the published version of the manuscript.

Funding: This work was partly funded by the Deutsche Forschungsgemeinschaft (DFG) via grant No. DR228/51-3 and by K. C. Wong Education Foundation (GJTD-2018-01).

Institutional Review Board Statement: Not applicable.

Informed Consent Statement: Not applicable.

Data Availability Statement: The data sets generated and analyzed during the current study are available from the corresponding author upon request.

Acknowledgments: We thank Vladimir Juričić and Run Yang for useful discussions and Gabriele Untereiner for technical support.

Conflicts of Interest: The authors declare no conflict of interest. The funders had no role in the design of the study; in the collection, analyses, or interpretation of data; in the writing of the manuscript; or in the decision to publish the results.

Appendix A

Electronic transport and magnetic susceptibility: temperature-dependent DC resistivity, $\rho(T)$, was measured in a custom-made setup at temperatures down to 2 K. To highlight the discussed feature in resistivity near T_s, we plot $\rho(T)$ on an enlarged scale in Figure A1a. To further confirm the T_s feature, we performed temperature-dependent measurements of magnetic susceptibility, $\chi(T)$, at 2 T down to 10 K with a commercial setup (MPMS, Quantum Design Inc., San Diego, CA, USA) based on a superconducting quantum interference device. The results of these measurements are shown in Figure A1b. To clearly observe the anomaly at T_s, we performed a polynomial fit of the $\chi(T)$ curve at $T > T_s$ and subtracted the fit from the experimental data. The value of $\Delta\chi(T)$ obtained in this way is shown in Figure A1c. For $T \ll T_s$, $\Delta\chi(T)$ remains almost constant.

Heat-capacity measurements: heat capacity was measured as a function of temperature, employing the relaxation method (PPMS, Quantum Design Inc., San Diego, CA, USA). The sample was attached with Apiezon N vacuum grease to the sapphire platform, and the heat capacity of this platform (including the vacuum grease) was measured in advance and then subtracted from the total heat capacity. Figure A1d displays our results of the specific-heat measurements. The data reveal a small λ-type anomaly at 290 K, which is associated with the antiferromagnetic ordering of Mn atoms. The Néel temperature is in good agreement with that reported by Guo et al. [6] from neutron powder diffraction data and is slightly higher than the findings in other reports [3,7]. The low-temperature C_p/T data can be well fitted with a power law, $C_p/T = \gamma + \beta T^2 + \delta T^4 + \varepsilon T^6$, with the Sommerfeld term $\gamma = 6.78$ mJ/(molK^2). The higher powers of this polynomial represent the lattice and magnon contributions. They are very small and amount to $\beta = 0.00126(1)$ J/(molK^4), $\delta = 2.04(3) \times 10^{-5}$ J/(molK^6), and $\varepsilon = -9.3(2) \times 10^{-8}$ J/(molK^8). Most importantly, C_p/T is featureless at T_s and in agreement with a previous report [3].

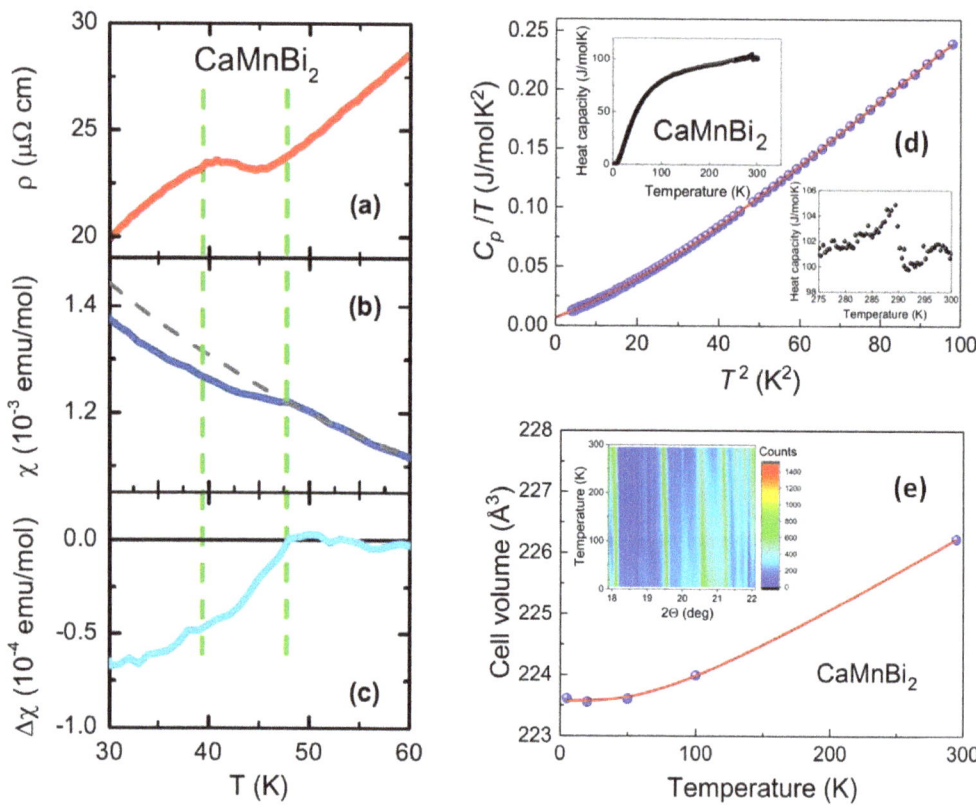

Figure A1. Characterization measurements of CaMnBi$_2$. DC resistivity $\rho(T)$ (**a**), magnetic susceptibility $\chi(T)$ (**b**), and the deviation of $\chi(T)$ from its high-temperature behavior (**c**). The data in panels (**a**–**c**) are shown at the temperatures near T_s to highlight the presence of a transition. Molar specific heat (**d**). The main frame shows a Sommerfeld plot (blue circles) with a fit (red line) to a polynomial in T^2 (see text). The insets provide an overview on a linear temperature scale and a magnification around the 290 K anomaly. The unit cell volume is shown as a function of temperature in panel (**e**). The red solid line represents a fit of the experimental data to Equation (A1) with the parameters given in the text. The inset displays a section of the diffraction pattern ($\lambda = 0.709319$ Å) versus Bragg angle 2Θ and temperature. The Bragg reflections shown are indexed as 200 at 18.15°, 114 at 19.58°, 105 at 20.60°, 211 at 20.65°, 203 at 21.30°, and 212 at 21.63°.

X-ray measurements: in order to check the structural aspect, we performed temperature-dependent X-ray powder diffraction measurements at 295, 100, 50, 20, and 5 K. The X-ray patterns were collected on a CaMnBi$_2$ sample contained in a 0.3-mm diameter quartz glass capillary under He exchange gas using Mo $K\alpha_1$ radiation. Temperatures between 295 and 5 K were adjusted in a home-built cryostat. As revealed in Figure A1e, there are no visible splittings or broadenings of the Bragg reflections, which would be indicative of a structural phase transition. The tetragonal lattice parameters were obtained from Rietveld profile refinements of the diffraction patterns assuming the space group P4/*nmm* (No. 129) and the atom and lattice parameters reported by Brechtel et al. [31] as starting parameters. They perfectly follow a simple Debye law:

$$V(T) = V_0 + I_V T \frac{T}{\Theta_D^3} \int_0^{\Theta_D/T} \frac{x^3}{e^x - 1} dx, \quad (A1)$$

with $V_0 = 223.58(3)$ Å, $\Theta_D = 279(4)$ K, and $I_v = 0.0130(7)$ Å (here, V_0 is the unit-cell volume at 0 K, Θ_D is the Debye temperature, and the pre-factor I_v is a linear function of the Grüneisen parameter in the Debye approximation [32]). As seen from Figure A1e, no anomalies in the thermal expansion, which could indicate a structural phase transition, were detected. This is consistent with the absence of broadenings or splittings of the Bragg reflections. Thus, any detectable structural transition at T_s is excluded.

References

1. Park, J.; Lee, G.; Wolff-Fabris, F.; Koh, Y.Y.; Eom, M.J.; Kim, Y.K.; Farhan, M.A.; Jo, Y.J.; Kim, C.; Shim, J.H.; et al. Anisotropic Dirac Fermions in a Bi Square Net of SrMnBi$_2$. *Phys. Rev. Lett.* **2011**, *107*, 126402. [CrossRef] [PubMed]
2. Wang, K.; Graf, D.; Wang, L.; Lei, H.; Tozer, S.W.; Petrovic, C. Two-dimensional Dirac fermions and quantum magnetoresistance in CaMnBi$_2$. *Phys. Rev. B* **2012**, *85*, 041101(R). [CrossRef]
3. He, J.B.; Wang, D.M.; Chen, G.F. Giant magnetoresistance in layered manganese pnictide CaMnBi$_2$. *Appl. Phys. Lett.* **2012**, *100*, 112405. [CrossRef]
4. Lee, G.; Farhan, M.A.; Kim, J.S.; Shim, J.H. Anisotropic Dirac electronic structures of AMnBi$_2$ (A = Sr, Ca). *Phys. Rev. B* **2013**, *87*, 245104. [CrossRef]
5. Feng, Y.; Wang, Z.; Chen, C.; Shi, Y.; Xie, Z.; Yi, H.; Liang, A.; He, S.; He, J.; Peng, Y.; et al. Strong Anisotropy of Dirac Cones in SrMnBi$_2$ and CaMnBi$_2$ Revealed by Angle-Resolved Photoemission Spectroscopy. *Sci. Rep.* **2014**, *4*, 5385. [CrossRef] [PubMed]
6. Guo, Y.F.; Princep, A.J.; Zhang, X.; Manuel, P.; Khalyavin, D.; Mazin, I.I.; Shi, Y.G.; Boothroyd, A.T. Coupling of magnetic order to planar Bi electrons in the anisotropic Dirac metals AMnBi$_2$ (A = Sr, Ca). *Phys. Rev. B* **2014**, *90*, 075120. [CrossRef]
7. Rahn, M.C.; Princep, A.J.; Piovano, A.; Kulda, J.; Guo, Y.F.; Shi, Y.G.; Boothroyd, A.T. Spin dynamics in the antiferromagnetic phases of the Dirac metals AMnBi$_2$ (A = Sr, Ca). *Phys. Rev. B* **2017**, *95*, 134405. [CrossRef]
8. Wang, K.; Wang, L.; Petrovic, C. Large magnetothermopower effect in Dirac materials (Sr/Ca)MnBi$_2$. *Appl. Phys. Lett.* **2012**, *100*, 112111.
9. Wang, A.; Graf, D.; Wu, L.; Wang, K.; Bozin, E.; Zhu, Y.; Petrovic, C. Interlayer electronic transport in CaMnBi$_2$ antiferromagnet. *Phys. Rev. B* **2016**, *94*, 125118. [CrossRef]
10. Corasaniti, M.; Yang, R.; Pal, A.; Chinotti, M.; Degiorgi, L.; Wang, A.; Petrovic, C. Fermi surface gapping in the Dirac material Ca$_{1-x}$Na$_x$MnBi$_2$. *Phys. Rev. B* **2019**, *100*, 041107. [CrossRef]
11. Yang, R.; Corasaniti, M.; Le, C.C.; Liao, Z.Y.; Wang, A.F.; Du, Q.; Petrovic, C.; Qiu, X.G.; Hu, J.P.; Degiorgi, L. Spin-Canting-Induced Band Reconstruction in the Dirac Material Ca$_{1-x}$Na$_x$MnBi$_2$. *Phys. Rev. Lett.* **2020**, *124*, 137201. [CrossRef]
12. Tanner, D.B. Use of x-ray scattering functions in Kramers-Kronig analysis of reflectance. *Phys. Rev. B* **2015**, *91*, 035123. [CrossRef]
13. Hosur, P.; Parameswaran, S.A.; Vishwanath, A. Charge Transport in Weyl Semimetals. *Phys. Rev. Lett.* **2012**, *108*, 046602. [CrossRef] [PubMed]
14. Bácsi, Á.; Virosztek, A. Low-frequency optical conductivity in graphene and in other scale-invariant two-band systems. *Phys. Rev. B* **2013**, *87*, 125425. [CrossRef]
15. Ashby, P.E.C.; Carbotte, J.P. Chiral anomaly and optical absorption in Weyl semimetals. *Phys. Rev. B* **2014**, *89*, 245121. [CrossRef]
16. Ahn, S.; Mele, E.J.; Min, H. Electrodynamics on Fermi Cyclides in Nodal Line Semimetals. *Phys. Rev. Lett.* **2017**, *119*, 147402. [CrossRef]
17. Carbotte, J.P. Optical response of a line node semimetal. *J. Phys. Condens. Matter* **2017**, *29*, 045301. [CrossRef]
18. Schilling, M.B.; Löhle, A.; Neubauer, D.; Shekhar, C.; Felser, C.; Dressel, M.; Pronin, A.V. Two-channel conduction in YbPtBi. *Phys. Rev. B* **2017**, *95*, 155201. [CrossRef]
19. Chaudhuri, D.; Cheng, B.; Yaresko, A.; Gibson, Q.D.; Cava, R.J.; Armitage, N.P. Optical investigation of the strong spin-orbit-coupled magnetic semimetal YbMnBi$_2$. *Phys. Rev. B* **2017**, *96*, 075151. [CrossRef]
20. Neubauer, D.; Yaresko, A.; Li, W.; Löhle, A.; Hübner, R.; Schilling, M.B.; Shekhar, C.; Felser, C.; Dressel, M.; Pronin, A.V. Optical conductivity of the Weyl semimetal NbP. *Phys. Rev. B* **2018**, *98*, 195203. [CrossRef]
21. Kemmler, R.; Hübner, R.; Löhle, A.; Neubauer, D.; Voloshenko, I.; Schoop, L.M.; Dressel, M.; Pronin, A.V. Free-carrier dynamics in Au$_2$Pb probed by optical conductivity measurements. *J. Phys.: Condens. Matter* **2018**, *30*, 485403. [CrossRef] [PubMed]
22. Maulana, L.Z.; Manna, K.; Uykur, E.; Felser, C.; Dressel, M.; Pronin, A.V. Optical conductivity of multifold fermions: The case of RhSi. *Phys. Rev. Research* **2020**, *2*, 023018. [CrossRef]
23. Maulana, L.Z.; Li, Z.; Uykur, E.; Manna, K.; Polatkan, S.; Felser, C.; Dressel, M.; Pronin, A.V. Broadband optical conductivity of the chiral multifold semimetal PdGa. *Phys. Rev. B* **2021**, *103*, 115206. [CrossRef]
24. Dressel, M.; Grüner, G. *Electrodynamics of Solids*; Cambridge University Press: Cambridge, UK, 2002.
25. Sachdev, S. *Quantum Phase Transitions*; Cambridge University Press: Cambridge, UK, 2011.
26. Van der Marel, D.; Molegraaf, H.J.A.; Zaanen, J.; Nussinov, Z.; Carbone, F.; Damascelli, A.; Eisaki, H.; Greven, M.; Kes, P.H.; Li, M. Quantum critical behaviour in a high-T_c superconductor. *Nature* **2003**, *425*, 271–274. [CrossRef] [PubMed]
27. Ioffe, L.B.; Millis, A.J. Zone-diagonal-dominated transport in high-T_c cuprates. *Phys. Rev. B* **1998**, *58*, 11631–11637. [CrossRef]
28. Van der Marel, D. Anisotropy of the optical conductivity of high-T_c cuprates. *Phys. Rev. B* **1999**, *60*, R765. [CrossRef]

29. Anderson, P.W. Infrared conductivity of cuprate metals: Detailed fit using Luttinger-liquid theory. *Phys. Rev. B* **1997**, *55*, 11785–11788. [CrossRef]
30. Schilling, M.B.; Schoop, L.M.; Lotsch, B.V.; Dressel, M.; Pronin, A.V. Flat Optical Conductivity in ZrSiS due to Two-Dimensional Dirac Bands. *Phys. Rev. Lett.* **2017**, *119*, 187401. [CrossRef]
31. Brechtel, E.; Cordier, G.; Schäfer, H. Zur Darstellung und Struktur von $CaMnBi_2$. *Z. Naturforsch. B* **1980**, *35*, 1–3. [CrossRef]
32. Sayetat, F.; Fertey, P.; Kessler, M. An Easy Method for the Determination of Debye Temperature from Thermal Expansion Analyses. *J. Appl. Cryst.* **1998**, *31*, 121–127. [CrossRef]

Article

Topological Properties in a Λ/V-Type Dice Model

Shujie Cheng and Xianlong Gao *

Department of Physics, Zhejiang Normal University, Jinhua 321004, China
* Correspondence: gaoxl@zjnu.edu.cn

Abstract: We studied a non-interacting Λ/V-type dice model composed of three triangular sublattices. By considering the isotropic nearest-neighbor hoppings and the next-nearest-neighbor hoppings with the phase, as well as the quasi-staggered on-site potential, we acquired the full phase diagrams under the different fillings of the energy bands. There are abundant topological non-trivial phases with different Chern numbers $C = \pm 1$, as well as higher ones ± 2, ± 3 and a metal phase in several regimes. In addition, we also checked the bulk–edge correspondence of the system by analyzing the edge-state energy spectrum.

Keywords: band structures; high Chern numbers; bulk-edge correspondence

1. Introduction

By means of an environment with a low temperature and strong magnetic field, Klitzing et al. discovered the quantum Hall effect in 1980 [1]. This discovery kicked off a wave of research on the quantum Hall effect, and a series of research on the topological features of condensed matter was inspired in the following decades [2–4]. These types of condensed matter are well classified according to their symmetry [5]. With these efforts, people have found some new topological quantum matter [6–8] with a quantum anomalous Hall effect (QAHE) [9], which releases the harsh condition of realizing a strong magnetic field.

A Chern insulator is a kind of insulator with QAHE that breaks the time-reversal symmetry. Its topological features can be directly reflected by the topological invariant, i.e., the Chern number (C). Thouless–Kohmoto–Nightingale–den Nijs (TKNN) first used the Chern number to describe the topological properties of a two-dimensional system [10]. In a gapped system, when the Fermi energy lies in a bulk band gap, the Chern number is always an integer and is equal to the quantized Hall conductance in units of e^2/h [11–13]. Chern numbers can be used to distinguish whether or not a system has topological properties. In other words, $C \neq 0$ ($C = 0$) corresponds to the topological nontrivial (trivial) phase. Afterwards, by developing TKNN's theory, Berry provided an alternative way to calculate the topological invariant with the Berry gauge field in the Brillouin zone [14]. Interestingly, the Chern numbers are linked to gapless edge states, forming the so-called bulk-edge correspondence [15]. The magnitude of the Chern number indicates the number of edge states.

In 1988, Haldane first theoretically pioneered the idea of breaking the time-reversal symmetry by applying a zero net magnetic flux through each unit cell in a hexagonal lattice and engineered a topological nontrivial model with $C = \pm 1$, which is known as the Haldane model [16]. This model opens a gate for people to study QAHE and has more or less influenced other two-dimensional systems that appeared later, such as the Checkerboard lattice [17], Kagomé lattice [18–21] and Lieb lattice [22–25]. Moreover, by considering the long-range tunneling [26–28] or more a complex magnetic flux [29–31], one can obtain the topological phase with a higher Chern number.

Recently, people have realized the Haldane model by trapping ultracold atoms in an optical lattice formed by three standing-wave laser beams [32–34] or in a periodically modulated optical honeycomb lattice [35]. In addition to these experiments, there have

Citation: Cheng, S.; Gao, X. Topological Properties in a Λ/V-Type Dice Model. *Crystals* **2021**, *11*, 467. https://doi.org/10.3390/cryst11050467

Academic Editors: Artem Pronin and Kwang-Yong Choi

Received: 30 March 2021
Accepted: 19 April 2021
Published: 22 April 2021

Publisher's Note: MDPI stays neutral with regard to jurisdictional claims in published maps and institutional affiliations.

Copyright: © 2021 by the authors. Licensee MDPI, Basel, Switzerland. This article is an open access article distributed under the terms and conditions of the Creative Commons Attribution (CC BY) license (https://creativecommons.org/licenses/by/4.0/).

been several works about the dice model [30,31] with a nonzero phase in the process of nearest-neighbor (NN) hoppings in the dice lattice [36–43]. In this paper, we will focus on a non-interacting dice model with a nonzero phase in the next-nearest-neighbor (NNN) term, but not in the NN term. We will consider a Λ/V-type on-site potential, which will give us a more fruitful phase diagram and exciting topological phenomena.

By analyzing the dispersions of the bands, in this paper, we uncover that the system possesses two different phases—a metal phase and bulk insulating phase, which are both in the 1/3 filling and 2/3 filling cases. In the bulk insulating phase, the topological properties are further investigated. After calculating the Chern number, we find that there is a topological trivial phase with $C = 0$ and topological nontrivial phases with $C = \pm 1$, $C = \pm 2$, and $C = \pm 3$, which are separated by the band-crossing lines. Then, we obtain the full phase diagram and find that the metal phase and topological phases are symmetrically distributed within the phases. The relative positions of these phases in the phase diagram will be inverted when we change the filling from 2/3 to 1/3, or vice verse. Finally, we also solve the edge-state spectrum and check the rule of bulk-edge correspondence.

This paper is organized as follows. In Section 2, we present the Hamiltonian of the dice model in both real and momentum space. In Section 3, we first analyze the band structures of the system. Next, we calculate the Chern numbers and numerically obtain the full phase diagram. Further, we check the bulk-edge correspondence through the edge-state spectrum. We summarize our work in the final section.

2. Model and Hamiltonian

Here, a non-interacting Λ/V-type dice model is studied, and it is shown in Figure 1. There are three interpenetrating triangular sublattices, denoted by R (red dots), B (blue dots), and G (green dots). The lattice constant a is set as $a = 1$. The Hamiltonian of our model has three parts:

$$\hat{H} = \hat{H}_1 + \hat{H}_2 + \hat{H}_3. \tag{1}$$

The first part $\hat{H}_1$ shows the isotropic hoppings with the same hopping amplitudes between nearest-neighbor sites, which pertain to various sublattices, and this part is presented as

$$\hat{H}_1 = \sum_{\langle \mathbf{R}_i, \mathbf{B}_j \rangle} t \left(\hat{c}_{\mathbf{R}_i}^\dagger \hat{c}_{\mathbf{B}_j} + H.c. \right)$$
$$+ \sum_{\langle \mathbf{R}_i, \mathbf{G}_\ell \rangle} t \left(\hat{c}_{\mathbf{R}_i}^\dagger \hat{c}_{\mathbf{G}_\ell} + H.c. \right) \tag{2}$$
$$+ \sum_{\langle \mathbf{B}_j, \mathbf{G}_\ell \rangle} t \left(\hat{c}_{\mathbf{B}_j}^\dagger \hat{c}_{\mathbf{G}_\ell} + H.c. \right),$$

in which t denotes the hopping amplitude, and it is regarded as the unit of energy, $\hat{c}_{\mathbf{R}_i}$, $\hat{c}_{\mathbf{B}_j}$, $\hat{c}_{\mathbf{G}_\ell}$ are the fermionic annihilation operators, and $\mathbf{R}_i$, $\mathbf{B}_j$, and $\mathbf{G}_\ell$ denote the coordinates of relevant sublattice sites R, B, and G, respectively. $\langle \cdots \rangle$ is the nearest-neighbor relation.

In the same R and B sublattices, we will consider the next-nearest-neighbor hoppings accompanied by a phase. Then, $\hat{H}_2$ can be expressed as

$$\hat{H}_2 = \sum_{\langle \mathbf{R}_i, \mathbf{R}_j \rangle} \left(t_2 e^{i\phi} \hat{c}_{\mathbf{R}_i}^\dagger \hat{c}_{\mathbf{R}_j} + H.c. \right)$$
$$+ \sum_{\langle \mathbf{B}_i, \mathbf{B}_j \rangle} \left(t_2 e^{i\phi} \hat{c}_{\mathbf{B}_i}^\dagger \hat{c}_{\mathbf{B}_j} + h.c. \right), \tag{3}$$

in which $t_2 e^{\pm i\phi}$ is the hopping amplitude, where ϕ is the phase, and $\pm$ represents the direction of the hoppings ($+$ is the clockwise direction and $-$ is the counterclockwise direction). References [30–34,44,45] tell us that the hopping terms in our toy models can be realized through laser-assisted tunneling. Moreover, the phase accompanied by the tunneling can be modulated with the momentum recoil. We think that this method is helpful in selectively engineering such a phase in specific hopping terms in experiments. At the very least, these are the most natural imperfections that may arise in the experimental implementation of such a model.

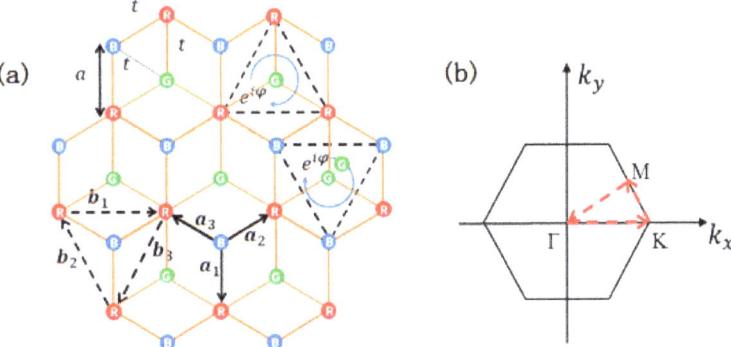

Figure 1. (a) Geometry of the dice lattice. R, B, and G are sublattice sites, and are marked with red, blue, and green dots respectively. The lattice constant a is taken as $a = 1$. The vectors a_n ($n = 1, 2, 3$) link the nearest-neighbor sites that pertain to different sublattices. The vectors b_n ($n = 1, 2, 3$) link the nearest-neighbor R sites or B sites. The circle arrows represent the next-nearest-neighbor tunnelings accompanied by a phase $e^{i\varphi}$. (b) The first Brillouin zone of the model. Γ, K, and M are high-symmetry points in the high-symmetry path, and are connected by three red dashed lines.

The final part describes the on-site potentials with a special configuration

$$\hat{H}_3 = \Delta \sum_{\mathbf{R}_i} \hat{c}^\dagger_{\mathbf{R}_i} \hat{c}_{\mathbf{R}_i} + \Delta \sum_{\mathbf{B}_i} \hat{c}^\dagger_{\mathbf{B}_i} \hat{c}_{\mathbf{B}_i} - 2\Delta \sum_{\mathbf{G}_i} \hat{c}^\dagger_{\mathbf{G}_i} \hat{c}_{\mathbf{G}_i}, \qquad (4)$$

in which Δ denotes the potential at the R and B sublattice sites, and -2Δ is the potential at the G sublattice sites. The configuration of the potential can be viewed as Λ/V-type ($\Delta < 0 / \Delta > 0$) of three levels in a super atom, which is composed of three sites and forms a three-band model in the lattice case. This potential configuration differs from that in other dice models [30,31] and can also be realized by tuning single-beam lattice depths [34,35].

We consider a system that has discrete translational symmetry; thus, the single-particle Hamiltonian can be written in momentum space [46–48] as

$$\hat{\mathcal{H}}(\mathbf{k}) = I(\mathbf{k}) + \mathbf{d}(\mathbf{k}) \cdot \vec{\lambda}, \qquad (5)$$

where $I(\mathbf{k})$ is a scalar, $\mathbf{d}(\mathbf{k})$ is a real vector with eight components, and $\vec{\lambda}$ denotes a vector consisting of Gell–Mann matrices [49]. As a matter of fact, the Chern number will not be affected by the scalar $I(\mathbf{k})$, and is only determined by $\mathbf{d}(\mathbf{k})$. In order to obtain the $\hat{\mathcal{H}}(\mathbf{k})$, we need to perform a discrete Fourier transformation on the three-component basis $(\hat{c}_{\mathbf{k},R}, \hat{c}_{\mathbf{k},B}, \hat{c}_{\mathbf{k},G})^T$:

$$\begin{aligned} \hat{c}_{\mathbf{k},R} &= \frac{1}{\sqrt{N}} \sum_{\mathbf{R}_j} e^{-i\mathbf{k}\cdot \mathbf{R}_j} \hat{c}_{\mathbf{R}_j}, \\ \hat{c}_{\mathbf{k},B} &= \frac{1}{\sqrt{N}} \sum_{\mathbf{B}_j} e^{-i\mathbf{k}\cdot \mathbf{B}_j} \hat{c}_{\mathbf{B}_j}, \\ \hat{c}_{\mathbf{k},G} &= \frac{1}{\sqrt{N}} \sum_{\mathbf{G}_j} e^{-i\mathbf{k}\cdot \mathbf{G}_j} \hat{c}_{\mathbf{G}_j}. \end{aligned} \qquad (6)$$

After the derivation, we acquire the components of the vector $\mathbf{d}(\mathbf{k})$, which are presented as

$$d_1 = d_6 = d_4 = \sum_n t\cos(\mathbf{k} \cdot a_n),$$
$$d_2 = d_7 = -d_5 = \sum_n t\sin(\mathbf{k} \cdot a_n),$$
$$d_3 = -2t_2 \sin\phi \sum_n \sin(\mathbf{k} \cdot b_n), \qquad (7)$$
$$d_8 = \sqrt{3}\Delta + \frac{2t_2}{\sqrt{3}}\cos\phi \sum_n \cos(\mathbf{k} \cdot b_n),$$

in which the six-unit vectors a_n and b_n ($n = 1, 2, 3$), which are shown in Figure 1a, are listed as

$$a_1 = \begin{pmatrix} 0 \\ -1 \end{pmatrix}, \quad a_2 = \frac{1}{2}\begin{pmatrix} \sqrt{3} \\ 1 \end{pmatrix}, \quad a_3 = \frac{1}{2}\begin{pmatrix} -\sqrt{3} \\ 1 \end{pmatrix},$$
$$b_1 = \begin{pmatrix} \sqrt{3} \\ 0 \end{pmatrix}, \quad b_2 = \frac{1}{2}\begin{pmatrix} -\sqrt{3} \\ 3 \end{pmatrix}, \quad b_3 = -\frac{1}{2}\begin{pmatrix} \sqrt{3} \\ 3 \end{pmatrix}. \qquad (8)$$

3. Results and Discussion

3.1. Band Structures

To begin, we study the band structures of the model described by Equation (1). The first Brillouin zone of this model is shown in Figure 1b, with Γ, K, and M being the high-symmetry points [50]. Without loss of generality, in the following numerical calculation, we set $t = t_2 = 1$. With the known components of $\mathbf{d}(\mathbf{k})$ in Equation (7), we can diagonalize $\hat{\mathcal{H}}(\mathbf{k})$ and obtain its eigenvalues at each momentum $\mathbf{k}$. According to this strategy, we finally acquire the energy dispersions along the high-symmetry path Γ-K-M-Γ with different Δ and phase ϕ.

As a matter of fact, the energy at each band has a maximal value or a minimal value at a high-symmetry point. According to this obvious feature, we numerically analyze the energy gap between two adjacent energy bands, and finally uncover that the system consists of a bulk insulating phase and a metal phase. Figure 2 shows the metal–insulator phase diagram at 1/3 filling, and Figure 3 shows that for 2/3 filling. The green dots, which are marked as a, b, c, and d, are the four chosen typical parameter points. The terms 1/3 filling and 2/3 filling mean that the Fermi energies are selected to ensure that these three bands are filled just enough by 1/3 and 2/3, respectively. There is no doubt that the system is in the metal phase (surrounded by the blue solid line and marked by M) when the gap is closed. The bulk insulating phase (marked by I) requires that the gap is be open. For instance, when the parameter is tuned to the a point, the gap is closed at 1/3 filling and is open at 2/3 filling. The consequence at the b point is the opposite of that at the a point. The system remains gapless at the c point and remains gapped at the d point. It is worth noting that the metal phase and bulk insulating phase are symmetrically distributed.

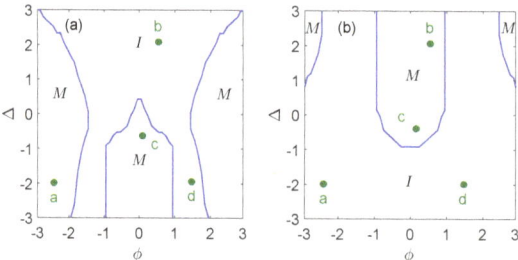

Figure 2. The metal-insulator phase diagrams in the cases of 1/3 filling (**a**) and 2/3 filling (**b**). M refers to the metal phase and I refers to the bulk insulating phase. In each case, there are four chosen typical points, a, b, c, and d, which are marked by green dots and are discussed in the main text.

Intuitively, the dispersion curves at these four chosen parameter points, (Δ_a, ϕ_a), (Δ_b, ϕ_b), (Δ_c, ϕ_c), and (Δ_d, ϕ_d), are plotted in Figure 3a–d, respectively. In these figures, we choose two Fermi energies to ensure the 1/3 filling (black solid line) and the 2/3 filling (black dashed line), respectively. In Figure 3a, because the top of the lowest band is higher than the bottom of the middle band, the Fermi energy crosses the middle band and forms a fully occupied lowest band and a partially occupied middle band. Accordingly, the system presents a metallic property in the 1/3 filling case. If the Fermi energy is located at the 2/3 filling line, the middle band is fully occupied and the highest band is empty. Then, in this case, the system will be in the bulk insulating phase. For the same reasons, one can easily comprehend that the system is a band insulator at 1/3 filling and a metal at 2/3 filling in the case shown in Figure 3b. Moreover, in Figure 3c,d, the system is stable in the metal phase and bulk insulating phase, respectively, no matter what the filling is. All of the results agree with our metal–insulator phase diagrams in Figure 2.

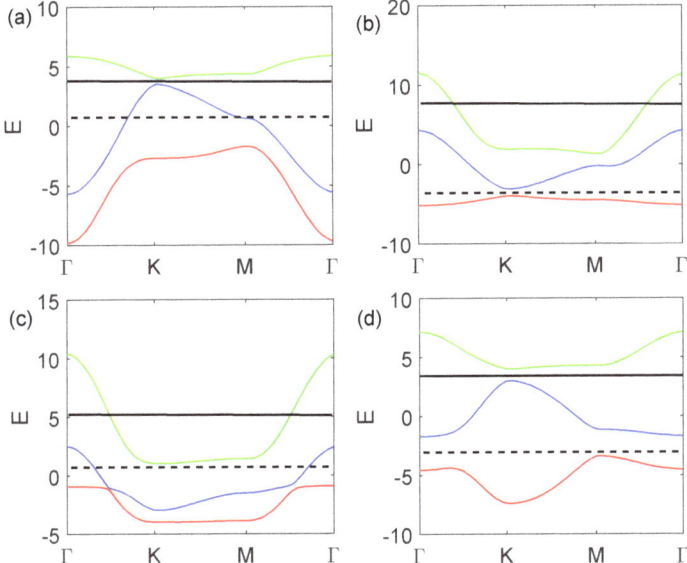

Figure 3. Dispersions of the Λ/V-type dice model along the high-symmetry path Γ-K-M-Γ. (**a**) $\Delta_a = -2$, $\phi_a = -2.5$, (**b**) $\Delta_b = 2$, $\phi_b = 0.5$, (**c**) $\Delta_c = -0.5$, $\phi_c = 0.1$, (**d**) $\Delta_d = -2$, $\phi_d = 1.5$. The red, blue, and green solid lines show the dispersions. The lower Fermi energy (black dashed line) and higher Fermi energy (black solid line) show the cases of 1/3 and 2/3 filling, respectively.

3.2. Chern Numbers and the Edge-State Spectrum

The nontrivial topological features of the Haldane model [16] and other dice models [30,31,43] motivate us to make it clear what topological phases exist in the bulk insulating region. According to the energy band theory [10,11,14], the n-th occupied band's Chern number is defined as a contour integral along the boundary of the first Brillouin zone,

$$C_n = \frac{1}{2\pi} \oint \mathbf{A}_n(\mathbf{k}) \cdot d\mathbf{k}, \quad (9)$$

in which $n \in \{1,2,3\}$ denotes the band index and $\mathbf{A}_n = -i\langle\psi_n(\mathbf{k})|\nabla_\mathbf{k}|\psi_n(\mathbf{k})\rangle$, with $|\psi_n(\mathbf{k})\rangle$ being the associated eigenvector of $\hat{\mathcal{H}}(\mathbf{k})$. The ascending order of n indicates the band from the bottom to the top. The topological properties of this model can be reflected by two quantities, i.e., $C_{\frac{1}{3}}$ and $C_{\frac{2}{3}}$, which satisfy $C_{\frac{1}{3}} = C_1$ and $C_{\frac{2}{3}} = C_1 + C_2$. We calculate the Chern number and obtain the full phase diagrams of the system, which are shown in Figure 4a,b for 1/3 and 2/3 filling of the system, respectively. There are several phase boundary lines in the bulk insulating phase, which are captured by the closing of the energy band. In Fact, the energy-crossing-lines also appear in the metal phase, but do not change the intrinsic properties of the metal phase. In each diagram, the black solid lines separate the topological nontrivial phase from the topological trivial phase, and the red solid lines distinguish the topological nontrivial phase with various $C_{\frac{1}{3}}$ and $C_{\frac{2}{3}}$.

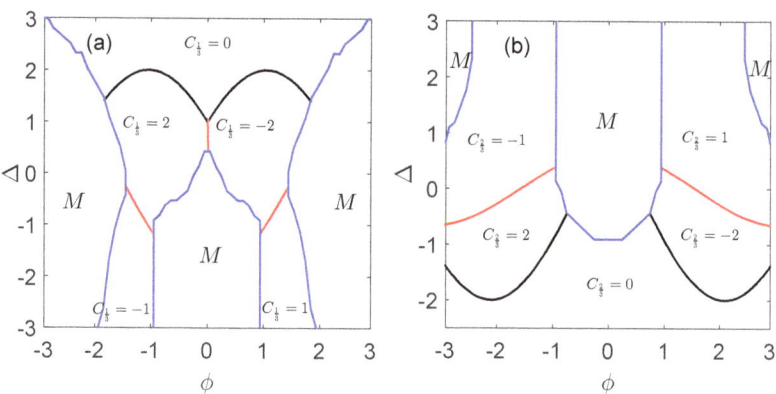

Figure 4. Two full phase diagrams with (**a**) 1/3 filling and (**b**) 2/3 filling, respectively. The blue solid lines and axes surround the metallic region (M), and the bulk insulating region consists of several topological regions. The black solid lines separate the topological nontrivial phase from the topological trivial phase, and the red solid lines distinguish the topological nontrivial phase with various $C_{\frac{1}{3}}$ and $C_{\frac{2}{3}}$.

As can be seen from the phase diagrams, abundant quantum phases exist in our model. In Figure 4a, intuitively, we know that, except for the metal phase, there are topological nontrivial phases with $C_{\frac{1}{3}} = C_1 = \pm 1$ and $C_{\frac{1}{3}} = C_1 = \pm 2$, as well as the topological trivial phase with $C_{\frac{1}{3}} = C_1 = 0$. A similar circumstance also appears in Figure 4. Furthermore, when the parameters are tuned continuously, the system will undergo abundant phases. We take $\Delta = -0.7$ as an example. As ϕ increases, at 2/3 filling, the system will undergo a closed circle with six different phases:

$$\begin{array}{ccc} C_{\frac{2}{3}} = -1 & \Rightarrow & C_{\frac{2}{3}} = +2 \\ \Uparrow & & \Downarrow \\ M & & M \\ \Uparrow & & \Downarrow \\ C_{\frac{2}{3}} = +1 & \Leftarrow & C_{\frac{2}{3}} = -2, \end{array}$$

where M stands for the metal phase. The distribution of the phase diagram in Figure 4b (2/3 filling) can be loosely regarded as the inversion of that with the 1/3 filling. Similarly, the system can also undergo rich phases when we tune the Fermi energy.

In the following, we check the rule of the bulk–edge correspondence. We keep the x direction of the system periodic and make the system possess a zigzag edge along the y direction. Therefore, k_x is a good quantum number. Finally, we solved the edge-state spectrum [4,15], which is plotted in Figure 5. We find that the system also obeys the rule of bulk–edge correspondence [15] for the reason that the magnitudes of $C_{\frac{1}{3}}$ and $C_{\frac{2}{3}}$ can be reflected from the intersections of the edge-state spectra. When we choose the parameter $(\Delta, \phi) = (-2, 1.5)$, the edge-state spectrum intersects at $k_x = \pm \pi / \sqrt{3}$ (see Figure 5a), which means that there is only a pair of edge modes, corresponding to $C_{\frac{1}{3}} = 1$. The edge-state spectrum is gapped at 2/3 filling, which means that there are no edge modes, corresponding to $C_{\frac{2}{3}} = 0$. Meanwhile, at this parameter point, the Chern number of the lowest band is $C_1 = -1$ and that of the middle band is $C_2 = C_{\frac{2}{3}} - C_1 = 0 - (-1) = 1$. In addition, it is known from the symmetry of the phase diagram that the Chern numbers become $C_1 = 1$ and $C_2 = -1$ at $(\Delta, \phi) = (-2, -1.5)$, and will also obtain the same edge-state spectrum as that in Figure 5a. When we select the parameter at $(\Delta, \phi) = (1, -1.3)$, there are two different intersections at 1/3 filling (see Figure 5b), which means that there are two pairs of edge modes, corresponding to $C_{\frac{1}{3}} = 2$. The spectrum intersects at $k_x = \pm \pi/\sqrt{3}$, which means that there is a pair of edge modes, corresponding to $C_{\frac{2}{3}} = -1$. By the definitions of $C_{\frac{1}{3}}$ and $C_{\frac{2}{3}}$, we get $C_1 = 2$ and $C_2 = -3$ in this case. Similarly, when we take $(\Delta, \phi) = (1, -1.3)$, we will know that $C_1 = -2$ and $C_2 = 3$ and we will obtain the same correspondence as that shown in Figure 5b.

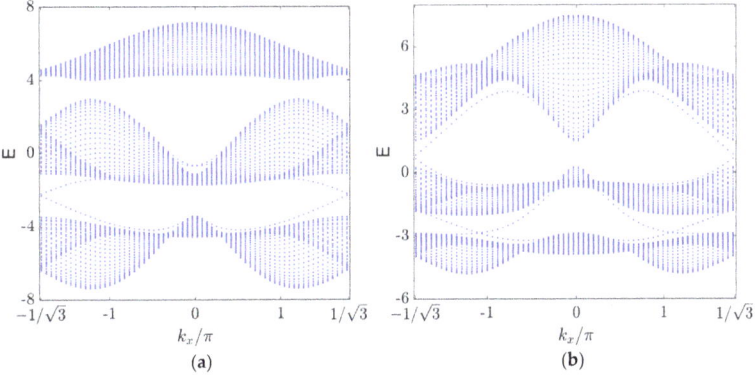

Figure 5. Two edge-state spectra of a cylindrical geometry with a zigzag edge. (**a**) $\Delta = -2, \phi = 1.5$. There is a pair of edge modes in the case of 1/3 filling, corresponding to $C_{\frac{1}{3}} = -1$, while there are no edge modes in the case of 2/3 filling, which corresponds to $C_{\frac{2}{3}} = 0$; (**b**) $\Delta = 1, \phi = -1.3$. There are two pairs of edge modes in the case of 1/3 filling, which corresponds to $C_{\frac{1}{3}} = 2$, and there is only a pair of edge modes in the case of 2/3 filling, which corresponds to $C_{\frac{2}{3}} = -1$.

4. Conclusions

To conclude, we have studied the band structures and topological properties of a Λ/V-type dice model. First, we investigated the energy spectrum characteristics under 1/3 filling and 2/3 filling. In the Δ-ϕ parameter space, the system can be divided into two parts: the metal phase and the bulk insulating phase. Furthermore, we calculated the Chern numbers according to the energy band theory in the bulk insulating phase and obtained a fruitful phase diagram. Interestingly, there are many topological nontrivial phases that are separated by some energy-level-crossing lines with different Chern numbers, such as $C = \pm 1$, $C = \pm 2$, and $C = \pm 3$. Finally, by solving the edge-state spectrum, we found that the system obeys the rule of bulk-edge correspondence.

In spite of the existence of dice lattice structures in several electronic materials, such as $SrTiO_3/SrIrO_3/SrTiO_3$ [51], $Ba_2CoRe_2O_{12}$ [52], and Gd_2CCl_2 [53–55], the high free modulation of the parameters in cold-atom experiments will be convenient for us to study the topological phases by manipulating the neutral atoms, which never occurred in the aforementioned research. For this reason, we hope that our system can be realized in cold-atom experiments and that phases with higher Chern numbers will be observed.

Author Contributions: Conceptualization, X.G. and S.C.; methodology, X.G. and S.C.; software, X.G. and S.C.; validation, S.C.; formal analysis, S.C.; investigation, S.C.; resources, X.G.; data curation, S.C.; writing—original draft preparation, S.C.; writing—review and editing, X.G. and S.C.; visualization, X.G. and S.C.; supervision, X.G.; project administration, X.G.; funding acquisition, X.G. All authors have read and agreed to the published version of the manuscript.

Funding: This research was funded by NSFC under Grants No. 11835011 and No. 11774316.

Institutional Review Board Statement: Not applicable.

Informed Consent Statement: Not applicable.

Data Availability Statement: The data presented in this study are available on request from the authors. The data are not publicly available due to intellectual property protection.

Conflicts of Interest: The authors declare no conflict of interest.

References

1. Klitzing, K.V.; Dorda, G.; Pepper, M. New Method for High-Accuracy Determination of the Fine-Structure Constant Based on Quantized Hall Resistance. *Phys. Rev. Lett.* **1980**, *45*, 494. [CrossRef]
2. Hasan, M.Z.; Kane, C.L. *Colloquium*: Topological insulators. *Rev. Mod. Phys.* **2010**, *82*, 3045. [CrossRef]
3. Qi, X.-L.; Zhang, S.-C. Topological Insulators and Superconductors. *Rev. Mod. Phys.* **2011**, *83*, 1057. [CrossRef]
4. Shen, S.-Q. *Topological Insulators*; Springer: Berlin, Germany, 2012.
5. Schnyder, A.P.; Ryu, S.; Furusaki, A.; Ludwig, A.W.W. Classification of topological insulators and superconductors in three spatial dimensions. *Phys. Rev. B* **2008**, *78*, 195125. [CrossRef]
6. Chang, C.-Z.; Zhang, J.; Feng, X.; Shen, J.; Zhang, Z.; Guo, M.; Li, K.; Ou, Y.; Wei, P.; Wang, L.-L.; et al. Experimental observation of the quantum anomalous Hall effect in a magnetic topological insulator. *Science* **2013**, *340*, 167–170. [CrossRef] [PubMed]
7. Chang, C.-Z.; Zhao, W.; Kim, D.Y.; Zhang, H.; Assaf, B.A.; Heiman, D.; Zhang, S.-C.; Liu, C.; Chan, M.H.W.; Moodera, J.S. High-precision realization of robust quantum anomalous Hall state in a hard ferromagnetic topological insulator. *Nat. Mater.* **2014**, *14*, 473–477. [CrossRef] [PubMed]
8. Deng, Y.; Yu, Y.; Shi, M.Z.; Guo, Z.; Xu, Z.; Wang, J.; Chen, X.H.; Zhang, Y. Quantum anomalous Hall effect in intrinsic magnetic topological insulator $MnBi_2Te_4$. *Science* **2020**, *367*, 895–900. [CrossRef]
9. Nagaosa, N.; Sinova, J.; Onoda, S.; MacDonald, A.H.; Ong, N.P. Anomalous Hall effect. *Rev. Mod. Phys.* **2010**, *82*, 1539. [CrossRef]
10. Thouless, D.J.; Kohmoto, M.; Nightngale, M.P.; den Nijs, M. Quantized Hall Conductance in a Two-Dimensional Periodic Potential. *Phys. Rev. Lett.* **1982**, *49*, 405. [CrossRef]
11. Niu, Q.; Thouless, D.J.; Wu, Y.S. Quantized Hall conductance as a topological invariant. *Phys. Rev. B* **1985**, *31*, 3372. [CrossRef]
12. Kohmoto, M. Topological Invariant and the Quantization of the Hall Conductance. *Ann. Phys.* **1985**, *160*, 343–354. [CrossRef]
13. Kohmoto, M. Zero modes and the quantized Hall conductance of the two-dimensional lattice in a magnetic field. *Phys. Rev. B* **1989**, *39*, 11943. [CrossRef]
14. Berry, M.V. Quantal phase factors accompanying adiabatic changes. *Proc. R. Soc. A* **1984**, *392*, 45–57.
15. Hatsugai, Y. Chern number and edge states in the integer quantum Hall effect. *Phys. Rev. Lett.* **1993**, *71*, 3697. [CrossRef]
16. Haldane, F.D.M. Model for a Quantum Hall Effect without Landau Levels: Condensed-Matter Realization of the "Parity Anomaly". *Phys. Rev. Lett.* **1988**, *61*, 2015. [CrossRef]
17. Sun, K.; Yao, H.; Fradkin, E.; Kivelson, S.A. Topological insulators and nematic phases from spontaneous symmetry breaking in 2D fermi systems with a quadratic band crossing. *Phys. Rev. Lett.* **2009**, *103*, 046811. [CrossRef]
18. Ohgushi, K.; Murakami, S.; Nagaosa, N. Spin anisotropy and quantum Hall effect in the *kagomé* lattice: Chiral spin state based on a ferromagnet. *Phys. Rev. B* **2000**, *62*, R6065. [CrossRef]
19. Xiao, Y.; Pelletier, V.; Chaikin, P.M.; Huse, D.A. Landau levels in the case of two degenerate coupled bands: Kagomé lattice tight-binding spectrum. *Phys. Rev. B* **2003**, *67*, 104505. [CrossRef]
20. Guo, H.M.; Franz, M. Topological insulator on the kagome lattice. *Phys. Rev. B* **2009**, *80*, 113102. [CrossRef]
21. Liu, X.P.; Chen, W.C.; Wang, Y.F.; Gong, C.D. Topological quantum phase transitions on the kagomé and square–octagon lattices. *J. Phys. Condens. Matter* **2013**, *25*, 305602. [CrossRef]
22. Weeks, C.; Franz, M. Topological insulators on the Lieb and perovskite lattices. *Phys. Rev. B* **2010**, *82*, 085310. [CrossRef]
23. Apaja, V.; Hvrkas, M.; Manninen, M. Flat bands, Dirac cones, and atom dynamics in an optical lattice. *Phys. Rev. A* **2010**, *82*, 041402(R). [CrossRef]
24. Goldman, N.; Urban, D.F.; Bercioux, D. Topological phases for fermionic cold atoms on the Lieb lattice. *Phys. Rev. A* **2011**, *83*, 063601. [CrossRef]
25. Tsai, W.-F.; Fang, C.; Yao, H.; Hu, J. Interaction-driven topological and nematic phases on the Lieb lattice. *New J. Phys.* **2015**, *17*, 055016. [CrossRef]
26. Yang, S.; Gu, Z.-C.; Sun, K.; Das Sarma, S. Topological flat band models with arbitrary Chern numbers. *Phys. Rev. B* **2012**, *86*, 241112. [CrossRef]

27. Wang, Y.-F.; Yao, H.; Gong, C.-D.; Sheng, D.N. Fractional quantum Hall effect in topological flat bands with Chern number two. *Phys. Rev. B* **2012**, *86*, 201101. [CrossRef]
28. Sticlet, D.; Pièchon, F. Distant-neighbor hopping in graphene and Haldane models. *Phys. Rev. B* **2013**, *87*, 115402. [CrossRef]
29. Hatsugai, Y.; Kohmoto, M. Energy spectrum and the quantum Hall effect on the square lattice with next-nearest-neighbor hopping. *Phys. Rev. B* **1990**, *82*, 8282. [CrossRef]
30. Goldman, N.; Anisimovas, E.; Gerbier, F.; Öhberg, P.; Spielman, I.B.; Juzeliūnas, G. Measuring topology in a laser-coupled honeycomb lattice: From Chern insulators to topological semi-metals. *New J. Phys.* **2013**, *15*, 013025. [CrossRef]
31. Andrijauskas, T.; Anisimovas, E.; Račiūnas, M.; Mekys, A.; Kudriašov, V.; Spielman, I.B.; Juzeliūnas, G. Three-level Haldane-like model on a dice optical lattice. *Phys. Rev. A* **2015**, *92*, 033617. [CrossRef]
32. Shao, L.B.; Zhu, S.-L.; Sheng, L.; Xing, D.Y.; Wang, Z.D. Realizing and Detecting the Quantum Hall Effect without Landau Levels by Using Ultracold Atoms. *Phys. Rev. Lett.* **2008**, *101*, 246810. [CrossRef]
33. Alba, E.; Fernandez-Gonzalvo, X.; Mur-Petit, J.; Pachos, J.K.; Garcia-Ripoll, J.J. Seeing Topological Order in Time-of-Flight Measurements. *Phys. Rev. Lett.* **2011**, *107*, 235301. [CrossRef]
34. Tarruell, L.; Greif, D.; Uehlinger, T.; Jotzu, G.; Essinger, T. Creating, moving and merging Dirac points with a Fermi gas in a tunable honeycomb lattice. *Nature* **2012**, *483*, 302–305. [CrossRef]
35. Jotzu, G.; Messer, M.; Desbuquois, R.; Lebrat, M.; Uehlinger, T.; Greif, D.; Esslinger, T. Experimental realization of the topological Haldane model with ultracold fermions. *Nature* **2014**, *515*, 237–240. [CrossRef]
36. Sutherland, B. Localization of electronic wave functions due to local topology. *Phys. Rev. B* **1986**, *34*, 5208. [CrossRef]
37. Vidal, J.; Mosseri, R.; Doucot, B. Aharonov-Bohm Cages in Two-Dimensional Structures. *Phys. Rev. Lett.* **1998**, *81*, 5888. [CrossRef]
38. Bercioux, D.; Urban, D.F.; Grabert, H.; Häusler, W. Massless Dirac-Weyl fermions in a $\mathcal{T}_3$ optical lattice. *Phys. Rev. A* **2009**, *80*, 063603. [CrossRef]
39. Möller, G.; Cooper, N.R. Correlated Phases of Bosons in the Flat Lowest Band of the Dice Lattice. *Phys. Rev. Lett.* **2012**, *108*, 045306. [CrossRef]
40. Rizzi, M.; Cataudella, V.; Fazio, R. Phase diagram of the Bose-Hubbard model with $\mathcal{T}_3$ symmetry. *Phys. Rev. B* **2006**, *73*, 144511. [CrossRef]
41. Burkov, A.A.; Demler, E. Vortex-Peierls States in Optical Lattices. *Phys. Rev. Lett.* **2006**, *96*, 180406. [CrossRef]
42. Bercioux, D.; Goldman, N.; Urban, D.F. Topology-induced phase transitions in quantum spin Hall lattices. *Phys. Rev. A* **2011**, *83*, 023609. [CrossRef]
43. Cheng, S.; Yin, H.; Lu, Z.; He, C.; Wang, P.; Xianlong, G. Predicting large-Chern-number phases in a shaken optical dice lattice. *Phys. Rev. A* **2020**, *101*, 043620. [CrossRef]
44. Dalibard, J.; Gerbier, F.; Juzeliūnas, G.; Öhberg, P. *Colloquium*: Artificial gauge potentials for neutral atoms. *Rev. Mod. Phys.* **2011**, *83*, 1523. [CrossRef]
45. Goldman, N.; Juzeliūnas, G.; Öhberg, P.; Spielman, I.B. Light-induced gauge fields for ultracold atoms. *Rep. Prog. Phys.* **2014**, *77*, 126401. [CrossRef]
46. Khanna, G.; Mukhopadhyay, S.; Simon, R.; Mukunda, N. Geometric phases for SU(3) representations and three level quantum systems. *Ann. Phys.* **1997**, *253*, 55–82. [CrossRef]
47. Sachdev, S. *Quantum Phase Transitions*; Cambridge University Press: Cambridge, UK, 2011.
48. Barnett, R.; Boyd, G.R.; Galitski, V. SU(3) Spin-Orbit Coupling in Systems of Ultracold Atoms. *Phys. Rev. Lett.* **2012**, *109*, 235308. [CrossRef]
49. Georgi, H. *Lie Algebras In Particle Physics: From Isospin To Unified Theories*; Benjamin/Cummings: Reading, MA, USA, 1982.
50. Setyawan, W.; Curtarolo, S. High-throughput electronic band structure calculations: Challenges and tools. *Comput. Mater. Sci.* **2010**, *49*, 299–312. [CrossRef]
51. Okamoto, S.; Xiao, D. Transition-Metal Oxide (111) Bilayers. *J. Phys. Soc. Jpn.* **2018**, *87*, 041006. [CrossRef]
52. Rawl, R.; Lee, M.; Choi, E.S.; Li, G.; Chen, K.W.; Baumbach, R.; dela Cruz, C.R.; Ma, J.; Zhou, H.D. Magnetic properties of the triangular lattice magnets $A_4B'B_2O_{12}$ (A = Ba, Sr, La; B' = Co, Ni, Mn; B = W, Re). *Phys. Rev. B* **2017**, *95*, 174438. [CrossRef]
53. Schleid, T.; Meyer, G. Crystal structure of digadolinium monocarbide dichloride (1T type), Gd_2CCl_2. *Z. Fur Krist.* **1994**, *209*, 371. [CrossRef]
54. Ryazanov, M.; Simon, A.; Mattausch, H. New synthesis route to and physical properties of lanthanum monoiodide. *Inorg. Chem.* **2006**, *45*, 2068–2074. [CrossRef] [PubMed]
55. Schleid, T.; Meyer, G. Synthesis and crystal structures of hydrogen and carbon stabilized lutetium monochloride, $LuClH_x$ and Lu_2Cl_2C. *Z. Fur Anorg. Undallgemeine Chem.* **1987**, *552*, 90–96. [CrossRef]

Article

Low-Energy Optical Conductivity of TaP: Comparison of Theory and Experiment

Alexander Yaresko [1,*] and Artem V. Pronin [2]

[1] Max-Planck-Institut für Festkörperforschung, Heisenbergstr. 1, 70569 Stuttgart, Germany
[2] 1. Physikalisches Institut, Universität Stuttgart, 70569 Stuttgart, Germany; artem.pronin@pi1.physik.uni-stuttgart.de
* Correspondence: a.yaresko@fkf.mpg.de

Abstract: The ab-plane optical conductivity of the Weyl semimetal TaP is calculated from the band structure and compared to the experimental data. The overall agreement between theory and experiment is found to be best when the Fermi level is slightly (20 to 60 meV) shifted upwards in the calculations. This confirms a small unintentional doping of TaP, reported earlier, and allows a natural explanation of the strong low-energy (50 meV) peak seen in the experimental ab-plane optical conductivity: this peak originates from transitions between the almost parallel non-degenerate electronic bands split by spin-orbit coupling. The temperature evolution of the peak can be reasonably well reproduce by calculations using an analog of the Mott formula.

Keywords: Weyl semimetals; band-structure calculations; optical response

1. Introduction

Weyl fermions [1] are known to be observed as elementary excitations in condensed-matter systems—the Weyl semimetals (WSMs) [2–8]. In WSMs, the valence and conduction bands touch each other at selected points of the Brillouin zone (BZ), the Weyl nodes.

TaP belongs to the currently most studied family of WSMs, which also includes NbP, TaAs, and NbAs. These materials are nonmagnetic non-centrosymmetric WSMs with 24 Weyl nodes of two different types, usually dubbed as W1 (8 nodes) and W2 (16 nodes) [5,9–13]. The available band-structure calculations predict that in TaP the W1 nodes are situated some 40 to 55 meV below the Fermi level E_F, while the W2 nodes are at 12 to 20 meV above it [11–13], see Figure 1.

The low-energy band structure of TaP and other WSMs determines their peculiar physical properties [14]. One way to experimentally probe the band structure at low energies is optical spectroscopy in the infrared (particularly, in the far-infrared) region [15]. The frequency-dependent conductivity, $\sigma(\omega) = \sigma_1(\omega) + i\sigma_2(\omega)$, of three-dimensional linear bands has been well studied theoretically using model Hamiltonians [16–23]. It has been shown that the interband portion of $\sigma_1(\omega)$ for a single isotropic Weyl band has to follow a linear frequency dependence [16–18]:

$$\sigma_1(\omega) = \frac{e^2}{12h}\frac{\omega}{v_F}, \tag{1}$$

where v_F is the band Fermi velocity (this formula is obtained assuming the electron-hole symmetry). Such linear behavior of $\sigma_1(\omega)$ at low energies has indeed been observed in a number of established three-dimensional Weyl and Dirac semimetals, as well as in candidate materials [24–30].

In many real materials of this type, however, the linear interband conductivity at low energies is (partly) masked by other features, such as intraband (Drude) conductivity or resonance-like interband contributions [30–35]. Particularly strong low-energy peak was

observed in TaP [30,35]. In Ref. [30], this peak was assigned to electron-hole pair excitations near the saddle points of the crossing bands, which form the Weyl nodes (Figure 1). To our knowledge, this assignment doesn't have a direct support from optical-conductivity calculations based on band structure. Also, the total number of states near the saddle points is relatively low. Hence, only relatively small kinks in the optical conductivity, rather than strong peaks, are expected in this situation [20,34]. On the other hand, our earlier study of the sister compound NbP [34] has demonstrated that the low-energy peaks, similar to the one in TaP, appear in NbP and are due to multiple transitions between almost parallel bands split by spin-orbit coupling (SOC). Based on our band structure calculations, we argue in this paper that the same explanation of its low-energy peak holds also for TaP.

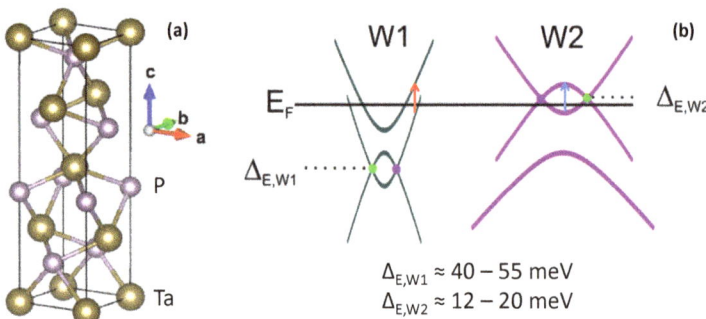

Figure 1. (a) Crystallographic structure of TaP and (b) a schematic diagram of its Weyl bands. Possible transitions between the saddle points of the merging Weyl bands and between the SOC-split bands are indicated as arrows.

2. Results and Discussion

In Figure 2, we plot our experimental optical spectra presented earlier in Ref. [35]. The measurements have been done on the isotropic ab plane of TaP (cf. Figure 1). The prominent low-energy peak is clearly seen in the real part of the optical conductivity at 50 meV (it corresponds to a deep in the optical reflectivity).

To gain insight into the origin of this peak, we carried out band structure calculations within the local density approximation (LDA) based on the experimental crystal structure of TaP [36]. The calculations were performed using the linear muffin-tin orbital (LMTO) method [37] with the Perdew-Wang exchange-correlation potential [38]. We used the relativistic PY LMTO computer code [39] with SOC added to the LMTO Hamiltonian in the variational step. BZ integrations were done using the improved tetrahedron method [40]. Additional empty spheres (E) were inserted at the 8b Wyckoff positions in order to minimize the effect of atomic sphere overlap. The Ta, P, and E states up to the maximal orbital quantum number $l_{max} = 3, 2,$ and, 1, respectively, were included into the LMTO basis set which is essential for calculation of the dipole matrix elements for the interband transitions involving the Ta d- and the P p-derived bands. When calculating the real part of the optical conductivity, we used the tetrahedron method on a dense $128 \times 128 \times 128$ k-mesh in order to resolve interband transitions between the SOC-split bands close to Weyl points [31,34]. No broadening has been applied to the computed spectra.

In Figure 3 we show the results of our band-structure calculations as well as the BZ of TaP. Four non-spin-degenerate bands, numbered 19 to 22, can be resolved in the vicinity of E_F (at every given $\mathbf{k}$ point, the bands are numbered with increasing energy staring from the lowest calculated band). Note that the bands in each of the two pairs, (19, 20) and (21, 22), are split by SOC because of the lack of inversion symmetry. Our results reproduce well the published band structures of TaP calculated using the full-potential codes [11,13].

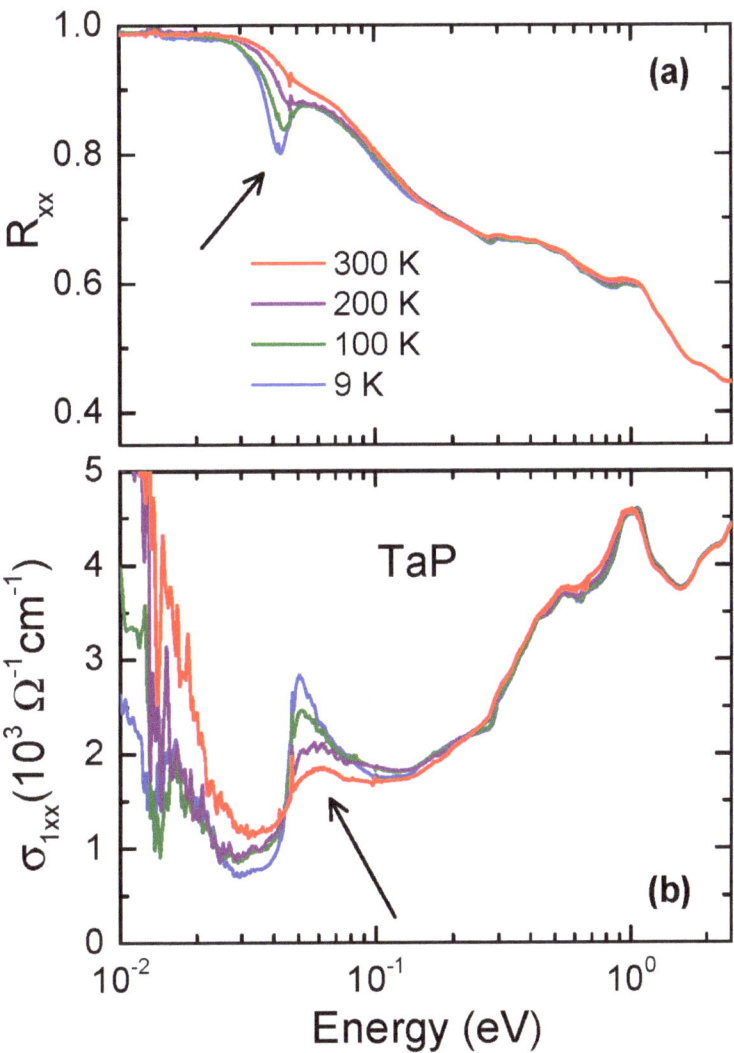

Figure 2. (**a**) Experimental in-plane reflectivity and (**b**) the corresponding real part of the optical conductivity of TaP at selected temperatures [35]. The arrows mark the feature discussed in this paper. The increased σ_{1xx} at low energies is due to intraband (Drude-like) absorption.

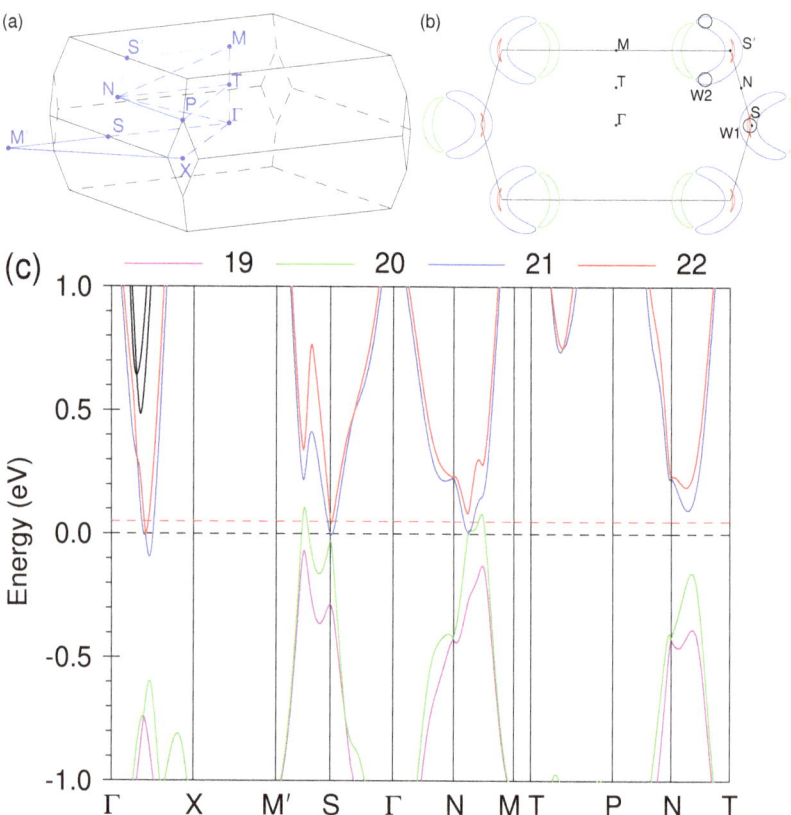

Figure 3. (a) Brillouin zone of TaP. (b) Fermi surface cross sections calculated for $\Delta E_F = 50$ meV. Black circles show approximate positions of projections of Weyl points onto $k_y = 0$ plane. (c) Band structure of TaP. Four bands closest to E_F (marked 19 to 22) are shown in different colors. Black and red horizontal dashed lines show the as-calculated position of E_F and the Fermi level shifted upwards by $\Delta E_F = 50$ meV, respectively.

Before we discuss the calculated optical conductivity spectra, we would like to note that in WSMs the match between the measured and the calculated optical conductivity at low frequencies is typically only qualitative: the calculations catch the major features observed in the experimental spectra, but are unable to reproduce the exact frequency positions of the features and their spectral shapes [13,15,30,31,34].

Another important point to be mentioned here is the unintentional (self-)doping, which is inherent to many real materials, where impurities, crystallographic defects, and vacancies may slightly change the position of E_F. Such unintentional doping, varying from sample to sample, has been shown to be relevant to TaP [41]. On the other hand, band structure calculations themselves have finite accuracy (cf. the spread in the calculated energy positions of the Weyl nodes, mentioned above). These considerations justify small variation of the position of E_F to get a better match between theory and experiment. Hereafter, we vary the Fermi-level position within $\Delta E_F = \pm 100$ meV.

Figure 4 presents the results of our interband-conductivity calculations starting from the self-consistent band structure shown in Figure 3. The black solid line in Figure 4 shows $\sigma_{1xx}(\hbar\omega)$ obtained with as-calculated E_F. The overall run of the experimental interband conductivity is well reproduced by this curve: $\sigma_{1xx}(\hbar\omega)$ increases with frequency and reaches a maximum at 1 eV (cf. Figure 2 and note that the intraband (Drude) contribution has not been taken into account in the band-structure computations). Nevertheless, no peak is visible in these computations at around 50 meV. A slight variation of E_F provides such a peak, but only if the Fermi level is shifted upwards (red and blue curves). Shifting E_F downwards does not change the σ_{1xx} spectra in the desirable way (magenta and cyan curves). The hight of the 50-meV peak reaches the experimental value of $2.5 \times 10^3 \ \Omega^{-1} \text{cm}^{-1}$ at $\Delta E_F = 50$ meV.

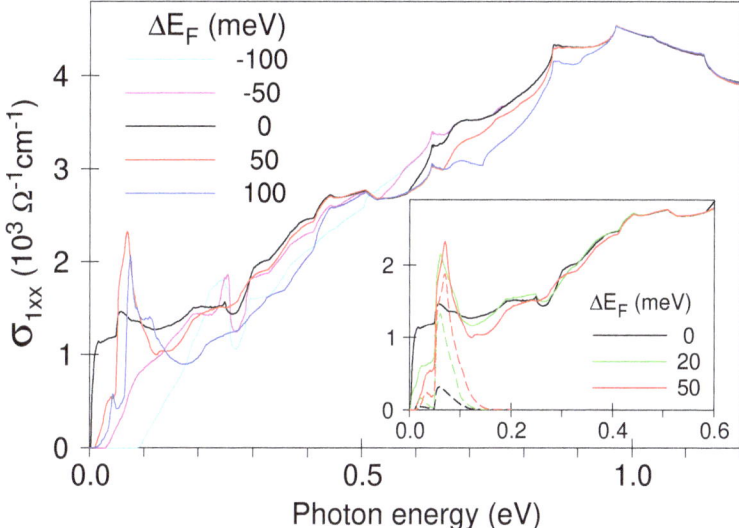

Figure 4. Low-energy optical conductivity of TaP calculated from its band structure. Lines of different colors correspond to different positions of the Fermi level, as indicated. The conductivity calculated for smaller positive ΔE_F is plotted in the inset. The contributions of $21 \rightarrow 22$ transitions are shown by dashed lines.

In the inset in Figure 4, we present an expanded view of the low-frequency optical conductivity calculated for small positive ΔE_F. It is obvious, that already a very small E_F shift of 20 meV is sufficient to produce the 50-meV peak. Note, that for all three curves yet another experimental feature—a broad shoulder at 0.3–0.5 eV—is also evident in the calculated spectra. Thus, we can conclude that a tiny shift of the Fermi level allows one to obtain a very reasonable overall description of the experimental $\sigma_{1xx}(\hbar\omega)$, including the strong peak at 50 meV.

To understand what interband optical transitions are responsible for this peak, one can take a look at Figure 3, where the original and shifted by 50 meV Fermi level positions are shown by black and red dashed lines, respectively. In the vicinity of Weyl points, i.e., near the S point and along the N–M line, band 21 is above the as-calculated E_F. The low-frequency interband conductivity is dominated by the transitions between the initial band 20 and the final band 21. The shift of E_F to higher energy leads to partial occupation of band 21. This suppresses the $20 \rightarrow 21$ transitions at low energy and, at the same time, allows transitions from band 21 to band 22, which remains mostly empty. As these SOC-split bands are almost parallel, the energies of such transitions are expected to be roughly the same for different momenta. Thus, a sharp peak may occur in $\sigma_{1xx}(\hbar\omega)$.

To confirm this observation, we performed band-resolved optical-conductivity calculations for the transitions between bands 21 and 22. The results of these calculations for three ΔE_F are plotted by dashed lines in the inset of Figure 4. It is apparent, that the $21 \rightarrow 22$ transitions provide the major contribution to the 50-meV peak, confirming our proposition. A $21 \rightarrow 22$ contribution coming from the **k** volume near the middle of the Γ–X line appears also for the as-calculated E_F, but it is too weak to be responsible for the 50-meV peak.

In order to model the experimentally observed temperature evolution of the 50-meV peak, we introduced a temperature dependence of the calculated interband optical conductivity by multiplying the interband transition probabilities with the factor $f(\varepsilon_{i\mathbf{k}})[1-f(\varepsilon_{f\mathbf{k}})]$, where $f(\varepsilon)$ is the Fermi-Dirac distribution function and $\varepsilon_{i\mathbf{k}}$ and $\varepsilon_{f\mathbf{k}}$ are the energies of initial and final states, respectively. Figure 5a shows that even this simple approach allows one to reproduce the experimentally observed reduction of the 50-meV peak with increasing temperature. A better agreement between theory and experiment is obtained, if the optical conductivity is calculated using an analog of the Mott formula [42], which is widely used to study the thermoelectric properties of metals. In this approximation,

$$\sigma(\omega) = \int \sigma(E,\omega)\left(-\frac{\partial f(E)}{\partial E}\right) dE, \qquad (2)$$

where $\frac{\partial f(E)}{\partial E}$ is the energy derivative of the Fermi-Dirac function and $\sigma(E,\omega)$ is calculated with E being the energy which discriminates between the initial and final bands, so that $E = E_F$ at $T = 0$. The results of these computations are shown in Figure 5b. We note that we compute the temperature dependence of the interband contribution only. In order to reproduce the upturn of the measured conductivity at low photon energies, one needs to consider the temperature dependence of the intraband Drude term, which is beyond the scope of this work.

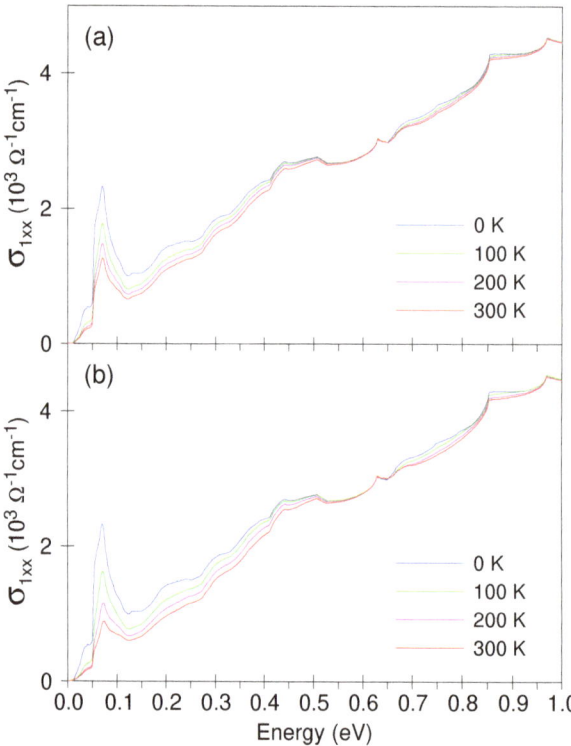

Figure 5. Temperature dependence of the optical conductivity calculated (**a**) by multiplying the interband transition probabilities with the Fermi-Dirac function and (**b**) using the Mott formula.

Finally, we would like to emphasize the importance of the transitions between the SOC-split bands. Such transitions can be considered forbidden in some models [20], while in the real WSMs they play an important role, as we have shown earlier for NbP [34].

These transitions are allowed, because the electronic bands can be characterized by their well-defined spin polarization, $\langle s \rangle \simeq \pm 1/2$, only for **k**-vectors faraway from the Weyl nodes; closer to the nodes, SOC is strong and spin polarization is much less perfect. Thus, transitions between *any* pair of bands are allowed there.

3. Conclusions

Summarizing, we have calculated the low-energy optical conductivity of the Weyl semimetal TaP (in the ab plane) and compared it to the experimental results. The best match between theory and experiment is found for a slightly shifted Fermi level (+20 to 60 meV). This shift confirms a small unintentional doping of TaP, discussed earlier [35,41], and offers a natural explanation of the strong low-energy (50 meV) peak reported in the experimental data [30,35]: the peak is due to transitions between the almost parallel non-degenerate electronic bands split by spin-orbit coupling.

Author Contributions: Conceptualization, A.Y. and A.V.P.; calculations, A.Y.; providing experimental data, A.V.P.; writing, A.Y. and A.V.P. All authors have read and agreed to the published version of the manuscript.

Funding: This research was funded in part by the Deutsche Forschungsgemeinschaft via grant number DR228/51-3.

Institutional Review Board Statement: Not applicable.

Informed Consent Statement: Not applicable.

Data Availability Statement: Data are available upon request to the corresponding author.

Acknowledgments: We thank Sascha Polatkan for technical assistance in manuscript preparation.

Conflicts of Interest: The authors declare no conflict of interest.

References

1. Weyl, H. Electron and Gravitation. I. *Z. Phys.* **1929**, *56*, 330–352. [CrossRef]
2. Murakami, S. Phase transition between the quantum spin Hall and insulator phases in 3D: emergence of a topological gapless phase. *New J. Phys.* **2007**, *9*, 356. [CrossRef]
3. Wan, X.; Turner, A.M.; Vishwanath, A.; Savrasov, S.Y. Topological semimetal and Fermi-arc surface states in the electronic structure of pyrochlore iridates. *Phys. Rev. B* **2011**, *83*, 205101. [CrossRef]
4. Burkov, A.A.; Hook, M.D.; Balents, L. Topological nodal semimetals. *Phys. Rev. B* **2011**, *84*, 235126. [CrossRef]
5. Huang, S.M.; Xu, S.Y.; Belopolski, I.; Lee, C.C.; Chang, G.; Wang, B.; Alidoust, N.; Bian, G.; Neupane, M.; Zhang, C.; et al. A Weyl Fermion semimetal with surface Fermi arcs in the transition metal monopnictide TaAs class. *Nat. Commun.* **2015**, *6*, 7373. [CrossRef] [PubMed]
6. Xu, S.Y.; Belopolski, I.; Alidoust, N.; Neupane, M.; Bian, G.; Zhang, C.; Sankar, R.; Chang, G.; Yuan, Z.; Lee, C.C.; et al. Discovery of a Weyl fermion semimetal and topological Fermi arcs. *Science* **2015**, *349*, 613–617. [CrossRef] [PubMed]
7. Burkov, A.A. Topological semimetals. *Nat. Mater.* **2016**, *15*, 1145–1148. [CrossRef]
8. Armitage, N.P.; Mele, E.J.; Vishwanath, A. Weyl and Dirac semimetals in three-dimensional solids. *Rev. Mod. Phys.* **2018**, *90*, 015001. [CrossRef]
9. Weng, H.; Fang, C.; Fang, Z.; Bernevig, B.A.; Dai, X. Weyl Semimetal Phase in Noncentrosymmetric Transition-Metal Monophosphides. *Phys. Rev. X* **2015**, *5*, 011029. [CrossRef]
10. Sun, Y.; Wu, S.C.; Ali, M.N.; Felser, C.; Yan, B. Prediction of Weyl semimetal in orthorhombic MoTe$_2$. *Phys. Rev. B* **2015**, *92*, 161107. [CrossRef]
11. Lee, C.C.; Xu, S.Y.; Huang, S.M.; Sanchez, D.S.; Belopolski, I.; Chang, G.; Bian, G.; Alidoust, N.; Zheng, H.; Neupane, M.; et al. Fermi surface interconnectivity and topology in Weyl fermion semimetals TaAs, TaP, NbAs, and NbP. *Phys. Rev. B* **2015**, *92*, 235104. [CrossRef]
12. Arnold, F.; Naumann, M.; Wu, S.C.; Sun, Y.; Schmidt, M.; Borrmann, H.; Felser, C.; Yan, B.; Hassinger, E. Chiral Weyl Pockets and Fermi Surface Topology of the Weyl Semimetal TaAs. *Phys. Rev. Lett.* **2016**, *117*, 146401. [CrossRef]
13. Grassano, D.; Pulci, O.; Conte, A.M.; Bechstedt, F. Validity of Weyl fermion picture for transition metals monopnictides TaAs, TaP, NbAs, and NbP from ab initio studies. *Sci. Rep.* **2018**, *8*, 3534. [CrossRef]
14. Wehling, T.O.; Black-Schaffer, A.M.; Balatsky, A.V. Dirac materials. *Adv. Phys.* **2014**, *63*, 1–76. [CrossRef]
15. Pronin, A.V.; Dressel, M. Nodal Semimetals: A Survey on Optical Conductivity. *Phys. Status Solidi B* **2021**, *258*, 2000027. [CrossRef]

16. Hosur, P.; Parameswaran, S.A.; Vishwanath, A. Charge Transport in Weyl Semimetals. *Phys. Rev. Lett.* **2012**, *108*, 046602. [CrossRef] [PubMed]
17. Bácsi, A.; Virosztek, A. Low-frequency optical conductivity in graphene and in other scale-invariant two-band systems. *Phys. Rev. B* **2013**, *87*, 125425. [CrossRef]
18. Ashby, P.E.C.; Carbotte, J.P. Chiral anomaly and optical absorption in Weyl semimetals. *Phys. Rev. B* **2014**, *89*, 245121. [CrossRef]
19. Tabert, C.J.; Carbotte, J.P.; Nicol, E.J. Optical and transport properties in three-dimensional Dirac and Weyl semimetals. *Phys. Rev. B* **2016**, *93*, 085426. [CrossRef]
20. Tabert, C.J.; Carbotte, J.P. Optical conductivity of Weyl semimetals and signatures of the gapped semimetal phase transition. *Phys. Rev. B* **2016**, *93*, 085442. [CrossRef]
21. Carbotte, J.P. Dirac cone tilt on interband optical background of type-I and type-II Weyl semimetals. *Phys. Rev. B* **2016**, *94*, 165111. [CrossRef]
22. Sánchez-Martínez, M.A.; de Juan, F.; Grushin, A.G. Linear optical conductivity of chiral multifold fermions. *Phys. Rev. B* **2019**, *99*, 155145. [CrossRef]
23. Carbotte, J.P.; Nicol, E.J. Signatures of merging Dirac points in optics and transport. *Phys. Rev. B* **2019**, *100*, 035441. [CrossRef]
24. Timusk, T.; Carbotte, J.P.; Homes, C.C.; Basov, D.N.; Sharapov, S.G. Three-dimensional Dirac fermions in quasicrystals as seen via optical conductivity. *Phys. Rev. B* **2013**, *87*, 235121. [CrossRef]
25. Chen, R.Y.; Zhang, S.J.; Schneeloch, J.A.; Zhang, C.; Li, Q.; Gu, G.D.; Wang, N.L. Optical spectroscopy study of the three-dimensional Dirac semimetal ZrTe$_5$. *Phys. Rev. B* **2015**, *92*, 075107. [CrossRef]
26. Sushkov, A.B.; Hofmann, J.B.; Jenkins, G.S.; Ishikawa, J.; Nakatsuji, S.; Das Sarma, S.; Drew, H.D. Optical evidence for a Weyl semimetal state in pyrochlore Eu$_2$Ir$_2$O$_7$. *Phys. Rev. B* **2015**, *92*, 241108. [CrossRef]
27. Xu, B.; Dai, Y.M.; Zhao, L.X.; Wang, K.; Yang, R.; Zhang, W.; Liu, J.Y.; Xiao, H.; Chen, G.F.; Taylor, A.J.; et al. Optical spectroscopy of the Weyl semimetal TaAs. *Phys. Rev. B* **2016**, *93*, 121110. [CrossRef]
28. Ueda, K.; Fujioka, J.; Tokura, Y. Variation of optical conductivity spectra in the course of bandwidth-controlled metal-insulator transitions in pyrochlore iridates. *Phys. Rev. B* **2016**, *93*, 245120. [CrossRef]
29. Neubauer, D.; Carbotte, J.P.; Nateprov, A.A.; Löhle, A.; Dressel, M.; Pronin, A.V. Interband optical conductivity of the [001]-oriented Dirac semimetal Cd$_3$As$_2$. *Phys. Rev. B* **2016**, *93*, 121202. [CrossRef]
30. Kimura, S.I.; Yokoyama, H.; Watanabe, H.; Sichelschmidt, J.; Suess, V.; Schmidt, M.; Felser, C. Optical signature of Weyl electronic structures in tantalum pnictides TaPn (Pn = P, As). *Phys. Rev. B* **2017**, *96*, 075119. [CrossRef]
31. Chaudhuri, D.; Cheng, B.; Yaresko, A.; Gibson, Q.D.; Cava, R.J.; Armitage, N.P. Optical investigation of the strong spin-orbit-coupled magnetic semimetal YbMnBi$_2$. *Phys. Rev. B* **2017**, *96*, 075151. [CrossRef]
32. Schilling, M.B.; Löhle, A.; Neubauer, D.; Shekhar, C.; Felser, C.; Dressel, M.; Pronin, A.V. Two-channel conduction in YbPtBi. *Phys. Rev. B* **2017**, *95*, 155201. [CrossRef]
33. Kemmler, R.; Hübner, R.; Löhle, A.; Neubauer, D.; Voloshenko, I.; Schoop, L.M.; Dressel, M.; Pronin, A.V. Free-carrier dynamics in Au$_2$Pb probed by optical conductivity measurements. *J. Phys. Condens. Matter* **2018**, *30*, 485403. [CrossRef] [PubMed]
34. Neubauer, D.; Yaresko, A.; Li, W.; Loehle, A.; Huebner, R.; Schilling, M.B.; Shekhar, C.; Felser, C.; Dressel, M.; Pronin Artem, V. Optical conductivity of the Weyl semimetal NbP. *Phys. Rev. B* **2018**, *98*, 195203. [CrossRef]
35. Polatkan, S.; Goerbig, M.O.; Wyzula, J.; Kemmler, R.; Maulana, L.Z.; Piot, B.A.; Crassee, I.; Akrap, A.; Shekhar, C.; Felser, C.; et al. Magneto-Optics of a Weyl Semimetal beyond the Conical Band Approximation: Case Study of TaP. *Phys. Rev. Lett.* **2020**, *124*, 176402. [CrossRef] [PubMed]
36. Willerstrom, J. Stacking Disorder In NbP, TaP, NbAs And TaAs. *J. Less-Common Met.* **1984**, *99*, 273–283. [CrossRef]
37. Andersen, O.K. Linear methods in band theory. *Phys. Rev. B* **1975**, *12*, 3060–3083. [CrossRef]
38. Perdew, J.P.; Wang, Y. Accurate and simple analytic representation of the electron-gas correlation energy. *Phys. Rev. B* **1992**, *45*, 13244–13249. [CrossRef]
39. Antonov, V.; Harmon, B.; Yaresko, A. *Electronic Structure and Magneto-Optical Properties of Solids*; Kluwer Academic Publishers: Dordrecht, The Netherlands; Boston, MA, USA; London, UK, 2004.
40. Blöchl, P.E.; Jepsen, O.; Andersen, O.K. Improved Tetrahedron Method for Brillouin-zone Integrations. *Phys. Rev. B* **1994**, *49*, 16223–16233. [CrossRef]
41. Besara, T.; Rhodes, D.A.; Chen, K.W.; Das, S.; Zhang, Q.R.; Sun, J.; Zeng, B.; Xin, Y.; Balicas, L.; Baumbach, R.E.; et al. Coexistence of Weyl physics and planar defects in the semimetals TaP and TaAs. *Phys. Rev. B* **2016**, *93*, 245152. [CrossRef]
42. Cutler, M.; Mott, N.F. Observation of Anderson Localization in an Electron Gas. *Phys. Rev.* **1969**, *181*, 1336–1340. [CrossRef]

MDPI
St. Alban-Anlage 66
4052 Basel
Switzerland
Tel. +41 61 683 77 34
Fax +41 61 302 89 18
www.mdpi.com

Crystals Editorial Office
E-mail: crystals@mdpi.com
www.mdpi.com/journal/crystals

www.ingramcontent.com/pod-product-compliance
Lightning Source LLC
LaVergne TN
LVHW070553100526
838202LV00012B/455